Written Language and Psent

Written Language and Psychological Development

LEONARD F. M. SCINTO
Applied Science Laboratories
Waltham, Massachusetts

1986

ACADEMIC PRESS, INC.
Harcourt Brace Jovanovich, Publishers

Orlando   San Diego   New York   Austin
London   Montreal   Sydney   Tokyo   Toronto

Acknowledgment is gratefully made for permission to use material from the following sources:

Haas, W. (ed.). *Writing without letters,* 1976; and Haas, W. *Phonographic translation,* 1970. Reprinted by permission of Manchester University Press.

Havranek, B. The functional differentiation of the standard language. In *A Prague School reader in esthetics, literary structure and style.* Edited by Paul L. Garvin. Copyright © 1964 by Georgetown University Press. Used with permission of the publisher.

Humphrey, N. *Consciousness regained,* 1982. Reprinted by permission of Oxford University Press.

Luria, A. R. *Language and cognition,* 1981. Reprinted by permission of John Wiley & Sons, Inc.

Vygotsky, L. S. The problem of the cultural development of the child. *Journal of Genetic Psychology,* 1928, pp. 415–434. A publication of the Helen Dwight Reid Educational Foundation.

Vygotsky, L. S. *Thought and language,* 1962. Reprinted by permission of the MIT Press.

ACADEMIC PRESS, INC.
Orlando, Florida 32887

United Kingdom Edition published by
ACADEMIC PRESS INC. (LONDON) LTD.
24–28 Oval Road, London NW1 7DX

LIBRARY OF CONGRESS CATALOGING-IN-PUBLICATION DATA

Scinto, Leonard F. M.
    Written language & psychological development.

    Bibliography: p.
    Includes index.
        1. Written communication.   2. Language acquisition.
3. Cognition.   I. Title.   II. Title: Written language
and psychological development.
P211.S43   1986   001.54'3   85-9160
ISBN 0-12-633250-9 (alk. paper)
ISBN 0-12-633251-7 (paperback)

PRINTED IN THE UNITED STATES OF AMERICA

86 87 88 89   9 8 7 6 5 4 3 2 1

But these were merciful men, whose righteousness
hath not been forgotten.

ECCLESIASTICUS XLIV

Contents

Coding Conventions   *xi*
Preface   *xiii*

Introduction   1

1 On Language and Its Manifestations   5

Definition of the Linguistic Sign   5
De Saussure and the Nature of the Linguistic Sign   8
Sound and Linguistic Sign   10
Psychological Definitions of Language   16
Toward a Substance-Neutral Definition of Language   20

2 Relation of Oral and Written Language   25

Introduction   25
Phylogensis and the Priority of Speech over Writing   26
Ontogenesis and the Priority of Speech over Writing   30
Structural Models of the Relation of Oral and Written Language   31
A Genetic Model of Oral and Written Language   38
Neurolinguistic Aspects of Oral and Written Language   42

3 Functional Differentiation of Oral and Written Language Norms   51

Introduction   51
Functional Features and Language Manifestions   56
Syntactic Differentiation of Oral and Written Norms   62

4 Developmental Models and the Nature of Written Language Acquisition   67

Introduction   67
The Prehistory of Writing in the Child   70
Biological and Cultural Lines of Development   73
Culture, Learning, and Development   76
The Nature of Written Language Acquisition   80
Studies of Written Language Acquisition   82

5 Written Language and Social Praxis   91

Introduction   91
Literacy and Cognition   93
Functional Differentiation and Social Praxis   95
Schooling and the Written Norm   98
Social Praxis and Written Language Acquisition   104

6 A Function Model of Written Text   107

Introduction   107
Definition of Text   108
Units of Text   110
Graph-Theoretic Models of Text and Module Delimitation   120
Combinatoric Text Modules and Graphs   122
Coefficients of Coherence and Compactness   124
The Acquisition of Strategies for Text Construction   129

7 Text Operations and Cognitive Functioning   139

Introduction   139
Function and Relation in Cognition   145
Function and Relation in Written Text   148
The Place of Written Monologic Text in Ontogenesis   157

8 Written Language and the Growth of the Mind   161

Introduction   161
Developmental Models and Culture   163
Written Language and Psychological Development   165
Language and Culture   170
Conclusion   172

References   175

Author Index   185
Subject Index   189

Coding Conventions

$T_2(=T_1)$	direct lexical copy
$T_2(proT_1)$	pronominalization
$T_2(domT_1)$	partial identity; synonym or member same lexical set
$T_2(\epsilon T_1)$	T_2 member of a larger set
$T_2(+T_1)$	T_2 definite reference of T_1 indefinite
$T_2(\sim T_1)$	T_2 contrary or opposite of T_1
$T_2(\varnothing T_1)$	T_2 not explicit in surface structure; ellipsis
$T_2(\equiv T_1)$	T_2 partial identity of T_1 but adds further specification
$T_n(contx)$	T_n derived from metalinguistic context, general
$R_n(contx)$	knowledge, and so forth
$T_n(ext)$	T or R incorporates an existential statement *it is* or
$R_n(ext)$	*there is,* or introduces a new object into discourse
$T_2(+tT_1)$	T_2 = temporal sequence after T_1
$T(-tT_1)$	T_2 = temporal sequence after T_1
$T_2(consq\ T1)$	T_2 = consequence of previous rheme
$T_2(impl\ R_1)$	T_2 = implication of rheme
$T_2(eg\ R_1)$	T_2 = illustration of rheme
$T_2(reas\ R_1)$	T_2 = reason or backing for rheme
$T_2(concl\ R_1)$	T_2 = conclusion of rheme
$R_2(\equiv R_1)$	as $T_2(\equiv T_1)$, above

Preface

'Αρχὴ μεγίστη τοῦ βίου τα γράμμτα
(Wax tablet: fourth- or
fifth-century schoolboy)

The theme that runs through this book is a concern I have felt for the need for a clearer understanding of the nature of written language, especially how written language is characterized with respect to oral language and the role the acquisition of written language might play in the later stages of the formation of individual mind. When this topic first began to occupy me, there was little concern within the broad mainstream of Anglo-American psychology about the nature and psychology of written language. However, within the past 5 years, there has been a major proliferation of works on writing, literacy, and written language. While this interest in the topic is welcome, the one unsatisfying aspect of this work was and continues to be to some extent the lack of a coherent theoretical framework within which to situate studies of written language, in particular developmental accounts of written language study. Indeed, there is little broad agreement as to what should constitute the object of study—that is, written language. What is written language? How is it different from oral language? What is acquired in acquiring written language? These are questions that have gone unasked for far too long. There is a need to ask these questions explicitly and in doing so to attempt answers that may provide some coherence to studies of written language in the many subdisciplines of psychology where written language is an important, if largely unexplored, variable. In the chapters that follow I address these and other questions about the psychology of written language, and the beginnings of answers emerge to fill the void that exists from leaving such questions unasked and assuming that somehow we all agree what the answers should be.

While the formulation of the issues in this book are primarily developmental and my central concern is to explore the question of the role of written language in the development of mind, the exposition should be of concern and interest to a set of diverse psychological disciplines. Written language, whether from the perspective of normality or pathology of functioning, should be of interest to neurolinguists with concerns about the loss of function due to trauma, to educators with concerns about the success or failure of the instructional process or instructional media, and to clinicians in learning disabilities, where assessments of written language function are often critical to issues of diagnosis and remediation. This book does not provide easy recipes about the psychology of written language, but it will, I trust, raise issues and stimulate debate about unquestioned assumptions about written language for a broad spectrum of psychologists, educators, and clinicians.

During the genesis of the ideas that are recorded in the following pages, I was fortunate to have around me colleagues and friends who were both stimulating and patient. To those at Harvard who first tolerated and at times encouraged my interest in the psychology of written langauge when such topics were hardly respectable and, in particular, to colleagues and friends at the University of Cambridge, where these ideas first bore fruit, I am affectionately grateful. In particular, I owe much to the critical eye of Dr. Addison Stone of Northwestern University. If this book is not the better for it, the fault is not his.

Introduction

In the long course of human inquiry, the topic and term *language* has been variously defined and more often than not abused, perhaps no more so than when preceded by qualifiers such as *natural, oral,* and *written.* When the focus of inquiry has been the role of language in human psychology, the discussion about what shall constitute language or what shall count as natural human language has indeed been the subject of much controversy. Yet in most accounts of the psychology of language there has been an almost tacit and unquestioned agreement to exclude from serious consideration the phenomena of written language. The concern of this work is to reexamine the topic of written language and its relation to what is ordinarily understood by the term *oral language,* to explore the process of its acquisition, and to examine the place of written language in the process of mental development.

Traditional accounts of the nature of language have viewed written language as a derivative symbol system, one that enjoys only a parasitic status with respect to oral language. The latter is seen, at least in mainstream accounts, as the natural instantiation of man's innate linguistic faculty. We shall see that some accounts of the nature of human natural language insist on vocal articulation as a sine qua non of the definition of the term *language.*

Chapter 1 takes up the question of the relation of written language to oral language and traces, through a number of philosophical and linguistic accounts, what may be termed the *phonocentric canon*. The often unquestioned and unstated assumption of this phonocentric canon asserts that the voice is somehow primary and central to language, and, by impli- cation, other instantiations of language are only secondary reflections of the voice. In contrast to this phonocentric canon, Chapter 1 argues that any definition of language must be substance neutral, that is, privilege no particular medium of expression, be it voice or graphic marks, in its definition. While oral language may enjoy a phylogenetic and ontogene- tic priority, this does not privilege oral language as a first-order symbol system and others as second-order systems only reflective of a first-order system.

In Chapter 2 this phonocentric canon is critically scrutinized, and it is argued that the vast preponderance of evidence from functional, analytic, neurological, and developmental considerations does not sustain the view of the naturalness of oral language and the unnaturalness of written language. In particular, the evidence from neurology points to oral and written language as equipollent systems that equally manifest man's lin- guistic capacity. Chapter 3 takes up certain functional principles of lin- guistic differentiation and reexamines oral and written manifestations of language in light of the principle of functional differentiation. Based on the early work of the Prague Linguistic Circle, this principle of differenti- ation argues that oral and written language manifestations fulfill function- ally distinct roles in any given linguistic community. Oral and written manifestations of language constitute complementary systems of lan- guage norms that can be clearly distinguished on the basis of various structural-functional characteristics. For example, on the plane of dis- course organization, written norms are usually manifested in monologic text forms, whereas oral norms usually are associated with dialogic forms of discourse organization.

Having made the argument for the equipollent status of oral and written language norms, the remainder of this book is an examination of the complex process of the acquisition of the written language norm, what is unique to this acquisition, how it differs from and complements oral language development, and the probable role the acquisition of written language may play in the development of mind. When a number of representative studies loosely grouped under the rubrics "literacy" and "writing" were examined in order to clarify what could be understood by the phrase "written language acquisition," it was found that there is little broad agreement as to what aspects a developmental model of written language acquisition should encompass. Given this lack of agreement, a model of written language acquisition that centers around a model of monologic text production is proposed.

Any account of written language development must be situated within a more general model of psychological development. At the very least, the general assumptions about the nature of psychological ontogenesis must be made explicit if remarks on the nature of written language development are to be intelligible and especially if questions about the role of written language acquisition in the construction of mind are to be posed. Chapter 4 explains some central features of a general model of psychological development. This discussion centers on those aspects of a general developmental model that are directly implicated in any account of written language acquisition. The prime issue addressed is the extent to which any model of psychological development must account for two broad lines in ontogenesis, the biological and the cultural. When considering the relation of oral and written manifestations of language in Chapters 1–3, the common distinction drawn between biological and cultural principles of psychogenesis is an analytic fiction. Genetic accounts of phylogenesis or ontogenesis must attend to the simultaneously dual nature of the genetic process, which is always an interfunctional composite of biological and cultural aspects. The arguments of Vygotsky and Luria are considered in explicating a model of psychological development that takes into account both biological and cultural lines of development. Language, and especially written language as partly constituted by cultural forces, represents in the developmental process the most visible and tangible aspect of the cultural line of development. Where the biological line may dictate a direct interaction between organism and environment, the cultural line proceeds by a logic of mediated interaction. The primary mediators are, it is argued, man's symbol systems — preeminently language, oral and written.

Scribner and Cole (1981), in a seminal study of the cognitive consequences of literacy, make the point that *literacy* is not a term that encompasses a unitary construct. They argue that within a given culture and across cultures there can be radically different manifestations of literacy. Taking up this point in light of the principles of differentiations of language function proposed in Chapter 3 and the nature of a cultural line of development, Chapter 5 looks at the written norm of language as partly constituted by particular cultural practices and institutions. In developed Western technological societies where the acquisition of literacy takes place primarily in formal scholastic settings, a particular functional variant of the written norm emerges. We can term this particular functional variant of the written norm the "scholarized" or intellectualized norm. Typically this scholarized norm places a premium on decontextualized monologic discourse. Particular functional variants of the written norm, it is argued, foreground and hence are unmarked for certain means of linguistic expression. This foregrounding or automatization of given linguistic means of expression for given types of written discourse is partly constituted by particular sociocultural practices. In the case of fully literate cultures with an institutional practice such as formal schooling, what can be properly understood by the acquisition of the written norm is the development of competence for producing communicatively adequate monologic text.

Chapter 6 proposes a model of monologic text based on structural-functional lines that is an outgrowth of the theoretical considerations put forward in Chapter 5. This model is presented in some detail in order to explain how the acquisition of the written norm may be approached at the level of text. Some empirical findings on the acquisition of strategies for text construction based on the model proposed earlier in the chapter are presented. These findings are suggestive of the course the acquisition of the written norm may take and are not presented as a definitive account of that acquisition. They do serve, however, to point up the correlation between competence in producing written text and other aspects of cognitive development.

In Chapter 7 the implications of the empirical findings presented in Chaper 6 are further explored. It is argued that a developmental sequence in the acquisition of written discourse can be discerned in children's production of written expository and narrative text. One result that clearly emerges is that competence in narrative text appears prior to competence in expository text. Explanatory constructs are explored to account for such findings. There follows an examination of the correlation between competence in producing written text and the onset of what Piaget terms "formal operational thinking." The summary results from the study presented in Chapter 6 are further analyzed and a model for analysis is proposed. The parallels between text construction strategies and the logic of operational thought are detailed. Again a number of explanatory constructs are proposed that might account for the parallels observed. Finally, it is argued that changes in the nature of operational thinking might plausibly be accounted for in part by the shift in the linguistic representational system at the child's disposal. With the appearance of ability to produce written monologic text comes a radical shift in the nature of the child's representational system from one that is less context dependent, hence more decontextualized and under intrapsychological control.

Chapter 8 draws together the themes that run through this work: the nature of the development of written language and the relation and consequences of that development for a more general model of ontogenesis. In particular, Chapter 8 draws together three themes: the distinctive nature of written language as partly constituted by cultural practice, the dual biological and cultural determinants of psychogenesis, and the mediated nature of much of ontogenesis.

1

On Language and Its Manifestations

Definition of the Linguistic Sign

Perhaps one of the most persistent traditions with respect to the nature of language within Western intellectual speculation is the close, almost exclusive identification of natural language with its vocal-auditory manifestation. Hand in hand with this linking of the spoken word and natural language has gone the relegation of written manifestations or, for that matter, any other substantive manifestations of language, to the realm of a secondary, artificial, or "nonnatural" limbo. Despite the sophistication achieved in explicating the nature and system of language over the past centuries, this view has persisted and become, with few exceptions, one of the foundations of the scientific linguistic enterprise. It would appear from a reading of most major Western texts on language that critical thinking on the issue of the relationship of oral and written manifestations of language has collapsed under the weight of tradition and folk theory. Indeed, this phonocentrism is not limited to treatments in linguistics but pervades both philosophical and psychological research as well.

Before we can begin to address the central questions of this work, the development of oral and written language in children and the respective roles of oral or written manifestations of language in the process of cognitive growth, we must reexamine the basis for this phonocentric canon and clarify the nature of the relation of the substantive manifestation of language to language as an underlying system of form. To this end we trace, within limits, the place of this identification of voice with language within the Western philosophical, linguistic, and psychological tradition. Through an examination of the nature of the linguistic system from a phylogenetic, axiomatic, neurological, and functional-communicative perspective, we attempt to formulate a more adequate account of the relationship of physical substance to the nature of linguistic form and hopefully arrive at a more critical account of natural language as an underlying system of signs and the substantive manifestation of this system in actual use.

The concept of the voiced language as primary, as somehow directly and immediately signifying the contents of the mind, enjoys a very long history. Aristotle, in *De Interpretatione,* defines spoken words as "symbols or signs of affections or impressions of the soul." But he relegates written language to a secondary or derivative role, saying that "written words are the signs of words spoken." He defines a noun as "a sound having meaning established by convention." Such a conception of the linguistic sign as sign is not very far from de Saussure's definition. The ancient tradition of the spoken word, the auditory sign, as primary is given more fully by Augustine in *De Dialectica* (V, 7, 11–23):

> A word is a sign of any sort of thing. It is spoken by a speaker and can be understood by a hearer. A thing is whatever is sensed or is understood or is hidden. A sign is something which is itself sensed and which indicates to the mind something beyond the sign itself. To speak is to give a sign by means of an articulate utterance. By an articulate utterance I mean one which can be expressed in letters. . . . Every word is a sound, for *when it is written it is not a word but the sign of a word* [emphasis added]. When we read, the letters we see suggest to the mind the sounds of the utterance. For written letters indicate to the eyes something other than themselves and indicate to the mind utterances beyond themselves. Now we have just said that a sign is something which is itself sensed and which indicates to the mind something beyond the sign itself. Therefore, what we read are not words but signs of words. For we misuse the term 'letter' [letter is to be understood as a spoken and not a written entity] when we call what we see written down a letter, for it is completely silent and is not part of an utterance but appears as a sign of a part of an utterance: whereas a letter as such is the smallest part of an articulate utterance. In the same way (we misuse the term 'word') when we call what we see written down a word, for it appears as the sign of a word, that is, not as a word but as the sign of a significant utterance. Therefore as I said above, every word is a sound.

We have quoted Augustine at such length because he neatly encapsulates the tradition of the nature of the sign and phonocentrism as it comes down to us from early formulations and persists in much Western thinking on the nature of language. The main tenets of phonocentrism are here; the immediacy of the identification of sound, an affirmation of its priority, the insistence that writing is not language but merely a secondary reflection of language, that the written word stands for something else, namely, the sound that is the word.

This secondary status ascribed to writing is given full play by Plato in the *Phaedrus*. Here we find no less mistrust of and even hostility to the written word. Plato subtly affirms the unnaturalness of written language, a theme that is later amplified by others. Thus the spoken word becomes identified with natural language, which is interior, in that it springs from the natural faculties of man, as opposed to writing, which is exterior. So Plato comments on the adverse psychological effects of writing when he states in the *Phaedrus* (281)

> For this invention of yours [writing] will produce forgetfulness in the minds of those who learn it, by causing them to neglect their memory, inasmuch as, from their confidence in writing, they will recollect by the *external* aid of *foreign* symbols, and not by the internal use of their own faculties. (p. 275; emphasis added.)

This theme is carried through much of classical and medieval writing on language. The concept of the exteriority of written language becomes contrasted with the personalist and immanent qualities of the voice, the *logos*. Knowledge by voice becomes the norm in classical times and continues to be honored long after literacy and writing become the major vehicle for the transmission and acquisition of knowledge. Ong (1958) writes of the audile-visual tension and the increasing influence of visualist metaphors for knowledge in the writings of Peter of Spain and in the dialectic of Peter Ramus. Yet despite what Ong sees as the unfortunate loss of the dialogicality of knowledge, namely, the substitution of the visual for the auditory sense and hence the depersonalization of man-language, the transmission of knowledge by dispute and the give-and-take of oral debate are the models that are preserved. We are left with the theme of the spoken language as somehow natural in contrast to writing and print. Dialectic is still defined as *ars bene decendi* or *ars bene disserendi* and rhetoric as *ars bene loquendi*. Indeed, the ancients' theme of writing as a secondary sign of a primary sign is echoed by Rousseau and Hegel.

But from where does this emphasis on the primacy of voice spring? We can only speculate that it is perhaps understandable that a predominantly preliterate or semiliterate culture should, through observation of the use of language, conclude that the natural expression of language is in fact the spoken word. Having become convinced of the naturalness of the human faculty for spoken language, it is not an unreasonable step, with the appearance of writing, to conclude that it is a mere recording of the spoken language. In fact there is perhaps some empirical foundation in the relation of the two manifestations of language that would appear to support such a conclusion. What is perhaps surprising is that this uncritical view of the nature of language persists as a dominant motif within literate and even print cultures. Indeed, for many the rise of phonology provides the basis for the scientificity of linguistics as a discipline. Derrida (1976) writes:

> Linguistics thus wishes to be the science of language . . . Let us first simply consider that the scientificity of that science is often acknowledged because of its *phonological* foundations. Phonology, it is often said today, communicates its scientificity to linguistics, which in turn serves as the epistemological model for all the sciences of man. (p. 29)

We shall examine where, how, and to what extent this folk theory assumes the mantle of scientificity and define the consequences for a theory of language. As Hjelmslev (1963) observes, language is a system of signs. This can command the assent of most theories of language. Where differences arise and where phonocentrism gains its foothold are in the definition of the substantive nature of the linguistic sign and its relation to other substantive manifestations of the linguistic sign.

De Saussure and the Nature of the Linguistic Sign

By common consent, de Saussure is acknowledged as a seminal figure of modern linguistic thinking, at least within modern Anglo–American linguistics. De Saussure's writing on the substantive nature of the linguistic sign and language forms the basis for later extrapolations and refinements. In his phonological prejudice in defining the nature of the linguistic sign and language is found the contemporary foundation that linguists such as Sapir, Bloomfield, and Jakobson incorporate as a fundamental canon of linguistic science. This has to a large extent impeded and frustrated critical thinking on the functional variation of oral and written language manifestation in the life of society and of individuals.

De Saussure begins his consideration of the nature of language by debunking it as solely a product of a social system of conventions. This conception of the dual origin of language as a product of social system and as an expression of certain natural dispositions reinforces the phonocentric definition of natural language. But this dualistic conception leads to a somewhat contradictory view of the place of substance in any definition of natural language for de Saussure. De Saussure (1959, p. 9) states that language is "both a social product of the faculty of speech and collection of necessary conventions that have been adopted by a social body to permit individuals to express that faculty." But while speaking of the faculty of speech, de Saussure is careful to distinguish what he means by language apart from the facts of speech. Language as social product, as system, stands apart from the facts of speech. It is for de Saussure "a self-contained whole and a principle of classification" (1959, p. 9). He carefully argues that language is not simply the product of some natural instinct nor should it be subordinated to any natural instinct for speech.

In distinguishing language from what in psychological terms might be called "verbal behavior," de Saussure sets up a tension that exists throughout his treatment of language in the *Cours* and that in the end belies the thread of phonocentrism that runs through this work and is reinforced in later treatments of language and speech. This tension is that of the natural or necessary manifestation of language in speech behavior. In wishing to distinguish language *(langue)* from the facts of speech *(parole)*, de Saussure must insist that there is no necessity for sound, a physical substance, to be part of *langue*. On the other hand, de Saussure is unwilling to fully accept the thesis that the choice of the substantive manifestation of *langue* in sound is truly arbitrary. This tension is clearly expressed when he writes that "no one proved that speech, as it manifests itself when we speak, is entirely natural, i.e., that our vocal apparatus was designed for speaking" (de Saussure, 1959, p. 10). Yet for de Saussure this does not mean that the vocal manifestation of *langue* is fully arbitrary either. He comments on Whitney:

> Whitney, to whom language is one of several social institutions, thinks that we use the vocal apparatus as the instrument of language purely through luck, for the sake of convenience: men might just as well have chosen gestures and used visual symbols instead of acoustical symbols. Doubtless his thesis is too dogmatic; language is not similar in all respects to other social institutions. (de Saussure, 1959, p. 10)

De Saussure goes on to say that "Whitney goes too far in saying that our choice happened to fall on the vocal organs; the choice was more or less imposed by nature" (p. 10). Here the natural is opposed to the conventional as dictated by society or culture. This theme of the natural as proof for the necessity of the phonic expression of language is present in most arguments for the primacy of spoken language. Spoken language is natural, whereas written language is secondary and conventional. For de Saussure, at least for the moment, there is, as it were, more than a fortuitous nature to the fact that language manifests itself through the vocal-auditory channel. Indeed, for him there is some kind of natural bond between language and its manifestation in speech. When de Saussure (1959) concludes that "we can say that what is natural to mankind is not oral speech but the faculty of constructing a language, i.e., a system of distinct signs corresponding to distinct ideas" (p. 10), he does not eliminate sound or the vocal manifestation of language from his definition of *langue* but rather excludes the here-and-now verbal act with all its concrete implications.   He gives sound as such, the phone, a different ontological status.

Sound and Linguistic Sign

To properly appreciate this association of sound as substance with the inner form of language, we must consider de Saussure's conception of the nature of the linguistic sign, in particular those aspects that touch on the association of sound and concept.   For de Saussure the nature of the sign is twofold: It represents the union (albeit arbitrary) of a concept and a sound-image.   The two entities that unite through an associative bond in the brain exist for de Saussure on a psychological plane:

> The linguistic sign unites, not a thing and a name, but a concept and a sound-image.   The latter is not the material sound, a purely physical thing, but the psychological imprint of the sound, the impression that it makes on our senses.   The sound-image is sensory, and if I happen to call it "material," it is only in that sense, and by way of opposing it to the other term of the association, the concept, which is generally more abstract. . . .
>
> The linguistic sign is then a two-sided psychological entity . . . . The two elements [concept and sound-image] are intimately united, and each recalls the other.   (de Saussure, 1959, p. 66)

Once sound-image and concept are united they are so intimately bound that de Saussure likens them to two sides of a sheet of paper.   One side cannot be cut without cutting the other.   For de Saussure the linguistic sign is a union of concept and sound without sounding, and language is speech without speaking.   While not wishing to identify language with the concrete event of speaking nor the sign with any particular sequence of sounded sounds, nonetheless de Saussure considers the linguistic sign and language united to sound by a natural bond.   Writing as derived, as coming after, has no part in this natural bond.   It remains outside and unrelated to the inner system of language.

Yet there seems to be an ambiguity here.   In wishing to distinguish language from speech, de Saussure (1959) claims that what is natural to man is language, not speech:

> The question of the vocal apparatus obviously takes a secondary place in the problem of speech.   One definition of *articulated speech* might confirm that conclusion.   In Latin, *articulus* means a member, part, or subdivision of a sequence;

applied to speech *[language]*, articulation designates either the subdivision of a spoken chain into syllables or the subdivision of the chain of meanings into significant units . . . . Using the second definition, we can say that what is natural to mankind is not oral speech but the faculty of constructing a language, i.e., a system of distinct signs corresponding to distinct ideas. (p. 10)

Sound in such a view is removed from the realm of the actual to some ill-defined ontological realm. Just what this status might be is left unspecified. Again we have the tension detected earlier, and this tension becomes even more apparent when we consider the role of difference in language. It is difficult to see why, if the actualization of speech is to be excluded from language, there is any need to create this conscious category of sound-image or to view *langue* as speech without speaking. It seems that this is to mix the facts of the diachronic plane—the historical fact of language as manifested in speaking, what Whitney (1875) sees as a truly arbitrary choice—with the attempt to determine the nature of language qua language on the synchronic plane. This mistake is essentially the one made by what we have called the folk theory of language, where verbal behavior is taken to be language and the linguistic sign the union of the content of thought and actualized sound.

However, what allows language to come into being, what is critical to the combination of linguistic signs, is the fact of difference and not their instantiation in any particular medium. Yet, in his writing on linguistic value, de Saussure affirms the union of sound and thought to produce language. It is here that we find the metaphor of language as a sheet of paper, thought being the front and sound the back. So de Saussure concludes that, in language, thought and sound cannot be divided. But the matter does not rest here.

Having defined the nature of the linguistic sign, de Saussure moves to a full consideration of linguistic value that allows the combination of signs to produce the system we know as language. On this point he clearly states the foundational premise (1959, p. 114): "Language is a system of interdependent terms in which the value of each term results solely from the simultaneous presence of the others." This opposition or difference between terms allows for meaning and significance in the system of signs. But if it is the fact of difference that accounts for the systematicity of language as a necessary complex of signs, what role does the sound substance play in this opposition?

It would seem that here de Saussure clearly opposes himself when he states (1959, p. 120), "The idea or phonic substance that a sign contains is of less importance than the other signs that surround it." Difference conceived in this way, as a source of linguistic value, can surely be given a written manifestation. What role can substance play in the fact of difference except an auxiliary one? As de Saussure (1959, p. 118) himself says of substance, "It is impossible for sound alone, a material element, to belong to language. It is only a secondary thing, substance to be put to use. All our conventional values have the characteristic of not being confused with the tangible element which supports them."

Derrida (1976) comments on de Saussure's concept of difference:

> By definition difference is never itself a sensible plenitude. Therefore, its necessity contradicts the allegation of a naturally phonic essence of language. It contests by the same token the professed natural dependence of the graphic signifier. That is a consequence Saussure himself draws against the premises defining the internal system of language. He must now exclude the very thing which had permitted him to exclude writing . . . . Without this reduction of phonic matter, the distinction between language and speech . . . for Saussure would have no rigor. (p. 53)

In the effort to define language as a virtual system, we must set it apart from the instances of its use. To do otherwise would deprive the essential distinction between *langue* and *parole* of any meaningful force. But in insisting on the *langue–parole* distinction, we must further divorce our definition of *langue* from any essential connection (on the synchronic plane) with a particular substantive manifestation, either on the level of the linguistic sign or the level of the combination of these signs from where linguistic value is ultimately derived. De Saussure (1959, p. 122) concluded his thoughts on value and difference by stating that "language, in a manner of speaking, is a type of algebra consisting solely of complex terms" and that "*language is a form and not a substance. . . .* This truth could not be overstressed, for all the mistakes in our terminology, all our incorrect ways of naming things that pertain to language, stem from the involuntary supposition that the linguistic phenomenon must have substance."

When de Saussure comes to consider specifically the graphic manifestation of language he is clear-cut in his exclusion of writing from language. The function of writing and its exclusion from language is clearly marked when he states, "Writing, though unrelated to its inner system [*langue*], is used continually to represent language" (de Saussure, 1959, p. 23). In contrasting language and writing he states, "Language and writing are two distinct systems of signs; the second exists for the *sole purpose* [emphasis added] of representing the first. The linguistic object is not both the written and the spoken forms of words; the spoken forms alone constitute the object" (de Saussure, 1959, pp. 23–24). This statement could almost be a paraphrase of Augustine's statement on writing quoted above. Nothing new is added, and the uncritical tradition is simply handed on. We should also note the teleological justification for the existence of a written system of signs. This too becomes a commonly repeated but unexamined theme. It is difficult to know why, having exluded sound from language in at least one respect, writing is cast farther out. Its total secondarity is assured. De Saussure's conclusion on the relation of writing to language is based on two critical assumptions: (1) the acceptance of the concept that after all there is some kind of natural bond between the sound stream and language, and (2) the fact that for de Saussure speaking always precedes writing. Since writing follows speech, it must then be derived from some analysis of spoken language. Yet why derivation on the diachronic plane should imply dependence on the synchronic plane is never spelled out. Clearly this limits what one can accept as the function of writing, which de Saussure sees as the sole purpose of representing language. It is this conclusion we must question when considering in more detail the relation of writing systems to spoken language and to language itself considered from a functional viewpoint. Yet, clearly, the critical point in this conception of the secondarity of writing is the notion that language must naturally, almost of necessity, be manifested in the sound stream.

Ultimately the tension between the need to separate any definition of language *(langue)* from its substantive manifestation and the incorporation of the phonic substance into the definition of language is never fully resolved by de Saussure. From these two contradictory themes in the *Cours* flow two opposable currents in linguistic thinking. One places a primacy on phonetic manifestations as essential to any definition of language (e.g., Sapir, Bloomfield, and Jakobson) and a second argues for a substance-free definition of language (Hjelmslev and Vachek).

For linguists such as Sapir, Bloomfield, and Jakobson, the phonic substance retains its essential place in any definition of language; this relegates written manifestations to the realm of secondarity. Indeed Jakobson makes what de Saussure called "an auxiliary discipline", that is, phonetics, the fundamental foundation of linguistic science. Hence the canon of phonocentrism is reinforced and extended. These linguists repeat the mistakes of the de Saussurian analysis. Ultimately all designations of natural language as being isomorphic with only phonic manifestations are based on diachronic considerations introduced onto the synchronic plane. Further, the error of taking written manifestations as filling the primary function of representing some underlying phonic code and, therefore, as derived are repeated in an uncritical fashion. As we have stated at the outset, this formulation, the trichotomy of language, speech, and writing, takes the shape of a well-established folk theory.

An examination of some post-de Saussurian formulations of this trichotomy makes the point abundantly clear. Martinet (1962) argues that language as communication must have a "phonic shape." He goes on to state, "This means that we should reserve the term 'language' for a medium of communication which is doubly articulated and whose outward manifestation is vocal" (p. 26).

Jakobson and Halle (1956) comment on the possibility that language may have at least two equipollent manifestations, speech and writing:

> In contradistinction to the universal phenomenon of speech, phonetic or phonemic writing is an occasional, accessory code that normally implies the ability of its users to translate it into its underlying sound code, while the reverse ability, to transpose speech into letters, is a secondary and much less common faculty. Only after having mastered speech does one graduate to reading and writing . . . . There is no such thing in human society as the supplantation of the speech code by its visual replicas, but only a supplementation of this code by parasitic auxiliaries, while the speech code constantly and unalterably remains in effect. One could neither state that musical form is manifested in two variables—notes and sounds—nor that linguistic form is manifested in two equipollent substances—graphic and phonic. (pp. 16–17)

Philip Tartaglia (1972), in a comprehensive review of problems in constructing language models, states, "Linguistics, however, is primarily concerned with the spoken language. The written language is usually only a reflection of the spoken language; the structure of the written language usually can only be understood in terms of the spoken language" (p. 91). The reasoning in these statements and the assumptions lying behind them are strikingly similar. Indeed they incorporate those basic elements necessary to sustaining the phonocentric canon.

In a statement on the phonic primacy of natural language, Wardhaugh (1976) succinctly summarizes the reasons that are generally put forward to sustain this phonocentric canon:

> That language is primarily speech is a basic concept in modern linguistics. In part the concept results from reaction to a previous overemphasis on philosophical and literary matters, but mainly it results from the *readily observable facts* [emphasis added] that while speaking is universal writing is not, that the written forms of language are based on their spoken forms not vice-versa, and that in the history of both species and individual the development of speech precedes that of writing. Linguists consider the primacy of speech to be a well established fact, so the "phonic bias" of much linguistic investigation is not at all surprising. (p. 23)

While we would admit to the fact of the priority and universality of spoken language on the diachronic plane, it is difficult to see how the secondarity and exteriority of the written manifestation of language flows directly from these "facts." There would seem to be a tacit implicational chain here that is not explicitly formulated and is badly in need of careful consideration.

While this phonocentric folk theory of language has enjoyed an almost unprecedented primacy in philosophical and linguistic conceptions of natural language, it has not gone altogether unchallenged. As we have noted, there is a second current flowing from de Saussure's analysis, which opposed the necessity of phonic substance as forming a part of the definition of language. Glossematics reaches strikingly dissimilar conclusions about the place of the phonic substance and the place of substance in general in a theory of natural language. Before considering the arguments for the central place of phonic manifestations of language and reexamining the trichotomy of language, speech, and writing from a fresh perspective, we consider the theory of language advanced by Hjelmslev in respect to the relation of substance to form.

In considering what may properly be placed under the terms "language" and "nonlanguage," Hjelmslev (1963) in his *Prolegomena* begins his consideration of this topic by laying down de Saussure's distinction between substance and form as the first principle in any such determination. Hjelmslev follows de Saussure in stating that substance in and of itself can never serve as the *definiens* for language. Given the arbitrary nature of the association of substance and form in the sign, Hjelmslev sees as following from this the possibility of more than one substance being ordered to one and the same linguistic form. Indeed, he sees this as a logical necessity of the arbitrary relation between form and purport ("purport" is to be read as "substance").

Hjelmslev (1963) comments on the supremacy of phonetics as follows: "The long supremacy of conventional phonetics has, moreover, had the effect of restricting the linguists' conception even of 'natural' language in a way that is demonstrably unempirical, i.e., inappropriate because nonexhaustive. It has been supposed that the expression–substance of a spoken language must consist exclusively of 'sounds' (p. 103).

For Hjelmslev and the glossematic school, the units or entities of language are algebraic in nature (see de Saussure, 1959, p. 66, quoted above). Form and substance, or expression–substance in Hjelmslev's terminology, are related as constant to variable. What is critical is linguistic form based on difference and not a particular instantiation of the form in a given expression content. Hjelmslev (1963) writes,

Substance is thus not a necessary presupposition for linguistic form, but linguistic form is a necessary presupposition for substance. *Manifestation,* in other words, is a selection in which the linguistic form is the constant and the substance the variable; we formally define manifestation as a selection between hierarchies and between derivates of different hierarchies. The constant in a manifestation (the *manifested*) can, with . . . Saussure, be called the *form;* if the form is a language, we call it the *linguistic schema.* The variable in a manifestation (the *manifesting*) can, in agreement with Saussure, be called the *substance;* a substance that manifests a linguistic schema we call a *linguistic usage.* (p. 106)

From a formal and axiomatic point of view, in order to maintain the distinction between *langue* and *parole,* between language and the facts of speaking, the distinction between form and substance must be maintained. The inevitable conclusion is that there is no necessity to consider phonic substance as either primary or privileged in the definition of language. Indeed, as Hjelmslev concludes, (1963, p. 109), "Language may be defined as a paradigmatic whose paradigms are manifested by all purports [substance]."

Hjelmslev and the glossematic school open the possibility for a fresh consideration of the question of the relation of various substantive manifestations to linguistic form. In breaking the hold of an exclusively phonocentric definition of language, the premises of this view and the resulting definition of natural language may be critically reexamined. However, before undertaking such an examination, we briefly survey conceptions of language that have been and are to be found in psychological approaches to the question.

Psychological Definitions of Language

Two major differences can be observed between linguistic or philosophical treatments and psychological treatments of language. While linguistics or the philosophy of language is primarily concerned with explicating the structural principles of language as virtual system, psychology has as its focus language and speech as instantiated behavioral variables. Despite the enterprise of explicating underlying competence, the primary data of psychological considerations are facts of *parole.* Psychology is concerned with actual instances of language in use and is less concerned with explicating the nature of language as virtual system. While it is always somewhat dubious to make such sweeping generalizations, it is broadly true that where linguistics and philosophy deal primarily with research into questions of *langue* as system, psychology primarily concerns itself with aspects of *parole.* The terms *langue* and *parole* should not be read as equivalents for competence and performance. The distinction being drawn here is that by and large psychology begins its analysis of language with a concern for language as behavior and not language as entity. In practice, however, this distinction is often blurred. But by and large the concerns of linguistics proper are not central concerns of the psychology of language.

A further difference arises when we attempt to survey approaches to language in psychology. Given the number of subdisciplines of psychology and their specialized research, it is difficult to characterize a unified treatment of language. Various subdisciplines characterize differently and emphasize diverse aspects of what we might wish to think of as a unified phenomenal entity. Neuropsychology may have as its focus the correlation of gross overt verbal behavior with neural structures, while genetic psychology focuses on distinctions of grammar and lexicon in trying to characterize the process of ontogenesis.

However diverse the particular orientations toward language within the subdivisions of psychology, certain tentative generalizations do emerge. Often the distinction between language and speech, at least within mainstream American psychology, is collapsed, and the terms are used somewhat interchangeably. It is also generally true that whether the term *language* or *speech* is employed, the understanding is generally of a verbal manifestation. Careful distinctions between oral and written language are in general not made unless research is particularly focused on such topics, as is sometimes done in neurolinguistic research on agraphia. Certainly developmental psycholinguistics, which takes as its focus the ontogenesis of language, has often blurred or ignored such distinctions. Surveying a number of textbooks and studies, we rarely found any attempt at actual definition of language as an entity. Psychology has largely imported its definitions of language as system from linguistic speculations on the subject. With this takeover has come the importation of the phonocentrism of which we have spoken. There is one notable early exception. Vygotsky recognized in his work on the mental development of children that the acquisition of written language is not simply the acquisition of a notational variant of spoken language. He comments (1978) on the attitude of psychology toward writing:

> One-sided enthusiasm for the mechanics of writing has had an impact not only on the practice of teaching but on the theoretical statement of the problem as well. Up to this point psychology has conceived of writing as a complicated motor skill. It has paid remarkably little attention to the question of written language as such, that is, a particular system of symbols and signs whose mastery heralds a critical turning point in entire cultural development of the child. (p. 106)

On the process of the acquisition of written language, Vygotsky (1978) argues that there is a gradual differentiation of written language from spoken language to the point where, for the child, writing assumes the status of a truly independent system.

> A feature of this system is that it is second-order symbolism, which gradually becomes direct symbolism. This means that written language consists of a system of signs that designate the sounds and words of spoken language, which, in turn, are

signs for real entities and relations. Gradually this intermediate link, spoken
language, disappears, and written language is converted into a system of signs that
directly symbolize the entities and relations between them. (p. 106)

There is a good deal of evidence to support such a view from work in both
neuropsychology and genetic psychology. But Vygotsky's position is
certainly not typical of the attitude of psychology toward written language. By and large psychology adopts the prevailing phonocentric view
of linguistics.

A major attempt at defining language qua language within a psychological framework has been undertaken by Osgood (1979). According to
Osgood, for any communicative system to be designated a language it
must have "non-random recurrent signals in *some channel* [emphasis
added], producible by the same organisms that receive them, which dis-
play non-random pragmatic, semantic, and syntactic dependencies that
are combinatorially productive" (p. 20). Clearly, written language fits
these criteria. However, for Osgood such criteria admit far too much
communicative behavior as language, and so to distinguish human language from language in general, he proposes further criteria: "For something that is a language [by the above-mentioned criteria] to be called a
human language, it must have the following structural characteristics: it
must . . . involve use of the vocal-auditory channel" (p. 20). Osgood
goes on to comment on this particular criterion in the following terms:
"*All natural human languages use vocalization for production and au-
dition for reception.* This of course refers to the primary communication
system for humans, there being many other derived systems—the most
general being writing . . . but also drum signals, smoke signals, and
Morse Code" (p. 20).

In an effort to uniquely define human language, Osgood falls prey to
the phonocentric canon: He excludes the signing of deaf-mutes as a natural language because no use is made of the vocal–auditory channel.
Clearly by implication we would likewise have to argue that aphasics who
have lost, for example, the capacity for speech are deprived of natural
language. The absurdity of this invocation of the vocal–auditory criterion can nowhere be better appreciated than in these remarks in which all
but vocal–auditory manifestations of language are condemned to the
limbo of non-naturalness. According to Osgood, they may indeed be
language but certainly not natural human language.

Osgood is in agreement with others such as Glucksberg and Danks
(1975, p. 23), who define language as "that verbal communication system
developed and used by humans," and Sebeok (1977, p. 1056), who states
that "the subject matter of linguistics is confined to verbal messages
only." All of these illustrate that use of a particular substantive manifesta-

tion to define human language qua human language eliminates vast numbers of human beings from having language on the basis of a rather arbitrary analytic criterion.

In attempting to define language and human communicative behaviors from a biological perspective, Dingwall (1979) comments on such phonocentric definitions of language in the following terms:

> Such definitions are inappropriate for interdisciplinary fields such as psycholinguistics and neurolinguistics which study a behavior rather than an entity. . . . Human communicative behavior is not an entity such as language which one either possesses in its entirety or not at all. Rather, it is a mosaic of structures, skills and knowledge that does not develop in children as a whole, does not disappear in dysphasics as a whole, and undoubtedly did not evolve as a whole. (pp. 53–54)

While language behavior clearly involves a wider scope of research interests than the attempt to define *langue* as virtual system, in none of the definitions of language that posit output modality as an essential defining criterion for language has any convincing independent reason been offered as to why such a criterion should be maintained. Clearly the appeal is to the universality of vocal-auditory manifestation as a behavioral observation about language in use. But why include such behavioral observation in a definition of an abstract entity when other behavioral facts, such as pragmatic constraints, have been and continue to be ignored? There seems little justification for such picking and choosing. Indeed, the appeal to actual speech behavior is a uniquely uncritical one in that the mere observation of language as spoken is never examined in light of other behavioral facts of language use nor is the verbal behavior very carefully scrutinized.

Any account of speech behavior within developmental, neurophysiological, or other branches of psychology must account for performance in the vocal-auditory domain as it relates to the underlying system of *langue,* but not as the exclusive behavioral manifestation of this *langue.* Also present and of equal research interest should be graphic and gestural manifestations. Conclusions about the relation of oral and written language can ultimately only come from careful empirical work on lines of ontogenesis followed by oral and written language.

The adjective *natural* is often applied to vocal-auditory manifestations of language. But as Dingwall has observed, this universality is perhaps at best a spurious or ideal conception. In psychological terms, holding to such a strict notion of universality often leads to absurd conclusions such as that the deaf or dysphasics have no language. At best the observation of the universality or naturalness of vocal-auditory manifestations should lead us to privilege such a manifestation of language from a diachronic, evolutionary, or ontogenetic perspective but not at the expense of other manifestations. The phone as instantiated language is at best *primus inter parens*. The term *derived,* which can be used with respect to the written manifestation in certain ontogenetic or diachronic accounts of language (see below), must be carefully defined and should in no case imply a secondarity or complete systematic dependence on some primary manifestation of language.

In summary, then, while properly addressed to language as behavior and not language as entity, psychology, as Dingwall points out, has too often accepted phonocentric definitions of language. This, when confounded with psychology's primary concern with language as behavior in vocal-auditory sense modalities, has led to a general conflation of the terms *language* and *speech*.

Toward A Substance-Neutral Definition of Language

We have argued that, by and large, attempts at defining and explaining language qua language have tended to incorporate and accord a central place to sound, the vocal-auditory dimension of speech events. This tendency has formed part of the conceptual baggage of language theorizing in Western intellectual thought since classical times. We have now to ask to what extent, if any, it is possible or desirable to arrive at a substance-neutral definition of language qua language. If we wish to characterize the notion of form, difference, and value as *langue* in de Saussure's sense, then clearly a substance-neutral characterization is desirable and necessary. The more we can reduce the necessity of accounting for the facts of any actual speech situation or behavior in a theory of *langue,* the closer we approach the description of *langue* as a type of algebra, as pure form. De Saussure (1959, p. 122) saw clearly the dangers of the "supposition that the linguistic phenomenon must have substance." If for a theory of *langue* a substance-free or substance-neutral characterization of language is desirable, is such an enterprise possible? There have been some notable attempts to arrive at a substance-neutral definition of language within linguistics. In particular, Hjelmslev and others of the glossematic school take the de Saussurian injunction about language as form to its ultimate conclusion and indeed demonstrate that any particular substance need not be accounted for by a theory of *langue* as a system of form and difference. Our only purpose in insisting on a substance-neutral characterization of *langue* is to clear away the burden of phonocentrism and the limitations this has imposed on functional considerations of the role of phonic and graphic manifestations of language in actual use. What is important to recognize is simply that any given substance need not be a defining and limiting characteristic of *langue*. By this we mean that *langue* as underlying system can be manifested in a number of substances — acoustic, graphic, or visual. Our purpose is not to arrive at such a characterization of language but simply to point to its possibility and necessity in order to consider from an unencumbered perspective the question of phonic and graphic manifestations of language.

While we argue that *langue* must and can be characterized irrespective of its substantive manifestation, what of *parole,* the actual behavioral manifestation of *langue?* When we consider *parole,* actual language behavior, questions about the instantiated use of a given substance become crucial. So if we wish to study speech production, we must account for the actual empirical dynamic aspects of the vocal-auditory apparatus. If we are engaged in questions regarding actual language acquisition in a population of normal subjects, we must again account for the acquisition and use of speech. But as we have argued earlier, such behavioral considerations do not privilege any particular behavioral manifestation over another. Questions of actual language behavior must take into account in their characterizations of such behavior the substantive manifestation of language, but not at the expense of generalizing about behavior in one manifestation to another, nor at the expense of making any particular manifestation the universal standard for all others. Following chapters demonstrate that various substantive manifestations of language stand in complex marking relations with each other and are correlated with specific facts of use in social praxis and also correlated with particular organizational patterns based on such use and social praxis. The principles that underlie the research on *langue* and *parole* constitute distinct areas of analysis, and it is incorrect to confuse the two as is done when substance becomes a defining criterion of *langue,* an abstract entity.

In addition to Hjelmslev and the glossematic school, the Prague Linguistic Circle formed a notable exception in the treatment of written language within the general discipline of linguistics. As early as the late 1930s, Prague linguists recognized the independence of the written norm as a proper concern of theoretical linguistics.

In two papers that appeared in 1932, Artymovyc asserts that written language enjoys a status independent of the spoken language. Havranek, in an article published in 1929, considers the relation of writing to speech and its influence on certain aspects of language as spoken. The idea of considering written and spoken manifestations as independent instantiations of *langue* is clearly in line with and follows from the principle of a functional-structural approach to language advanced by the Prague School

(Vachek, 1966). It is perhaps somewhat ironic that the Prague School, which was largely responsible for major advances in the field of phonology with such figures as Trubetzkoy and Jakobson, should also have produced Vachek, one of the foremost linguists to attack the question of written language. In 1959, and in a number of earlier papers, Vachek produced a seminal thesis on the place and functional role of written language within the framework of other functional language norms.

Prague linguists view language *(langue)* as a system, in fact a system of systems. Language is in particular a functional system. The Prague group stated in their manifesto to the first Congress of Slavic Philologists (1929/1978, p. 1), "From the functional standpoint, language is a system of instrumental means of expression. No language phenomenon can be understood without considering the system of which it is a part."

This functional principle in conjunction with the principle of differentiation of various language manifestations, both the functional ends and linguistic means of such manifestations, leads the Prague School to consider the written manifestation of language as a legitimate and independent language phenomenon fulfilling its own particular role in diachronic and synchronic terms. Mathesius (1975), the seminal figure in the formation of the Prague group, writes:

> At present, however, it is admitted that a written utterance is a form of language *sui generis* just as a spoken utterance, each having its specific function . . . . Although the written utterance has developed on the basis of speech, it is not a mere mechanical projection of the latter. In cultural languages written language has attained considerable autonomy with respect to speech. (p. 15)

Language as spoken and language as written are equivalent systems with respect to language as underlying system, each fulfilling specific communicative and social functions within a given language community.

While the glossematic school and the Prague group both recognize that spoken language and written language exist as at least potentially independent language norms, Prague functional approaches (unlike the glossematic position, which argues that each may exist independently of each other) admit that the two language norms stand in relation to each other both diachronically and synchronically. Spoken language is qualified as the unmarked member of an opposition and written language as the marked member. Both diachronically and synchronically the two norms share certain structural correspondences. We explore this structural correspondence and its consequences from a psychological perspective at a later point.

The unique contribution of the Prague group's analysis of the substantive manifestation of language lies not only in their recognition of written language as other than a mere reflection of spoken language but in the further recognition that the two language norms fulfill very different functions within any given communicative act. It is this functional dimension and the further principle that various functions have nontrivial structural consequences that permit us to develop a balanced approach to the question of the roles played by these norms in the exfoliation of cognitive structures during the course of development.

Both the glossematic and the Prague approaches illustrate that while a phonocentric conception of language has dominated work in structural linguistics and to a degree work on the psychology of language, it has not gone unchallenged. The work of both of these groups demonstrates that the phonocentric conception is not as fundamental to a description of language as an abstract entity as the great burden of work in descriptive linguistics would seem to suggest. The work of the Prague group, Hjelmslev, and others, leaves open the possibility of a substance-neutral approach to defining language as form in structural linguistics. The Prague group's notion of the mutually constitutive roles of structure and function in defining language also opens the possibility for a psychology of language and language manifestation in actual communicative behavior that is founded more solidly on empirical considerations of the use of language without excluding on a priori grounds what might be relevant facts.

In Chapter 2 we undertake to reevaluate the question of the relation of oral and written manifestations of language to *langue* and their relation to each other. We consider the structural, neurological, functional, and behavioral evidence from diachronic, synchronic, and ontogenetic perspectives in order to determine if the phonocentric canon may be maintained or if in fact oral and written manifestations constitute equipollent but distinct language manifestations.

2

Relation of Oral and Written Language

Introduction

In Chapter 1 we proposed that in defining the relation between oral and written language manifestations much of Western linguistic analysis has accepted the phonocentric canon in largely unquestioned fashion. This bias in favor of the primacy of speech as the natural manifestation of language reduces written and other non – vocal-auditory manifestations to a secondary status. Indeed, some have argued that only vocal-auditory manifestations can enjoy the status of natural human language.

While we have pointed to attempts within linguistic treatments of language to reassess the nature of the relation of various substantive language manifestations to an underlying system of language, we here consider in detail the structural and psychological basis of the relation between vocal-auditory and graphic instantiations of language in order to lay down a more considered basis for an account of the functional role of oral and written language in psychological development. The trichotomy of language, speech, and writing has been characterized as filling particular slots in a structural configuration portrayed by the diagram below:

$$\text{Langue} \longrightarrow \text{Speech} \longleftrightarrow \text{Writing}$$

Writing, in such a linear configuration, refers to or symbolizes only speech that in turn mediates and relates writing to the system *langue.* Writing stands in direct relation only to speech, of which it is a concretization.

This view of the relation of writing to language and writing to speech is based on a set of arguments that fall into three classes: phylogenetic–ontogenetic, structural, or neuropsychological. We take up each of these arguments in turn. In Chapter 3 we consider the functional basis for arriving at an explication of the relation of writing to speech and language. Only by introducing functional considerations can we arrive at a valid disposition of writing, speech, and language in any structural configuration.

In these discussions we reserve the term *language* for what de Saussure understood by the term *langue,* that is, language as a virtual system of form. By speech and writing or the terms *spoken language* and *written language* is understood the actual manifestation of language in a phonic or graphic substance respectively.

Phylogenesis and the Priority of Speech over Writing

Arguments based on the phylogenetic priority of speaking argue that speech is prior to the appearance of writing and further that it is universal to the species whereas writing is not. The conclusion is then drawn that writing or written language is derived from and secondary to speech. Insofar as we can be aware of the facts of the origin of language, we cannot deny the facts or logic of this argument. However, the argument is not allowed to rest here. The further interpretation is made that since writing is derived from speech, which is primary, prior, and universal, writing is therefore artificial and nonnatural and does not directly tap language as underlying form but represents only speech. On the face of it, this further conclusion is simply unwarranted. If on the basis of phylogenetic priority we were to conclude that all later developments in a given system were somehow artificial and nonnatural with respect to earlier developments, we would logically have to conclude that the neocortex in man, because phylogenetically later, is in some sense nonnatural with respect to the brain stem, which precedes it phylogenetically. The same can be said for the conclusions of nonnaturalness based on arguments of species universality. If we were to allow the logic of such conclusions, we would have to argue that many of the species accomplishments are clearly not natural because not species-universal. A case in point might well be Western mathematics, say algebra. Certainly such a system is not species universal, but one can hardly argue that it is not natural.

Clearly the difficulty lies in how we are to construe the use of the word *natural*. The arguments based on naturalness certainly do not use this term in any rigorously defined fashion. Careful examination of these arguments indicates that what is natural is simply that which is manifested in a species-universal fashion. But such a criterion does not hold up under scrutiny. Must, for example, a system or skill actually be manifested in a species-universal pattern to be natural? Or may it only be potentially universally manifestable by the members of a species to be natural? If we accept language as a cultural achievement of the species as well as a biological one, what is natural becomes even more blurred. Any particular set of cultural forms may be manifested by a given society or culture but not by all cultures. Nonetheless, we would hardly argue that such culture-specific manifestations are unnatural when we consider particular functional needs that may call forth particular manifestations of a given pattern, skill, or practice. We must admit that not all groups of the species exhibit the same functional needs at any given time and do not, therefore, exhibit universal patterns, skills, or practices. But they may, should the functional needs of the group demand similar solutions.

Language code is not a static system, it is a dynamic entity. As a cultural creation it has evolved and not sprung full grown for all time, as it were, from the head of Zeus. It continues to evolve, and written language in this respect is the development of a latent structural possibility of the system of language code. Clearly the spoken manifestation of the language code is phylogenetically prior to the written manifestation. But this fact does not logically imply that one manifestation is natural and one not natural. Phylogenetic priority is simply neutral with respect to the question of what is a natural manifestation of language code, particularly if language is seen in part at least as a cultural product. However, if we move to the biological plane, what constitutes natural in the arguments about the naturalness of spoken manifestations of the language code takes on a different shade of interpretation. On the biological plane, arguments of naturalness imply that what is natural is what is achieved by the species outside of the context of culture. Spoken language in this view is seen as natural because it is not dependent on cultural formation nor in some sense a cultural transmission. The typical argument made is that whereas the acquisition of written language is the subject of conscious instruction, spoken language is acquired without such deliberate instruction. When we consider the roles of instruction and development in the acquisition process, we consider this argument in greater detail. But clearly even spoken-language acquisition takes place in social-cultural settings; it has never been demonstrated that spoken language can be acquired without and outside of a social-cultural setting. Language in man may indeed have a mammalian–neurological base, but it is only realized when an enabling cultural setting is present.

To be sure, even admitting this dichotomy of biology and culture may be an analytical fiction. To draw such a distinction implies a particular model of man and a particular model of culture as something overlaid but separable from the biological organism. In such a conception the cultural realm is in a sense not natural. What is natural is biology. It is in this context, leaving aside the question of the merits of such a view of biology and culture, that the spoken manifestation of language is seen as natural and the written manifestation as nonnatural. Writing as a product of culture overlays speaking, which in such a biological view is an innate capacity of the organism. Here, arguments about phylogenetic priority achieve what force they might have primarily from the biological view of natural man. Such a conception must clearly see language as a biological fact and not a cultural fact in any primary sense. What is cultural about language is laid over the biological capacity, which in the position of someone like Chomsky is part of the genetic code, presumably for which there exists a particular polypeptide chain.

To view language as such a purely biological achievement is unacceptable, and further, to accept the strict dichotomy on which such a view rests does not sustain the scrutiny of current anthropological, psychological, and biological criticism.

Geertz (1973a) argues quite convincingly that biology and culture must be viewed as mutually constitutive processes. He argues that if hominid phylogeny is spread out along an appropriate time scale we gain a different perspective on the nature of evolutionary processes since the appearance of australopithecus. This allows us to see that in fact cultural accumulation was far advanced well before organic development ceased and in fact that this accumulation played an active role in organic development as opposed to simply being the result of such development. In this sense culture is not an epigenesis of biological evolution but plays a formative role in organic development itself. Geertz (1973a) goes on to comment that cultural accumulations

> must have acted to shift selection pressures so as to favor the rapid growth of the forebrain as, in all likelihood, did the advances in social organization, communication, and moral regulation which there is reason to believe also occurred during this period of overlap between cultural and biological change. *Nor were such nervous system changes merely quantitative; alterations in the interconnections among neurons and their manner of functioning may have been of even greater importance than the simple increase in their number* [emphasis added]. Details aside,

however—and the bulk of them remain to be determined—the point is that the innate, generic constitution of modern man (what used, in a simpler day, to be called "human nature") now appears to be both a cultural and a biological product in that "it is probably more correct to think of much of our structure as a result of culture rather than to think of men anatomically like ourselves slowly discovering culture" [Washburn 1959]. (pp. 66–67)

Geertz sums up this interactionist position on biology and culture when he states:

> The fact that these distinctive features of humanity emerged together in complex interaction with one another rather than serially as for so long supposed is of exceptional importance in the interpretation of human mentality, because it suggests that man's nervous system does not merely enable him to acquire culture, it positively demands that he do so if it is going to function at all. Rather than culture acting only to supplement, develop, and extend organically based capacities logically and genetically prior to it, it would seem to be an ingredient to those capacities themselves. A cultureless human being would probably turn out to be not an intrinsically talented though unfulfilled ape, but a wholly mindless and consequently unworkable monstrosity. (Geertz, 1973a, pp. 67–68)

With the rejection of the dualism of the biology–culture split, arguments about the naturalness of speaking and nonnaturalness of writing as a cultural product evaporate. Man's capacity for symbol use does not stop with speech but continues to evolve within the matrix of culture and is never divorced from his "organically based capacities," in Geertz's terminology.

On the relation between the biological and the cultural, Luria (1973), writing about the functional organization of the neural system, argues that perception, speech, thinking, and other functions are not examples of isolated faculties that are the direct function of initial cell groups having locations in specific areas of the brain. Rather,

> The fact that they were all formed in the course of long historical development, that they are social in their origin and complex and hierarchical in their structure and that they are all based on a complex system of methods and means . . . implies that the fundamental forms of conscious activity must be considered as complex functional systems. (Luria, 1973, pp. 29–30)

The tendency to regard such functions as isolated organizations is recorded in Fodor's (1982) analysis in *The Modularity of Mind.* In contrast to Fodor's formulation, Luria argues for the importance of the mediating role of such external social-cultural practices as sign use for the formation of functional connections between neural systems. He states that

> it becomes perfectly clear that these external aids or historically formed devices are *essential elements* in the *establishment of functional connections between individual parts of the brain,* and that by their aid, areas of the brain which previously

were independent become the *components of a single functional system.* This can be expressed more vividly by saying that historically formed measures for the organization of human behavior tie new knots in the activity of man's brain, and it is the presence of these functional knots, or, as some people call them, 'new functional organs' (Leontiev, 1959), that is one of the most important features distinguishing the functional organization of the human brain from an animal's brain. (Luria, 1973, p. 31; emphasis added)

Insofar as such nonorganic factors are constitutive of functional neural organization and since the process of development continues, there is little reason to accept arguments about the phylogenetic priority of speech over writing as leading to the conclusion that writing is not a natural expression of man's capacity for language. The later appearance in time of graphic manifestations of language tells us little of the actual functional or neural relationship of spoken and written language.

Ontogenesis and the Priority of Speech over Writing

Closely related to these priority arguments on the phylogenetic plane are similar arguments advanced on the ontogenetic plane. They are based on assumptions similar to those underlying arguments on the phylogenetic plane, namely that there is a natural as distinct from a learned or social-cultural order. Insofar as speech comes naturally to man and writing must be consciously taught, it is concluded that speech is natural and writing is simply a nonnatural, learned or a cultural overlay. Again this dichotomy between innate potential and learned capacity is simply not maintainable under any rigorous analysis. Working in a neuropsychological and neurolinguistic framework on the development of uniquely human abilities such as language, Milner (1976) comments that neural and behavioral data indicate

1. At birth man is functionally a decorticate mammal; his humanity is present entirely as potential.
2. The development and expression of that potential is dependent upon the growing normal individual human organism's suitably enabling transactions with its environment. (p. 99)

Ontogenesis requires, whether for speech or writing, a social context, a suitable environment. That the capacity for a written manifestation of language normally but not always occurs later in development does not render it necessarily either secondary or nonnatural. The acquisition of spoken language does not happen spontaneously nor easily, as efforts at understanding this process of acquisition have proven. Temporal priority does not confer on any developmental milestone a particular claim to naturalness. Spoken manifestations of language are clearly prior to written manifestations of language both phylogenetically and ontogenetically. But this fact itself tells us little of the nature of the diachronic or synchronic relation of these manifestations either to each other or to the system of language code.

The phylogenetic and ontogenetic priority of one particular manifestation of the language code does, however, make the question of the nature of the relation of oral and graphic manifestations to each other and to the language code nontrivial. This question can be put in the following way: Is the written manifestation of language related to the underlying language code only through the oral manifestation of language? And further: To what extent do oral and written manifestations of language constitute independent, isomorphic, or equipollent instances of language code, and to what extent does oral and written language acquisition constitute independent, isomorphic, or parallel domains of linguistic development? Arguments about temporal priority are insufficient to answer these questions. In order to come to some reasonable conclusions, structural, functional, neurological, and developmental considerations must be taken into account.

Structural Models of the Relation of Oral and Written Language

Three accounts of the relation of language, speech, and writing to one another have been posited. As we have seen, the traditional phonocentric canon maintains that speech is the natural instantiation of the language code. The most extreme view in this framework sees the oral manifestation of language as a necessary part of the definition of the language code itself. Within this view, written manifestations of language are only graphic representations of speech and derive meaning only through mediation by the phonological component of language. Written manifestations of language do not directly access the language code but only mimic the spoken manifestation of language. In contrast to such phonocentric conceptions, and lying at the other extreme, is the position that the language code can be manifested equally by various substantive manifestations. Such a position maintains that oral and written manifestations exist independently of each other and that both are direct instantiations of the underlying language code. This position has received its clearest and most extensive treatment in the work of the glossematic school and especially in the writings of Hjelmslev (1963) discussed in Chapter 1 of this volume. Uldall, a prominent exponent of the glossematic school, writes that "The system of speech and the system of writing are . . . only two realizations out of an infinite number of possible systems, of which no one can be said to be more fundamental than any other" (Uldall, 1944, p. 16). An earlier version of such a thesis of the independence of the two manifestations, spoken and written, was put forth by Artymovyc (1932a, 1932b).

These positions both rest ultimately and solely on structural-analytic considerations and are argued on this basis. However, these positions do not exhaust the possibilities for the ways in which language, speech, and writing may be related. Somewhat intermediate between the two views lies the position adopted by members of the Prague Circle, which we have referred to earlier. The clearest accounts of the Prague conception, which may be termed a functional-structural view, are to be found in the writings of Vachek (1942, 1948, 1959, 1965). This functional-structural position sees oral and written manifestations of language as structurally related but functionally fulfilling independent but complementary ends within the linguistic life of a given community. Oral and written manifestations of language exist in complementary distribution with each other, the written manifestation appearing as the marked member of the opposition. A further consequence of this functional-structural approach leads to the view that oral and written manifestations of language represent systematic and normative options within the language code. We discuss more fully this systematic and normative quality of the two manifestations later. At present we only point out that this functional approach requires that when we consider the nature of the relation of the manifestations of the language code to each other and to the code itself we must account for the actual use of these manifestations if we are to reach any sound conclusions.

We can roughly characterize these three approaches in the following figure:

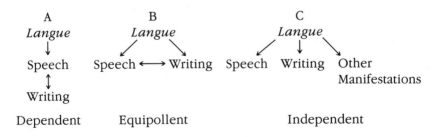

In this figure we characterize A as *dependent:* written language accesses the underlying language system only through the spoken language. B is termed *equipollent:* spoken and written language mutually access the underlying code independently and are themselves linked by systematic translation rules. C we term *independent:* various language manifestations access the underlying code independently and make no reference to each other.

C (independent) fairly represents the position of some glossematic writers, where oral and written manifestations are independent of each other. While this may be true for some members of a language community from a synchronic point of view and for some nonphonological scripts, it can hardly be sustained for the relation of oral and written manifestations of language in the case of phonetic scripts and especially from a diachronic point of view. Historical scholarship on the origin and development of the major phonetic scripts (Haas, 1976; Pulgram, 1976) seems to agree that such scripts were not developed independently of the spoken language. In these cases we can speak of a "derived" script, to use a term employed by Haas. Haas (1976a) defines derived and underived scripts according to whether there is a regular correspondence between graphemes and phonemes. If there is such a regular correspondence, the script is said to be derived. If no such correspondence holds, the script is underived.

It is in this limited sense that we can speak of the relation of written to oral manifestations of language as being derived. Often it is on this basis, though unexpressed, that arguments about the secondary character of writing are advanced and the claim made that written manifestations of language, to be meaningful, must be mediated by oral language. Further evidence for this position is drawn from the ontogenetic realm. It is argued that written forms are derived from oral forms. The child first has an oral language and from this, through formal schooling in the case of industrialized societies in the West, derives the written language. Haas (1976a) answers such speculation and arguments as follows:

> It has been said that only an underived pictographic script can be used to express meanings *directly,* while derived writing cannot convey its meaning except *indirectly,* i.e., *via* the spoken units to which the graphemes 'refer.' This fallacy seems to have its root in a confusion between (i) *acquisition* of it by learners, and (ii) the *use* of an established script in communication. The designer of a derived script, or the learner of it, may quite legitimately be said to be referring to the spoken units to which he assigns the graphic characters; and these characters may then be said to have 'referential meaning.' But these references or meanings do not enter the structures, and do not contribute to the meanings, of the utterances, spoken or written; a message in either medium is intelligible independently of the other. (pp. 145–146)

Haas speaks of the nature of the relation of spoken and written forms of language as one of "translation." The forms in either medium are in this

sense neither completely independent nor are they necessarily isomorphic. We consider at a later point the neurological foundation for arguments based on this idea of translation between the two media. Haas
(1976a) expands his notion of translation and the idea that correspondences between units do not enter structures when he gives the following
example in which he makes a distinction between intra- and interlingual
relations:

> The relations that characterize the word *cat,* spoken or written, as a *semantic
> constituent* of sentences, spoken or written, are *intra*-lingual (intrasystemic) rela-
> tions; *cat* has a referential meaning that contributes to the meanings of the utter-
> ances in which it occurs. But the references of ⟨c⟩ to [k], ⟨a⟩ to [ae], etc., are
> *inter*lingual (intersystemic); they do not contribute to the meanings of the sen-
> tences in which either the sounds [k], [ae], etc., or the graphemes ⟨c⟩, ⟨a⟩, etc.,
> occur. For the user of an established script, the designer's references are trans-
> formed into rules of optional translations. (p. 146)

In pointing up this distinction between intralingual and interlingual relations in oral and written manifestations of language, Haas clears the way
for a proper assessment of the nature of the relation between various
manifestations of the language code for the members of a given linguistic
community. In further discussing the relation of oral and written manifestations, we confine ourselves to the synchronic plane, that of an established script already in place in a fully expanded linguistic system. Such a
consideration of the nature of the relation is independent of the derivation
of a given script historically and even, for the moment, the acquisition of a
script ontogenetically. We return to the ontogenetic question later.

Of the three configurations of the relation of writing and speech proposed, A (dependent) and B (equipollent) appear to be the most plausible models of the actual relation of these systems in English and indeed in
the vast majority of script-speech systems of language. While C (independent) is a logical possibility, as with an underived script in Haas' use of this
term, we limit our consideration to those models that are appropriate to
derived systems, as these prove to be the most problematical. The figures
for A (dependent) and B (equipollent) instantiate two distinct possibilities: either written manifestations of language only derive meaningfulness through the mediation of the phonological medium, the case in the
dependent model; or they are meaningful, in a communicative and semantic sense, independently of the phonological medium but enjoy a
correspondence with this medium that may be called into play for purposes such as the acquisition of the written medium, as in the equipollent
model.

We have spoken of the correspondence of units in the written medium
to units in the oral medium. But this is not to imply that this correspon-

dence is one-to-one. As the many attempts at spelling reform in English have argued, the case is precisely the opposite (Stubbs, 1980; Venezky, 1970). In English the correspondence between graphemes and phonemes is many-to-many (Haas, 1970). There are two ways of characterizing this correspondence of graphemes to phonemes: As reference or as translation.

Model A implies that the graphemes in the written manifestation reference, that is, refer to, the phonemes in the oral manifestation. This is to say, graphemes are only signs of signs. On such a view the many-to-many correspondence of graphemes to phonemes is highly problematic, and on the face of it the calls for spelling reform seem plausible. Yet it is the very characterization (that graphemes refer to phonemes and are only signs of signs) that allows for the plausibility of such arguments. For a very full treatment of this referential position see the discussion in McIntosh (1961) and Hall (1964, 1966).

On the face of it this referential hypothesis poses great difficulties. If a grapheme ⟨c⟩ is said to refer to the phoneme [c] of *cider* and to [k] of *cat,* the phoneme sequence *cat* or *cider* would carry, in Haas' terms, a double semantic load. It would simultaneously refer to the corresponding phoneme sequence and to some piece of extralinguistic reality. This raises the very pertinent question of whether the grapheme sequence ever really refers to extralinguistic reality directly or only via the mediation of the corresponding phoneme sequence. The way out of this double semantic load question is to simply assert that in no sense does the grapheme sequence refer directly to extralinguistic reality. However, evidence from reading studies (Coltheart, 1980; Henderson, 1982) and neurolinguistic assessments of brain-damaged patients (Hecaen & Albert, 1978; Patterson, 1982) clearly demonstrates that, in the absence of phonological mediation, sequences of graphemes can refer directly to extralinguistic reality. We consider this evidence below. On the assumption that it can be demonstrated that sequences of graphemes can reference extralinguistic reality directly, this would lead us to hold suspect the referential view of grapheme–phoneme correspondence. Haas (1970) presents a critique of the referential position and the most lucid discussion of the nature of grapheme-phoneme correspondence to be found in the literature. We can summarize the points he makes here:

1. Correspondence between graphemes and phonemes is symmetric. Haas argues that representation in the context of grapheme-phoneme correspondence is symmetric. If graphemes represent phonemes, then logically phonemes simultaneously represent graphemes. One cannot argue from such a proposition that it follows that graphemes or grapheme

combinations cannot refer directly to extralinguistic reality. To be sure, to say that a grapheme refers to a given phoneme is a curious use of the word *refer*. Ordinarily we do not understand by the term *refer* such a symmetric relation. The sign refers to a segment of extralinguistic reality, but we do not say that a segment of extralinguistic reality refers to a linguistic sign.

2. If we construe graphemes as signs that stand for phonemes, how do they contribute to the meanings of the expressions composed of them? The answer is simply they do not. Phonemes are not objects of which graphemes are the representamina. Rather, graphemes are interpretants of phonemes, to use Peirce's (1931 – 1958) terminology. But then on the other hand, phonemes are the interpretants of graphemes. The relation is again symmetric. The relation between phonemes and graphemes is one of correspondence between type and type and not that of object to representamen. We cannot say in any fully legitimate sense that the correspondence between phonemes and graphemes instantiates a proper sign relation. They are mere recordings in another medium. In such a view we would as likely argue that the acoustic print of a spoken utterance is a sign standing for the spoken utterance. Whereas the acoustic print has no semantic value of its own, sequences of graphemes clearly do, and this independently of any corresponding phonetic realization. If graphemes were mere recordings of phonemes in another medium, we would have to construe the nature of their relations as score to actual musical sounds. On this point Haas (1970) states,

> Here we might note, lies an important difference between language and the 'language' of music. The 'meaning' of a piece of music is obviously motivated by its component sounds. The bond between musical meaning and musical expression is not arbitrary; the auditory medium cannot be replaced without losing the 'message'. Consequently, a musical score cannot convey its meaning directly but can convey it only *via* an actual or imagined musical performance. Nor can those who are born deaf learn to understand music by reading its score, as they can learn to understand talk by reading its text. (p. 13)

Letters do not stand for the sounds of speech as printed notes stand for the sounds of music. The problem of the double semantic load remains.

3. Graphemes stand in combination with each other as phonemes stand in combination with each other. The combination of graphemes is dissimilar to the combination of morphemes in a sentence. Haas concludes that to apply the term *refer to* to the correspondence of graphemes to phonemes is inappropriate. It is at best, as we have argued above, a curious sense of the expression *refer to*. More appropriately one could say that graphemes record phonemes. But because of the symmetric nature of this relation, one could as well say that phonemes record graphemes.

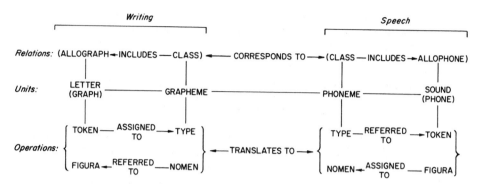

Figure 2.1   Three relations between speech and writing. Reproduced from Haas (1970) with permission of Manchester University Press.

With such an analysis, the simple referential model of grapheme-to-phoneme relation ceases to be plausible.   Clearly the nature of the relation, and certainly there is a relation, is much more subtle and complex even on purely structural grounds.   The symmetric nature of the correspondence between graphemes and phonemes has been construed as that of translation.   Haas (1970) fully develops the concept, defining translation as "a matching of expressions in their functions" (p. 18).

In explaining translation between phonemes and graphemes, Haas (1970) isolates three relations within the operation.   He states that in the process of reading aloud or writing down, we are involved in a relation of correspondence between graphemes and phonemes and two class-inclusion relations, one between graphemes and letters and one between phonemes and sounds.   Haas states that correspondence is generated in translation and inclusions are generated either by operations of classification or by assignment of reference.   This scheme is captured in Figure 2.1.

Haas explains more fully what this process of translation involves in the process of reading aloud or writing from dictation.   Note that it is a matching of type to type or interpretant and not of token to token or even token to type between these media of expression.

Haas (1970) summarizes:

> Let us note that the two classificatory operations of reference do not imply or establish any relation between writing and speech.   The one assigns letter-shapes to graphemes, the other assigns sounds to phonemes.   It is a very different operation that matches assigned graphs with assigned sounds.   This operation, of translation, presupposes the assignments of class; we cannot match the enormous number and variety of individual graphs with the enormous number and variety of individual sounds.   We are matching typical graphs with typical sounds.   The two operations of reference are presupposed.   But what we translate is clearly not these presupposed assignments or 'referential meanings'; it would be ludicrous to suggest that, in using an alphabetic script, we are engaged in matching allographic

ranges (capitals, lower case, italic, and various styles of handwriting) with allo-
phonic ranges or variation (aspirated, unaspirated, etc., and various idiosyncratic
pronounciations). The translatability of letters and of sounds concerns another,
third, aspect of them, besides their *figura* and *nomen;* it concerns what ancient
grammarians referred to as their *potestas*—that is, their linguistic value, as constituent elements. What we have to match in translating from one medium into the
other, is the powers which the elements (units) have, in each, for combining with
one another in constituting significant utterances. (p. 27)

On this account, oral and written manifestations are clearly related at
the level of graphemes and phonemes on the basis of a structural correspondence of each serving as the interpretant of the other. However,
such a picture of this relation makes no claim, and indeed no claim can
reasonably be made, about the strict dependence, in any logical sense, of
graphemes on phonemes. At the level of combination, such graphemes
and phonemes form a system about which this correspondence makes no
claims. The temporal priority, which we admit for the oral manifestation
of language on diachronic and ontogenetic planes, implies, as we have
argued, no logical priority. The very symmetric nature of correspondence militates against any interpretation of logical dependence of one
manifestation upon another. The notion of translation, which allows us
to move freely from one medium to another, is parallel to translation
between languages. We would hardly claim in the case of interlingual
translation any logical priority of one language over the other simply
because we can translate between them. Likewise, we cannot assess any
logical dependence of meaningfulness of one system on the other in
translation at the level of graphemes and phonemes.

The critical question of the independent status of oral and written manifestations of language simply cannot be answered at the level of assessing
the nature of the correspondence between orthography and phonology.
Considerations of orthography and phonology only allow us to say that the
two systems admit of translation between each other. We cannot determine to what extent a fully expanded system of written language can
indeed function qua language apart from oral language. Ultimately we
shall have to look to the actual use of oral and written manifestations of
language in order to draw any such conclusions.

A Genetic Model of Oral and Written Language

Apart from such structural considerations as the derivation of writing
from an analysis of oral language and the relation of graphemes and
phonemes, arguments for the validity of the model of dependence (A) are
often advanced on ontogenetic grounds. It is argued that whereas

speech, that is, oral language, is acquired naturally and precedes the acquisition of written language, which is consciously learned, written language is dependent on oral language for its development and continued use.

Such arguments are reminiscent of those advanced on the basis of diachronic considerations and are often linked to them. At the heart of such arguments lies the distinction between what is due to some natural capacity and what represents an acquired characteristic. We dealt with this dichotomy above when we considered the split between biology and culture at the heart of diachronic arguments for the primacy of oral language and the dependent status of written language. As we have pointed out with respect to diachronic arguments, such a sharp distinction between biology and culture is naive in the extreme. The same may be said of such a distinction between natural versus acquired capacities for oral and written language in ontogenesis. To deny such a sharp distinction is not to deny either that there is a neurological basis for language or that there must be present certain neurological milestones for the acquisition of either oral or written language. However, the biological and cultural lines of development do not develop either in isolation from each other or sequentially, first the biological and then the cultural.

In writing of the functional organization of the brain and the development of the systemic structure of brain organization in higher mental functions, Luria (1973) comments on the role of social–cultural factors:

> It is this principle of construction of functional systems of the human brain that Vygotsky (1960) called the principle of 'extracortical organization of complex mental functions,' implying by this somewhat unusual term that all types of human conscious activity are always found with the support of external auxiliary tools or aids. (p. 31)

In the ontogenesis of higher mental activities, among which we must include language, brain and culture interact and are interfunctionally codetermining systems in this process. Luria (1980) elaborates on this notion of the sociohistorical origin of higher mental functions and ontogenesis:

> The higher forms of human mental activity are sociohistorical in origin. In contrast to the animal, man is born and lives in a world of objects created by the work of society and in a world of people with whom he forms certain relationships. From the very beginning this milieu influences his mental processes. The natural reflexes of the child (sucking, grasping, etc.) are radically organized as a result of the handling of objects. New motor patterns are formed, creating what is virtually a "mold" of these objects, so that the movements begin to match the properties of the objects. The same applies to human perception, formed under the direct influence of the objective world of things, themselves of social origin. (p. 30)

We have addressed the issue of priority in our earlier remarks on arguments about the dependent status of written language manifestations from a phylogenetic and ontogenetic point of view. Luria's researches and those of Vygotsky (1965) and Leont'ev (1959) on the functional organization of higher mental activity address the issue of this dichotomy between biology and culture, a theme on which we later elaborate in a discussion of language acquisition. If anything is to be learned about the relation of oral and written manifestations of language by addressing the issue of ontogenesis, it will not come from considerations of either the priority or naturalness of oral manifestation of language.

This is not to say that we can learn nothing from genetic considerations. In many respects genetic studies are the only clear guide in understanding the complex structure of mature and fully developed psychological systems. However, we must avoid characterizing as a steady-state functioning system one still in the process of development. An example of such would be to characterize the functional ends of mature language use in terms of the functions available to a child at, say, the age of four years. Clearly the child's capacity for and use of language differs radically from that of the adult. Equally absurd would be a characterization of normal, fully developed language functioning on the basis of observations of language functioning in individuals suffering from degenerative dementia.

With these cautions in mind, what can ontogenetic studies of language tell us about the nature of the relation of oral and written manifestations of language? While the picture from behavioral or neurological ontogenetic studies is far from clear or complete, certain findings seem sound enough to accept as facts. In normal development, oral language appears prior to written language or language manifested in some other modality. It is equally clear that speech plays a critical role in early states of acquiring written language, in either expressive (writing) or receptive (reading) modes. As development proceeds, however, reliance on the oral manifestation of language lessens. This is in line with findings on the functional interconnection of cerebral centers. As Weigl (1975) has pointed out:

> Once established, the higher psychic processes function differently from the way they functioned during the formative period. Whereas during acquisition various functional cerebral systems interacted, there is a gradual reduction in this functional complexity once a certain degree of mastery has been attained. Certain intracerebral connections are no longer needed once the function is perfected; however, such connections continue to be potentially available and may be reactivated in case of need. (p. 386)

Most genetic studies point to the fact that oral language does play some mediating role in early stages of the acquisition of receptive and expressive written language manifestations. This should not be surprising, especially in the case of acquiring competence in a script derived in the first instance from an analysis of oral language. While such would be the case in normal development within linguistic communities with phonologically derived scripts, it is less likely to be the case in communities with nonderived scripts (Li & Thompson, 1982). But even in linguistic communities with phonologically derived scripts, where the acquisition of that script is facilitated by the translation rules between script and phonology, this genetic fact does not necessarily characterize steady-state language functioning. As we have seen above, Weigl (1975) observes that once certain developmental milestones are passed and knowledge of a script is complete, there is no a priori reason to assume that written language must always be mediated by the translation rules that relate it to oral language. Beyond normal development, where oral language represents a primary expression of language-code competence and a base on which other systems are acquired, written language can be acquired without such a primary system first being in place. Studies of populations with certain sensory defects, particularly the congenitally deaf, show that language in other modalities is possible in the absence of a primary acquisition of oral language.

However, if we limit ourselves to the case of normal development, the conclusion is inescapable, based on accumulated findings, that translation rules do play a central role in relating the use of a phonologically derived script to the underlying system of language code. But this fact is on a par with that of the diachronic fact that such scripts were in the first instance based on an analysis of the phonological system. These two facts do not tell us much about the actual functioning and hence relation of oral and written manifestations of language as fully articulated and functioning systems beyond what we have seen Haas argue so cogently, namely, that there exist translation rules that allow us to move freely between the two. When we move out of the realm of such phonologically derived scripts, the case is of course much altered. Yet these diachronic and genetic considerations do provide a partial answer to the question of how written and oral manifestations are related. For phonologically based writing systems, we can conclude that at some historical period and at some genetic stage oral manifestations played a primary mediating role between written manifestations and the underlying language code. Further, normal language ability appears to include a translation component that allows for the free movement between oral and written manifestations of language, especially evident in the exercise of such tasks as writing from dictation and reading aloud. Based on structural, neurological, and ontogenetic considerations, we can summarize the conclusions about the relation of oral and written manifestations of language as follows:

1. Alphabetic-phonological scripts are derived, historically, from an analysis of oral language manifestations.
2. Phonemes and graphemes are symmetric interpretants of each other, and graphemes are not second-order signs of phonemes.
3. Phonemes and graphemes are related by a set of translation rules that allow for the free movement between these systems as evidenced by such behavioral tasks as writing from dictation and reading aloud.
4. There is neurological evidence to support the functional interaction of oral and written manifestations of language.
5. Evidence from normal development in language acquisition attests to the fact that oral manifestations of language are prior to written manifestations and that such oral manifestations play a central and perhaps decisive mediating role in the acquisition of written manifestations of language, at least in linguistic communities that use a phonologically derived script system.

If we once again consider the three models proposed earlier for the representation of the relation of oral and written manifestations, we can perceive diachronic and ontogenetic movement between models A (dependent) and B (equipollent) as depicted in Figure 2.2.

In order to verify such a characterization of the relation between oral and written manifestations of language where there is a movement from necessary phonological mediation to optional phonological mediation, we have to take into account evidence from other than diachronic or ontogenetic spheres.

Neurolinguistic Aspects of Oral and Written Language

If such a model of the relation of oral to written language is to be empirically grounded and if the concept of a movement from mediated to unmediated written language is to receive any support, we must look to studies detailing the impairment of language activity due to insult to the brain. Neurolinguistic studies of aphasic pathologies potentially provide some empirical evidence on these issues. But before sifting through some of these findings, certain caveats about the interpretation of these findings must be kept in mind.

The first caution has to do with the difference between the strict localization of mental functions in the cortex and what has been termed by

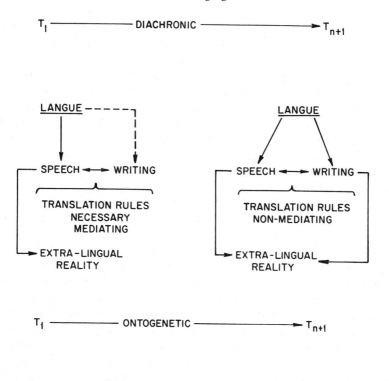

T_1 ———————— DIACHRONIC ————————→ T_{n+1}

T_1 ——————— ONTOGENETIC ———————→ T_{n+1}

– – – –► ; POTENTIAL CONNECTION

Figure 2.2   Diachronic and ontogenetic model of the relation of speech and writing. The dashed line indicates a potential connection.

Luria (1973, 1980) "mental functions with dynamic levels of localization." By strict or narrow localization of function can be understood the notion of a particular mental function being associated with a highly circumscribed set of cells or particular tissue. On the notion of function and dynamic levels of localization Luria (1980) writes:

> An important advance in modern physiology has been the radical revision of the concept of function, for this has led to new views concerning localization. In the light of modern data, function has ceased to be understood as a direct property of a particular, highly specialized group of cells of an organ. Since Pavlov advanced his reflex theories, the word "function" has come to mean the product of complex reflex activity comprising: uniting excited and inhibited areas of the nervous system into a *working mosaic*, analyzing and integrating stimuli reaching the organism, forming a system of temporary connections, and thereby insuring the equilibrium of the organism with its environment. This is why the concept of localization of functions has also undergone a radical change and has come to mean *a network of complex dynamic* structures or *combination centers* consisting of mosaics of distant points of the nervous system, united in a common task. (p. 21; emphasis added)

Such radically divergent concepts of localization lead to very different interpretations of data on language impairment due to certain focal lesions. If a strict or narrow concept of localization were sustainable, if oral and written language were located in different areas of the cortex, and further if oral and written manifestations of language constituted separate language manifestations, then we would expect lesions to speech areas to leave written manifestations unimpaired. But if it were the case that lesions in speech areas, under a strict or narrow concept of localization of functions, resulted in parallel impairment to written manifestations of language, we would be justified in concluding that written manifestations are mediated by the vocal-auditory system of language. Of course, since the model proposed in Figure 2.2 claims that oral and written manifestations of language both tap a language-code center equally and independently, we might conclude that where both oral and written manifestations are impaired due to certain focal lesions, it might be the case that what is in fact subject to impairment is this language-code center, affecting both manifestations. But in any case, in a strict localization view it should be logically possible to find cases where (1) one manifestation of language is impaired leaving the other intact, or (2) both manifestations are impaired (either due to lesions of some language-code area or to lesions of speech areas). It is difficult to disambiguate between the possibilities under (2) unless we also examine evidence on the particular location of lesions. There are those such as Weigl who have argued (Weigl & Bierwisch, 1970) that even in severe cases of aphasic disturbance, competence is not lost, in which case the possibilities under (2) are limited.

However, as we have said, such a strict or narrow concept of the localization of mental functions is not sustainable given empirical findings. (For a review of relevant evidence see Luria, 1973, pp. 19–34; 1980, p. 28.) The notion of the dynamic levels of localization and the complex functional or interfunctional organization of mental activities does not allow for such a clear-cut interpretation of the neurolinguistic evidence. Given the concept of the plasticity of neural systems and the idea of interrelated mosaics of areas of neural activity, evidence from lesions to particular areas and the behavioral correlates of such lesions are difficult to interpret. Were it the case that any given lesion had the effect of impairing both oral and written manifestations of language, several interpretations of such a result would be equally plausible. We do not wish to suggest that the evidence is totally ambiguous or that typologies of behavioral defects associated with lesions to certain areas are not possible. This is clearly not the case. However, a difficulty of interpretation is introduced that is not necessarily present in a strict localization theory of mental function. Where there is equal impairment of both oral and written manifestations, as in (2) above, we cannot simply or easily conclude that such evidence points to a mediational model of oral and written manifestations of language. Given that many cortical systems are brought to bear in such a complex higher mental activity as language, it cannot be assumed that partial or full destruction of any of these systems leads to the complete loss of a given higher mental function. Indeed, total loss of a function would, in light of careful clinical observation, appear to be somewhat unlikely. As Luria (1980) points out, the disturbance of any particular function may be due to lesions in widely different parts of the cerebral cortex, and very circumscribed lesions often lead not to disturbance of isolated functions but of entire complexes of unrelated functions.

Given these cautions about the possible interpretations of evidence from language impairment due to lesions and especially the last-quoted remarks of Luria, we examine the evidence to see what support, if any, there is for the model proposed in Figure 2.2.

We wish to answer a specific question: Does the written manifestation of language require the mediation of speech to be realizable as linguistic communication? Possible answers include the following:

1. Oral mediation is always necessary for written language manifestation.
2. Oral language mediation is necessary for acquiring written manifestations of language, but once a system of written language achieves a steady state of functioning, oral mediation is optional.

In each of these conceptions we refer only to the capacity and ability of individuals with normal and intact language competence; we exclude from consideration individuals with congenital impairments such as deafness or cerebral palsy. However, conclusions about the role of oral language in ontogenesis are affected by evidence from such atypical populations. This is especially true in light of the universalist nature of claims about the role of oral language detailed in earlier arguments.

The model we propose in Figure 2.2 reflects the second answer to the question posed above. What evidence is there from developmental neuropsychology and studies of aphasia that such a model is plausible? We have seen above that Weigl (1975) makes the general comment that the cerebral organization of higher psychic functions undergoes a fundamental change during the course of development. Certain once-necessary interactions between functional systems become unnecessary over the course of development.

This general statement on the cerebral organization of higher mental functions accords well with the developmental model we have proposed. Whereas oral language plays a fundamental mediating role in early stages of the acquisition of written language, once written language develops a degree of automaticity, the mediating role of oral language diminishes to the point where written language exists as a partial autonomous system that independently taps, as does oral language, a common language-code capacity. What links oral and written language manifestations at fully automated levels of functioning are the translation rules we have spoken of earlier. Experimental studies by Nasarova (1955), Sokolov (1967), Weigl (1964), Weigl, Bottcher, Lander, and Metze (1971), and others have demonstrated the validity of such a conclusion.

In summarizing his work and that of others on the organization of cortical systems in writing and reading, Luria (1980) concludes:

> The process of articulation (speaking aloud), which plays a decisive role in the early stages of education, has little to do with the highly automatized form of writing. A person capable of writing in this highly automatized manner can, therefore, do so even when articulation is excluded. . . . This all suggests that in different stages of writing development changes take place in its psychophysiological composition, so that *the part played by cortical systems in this activity does not always remain the same.* (p. 530; emphasis added)

Luria goes on to point out that when considering writing systems that are not as directly phonologically derived (e.g., Russian), the role of the phonological component as mediator, if existent at all, is reduced even in early stages of the acquisition of such a script. In speaking of receptive capacity for written language, Luria (1980, p. 531) concludes, "in the subsequent stages the process becomes transformed into the visual recognition of words and no longer depends exclusively on the analysis and synthesis of phonetic letters." For similar conclusions see Poulton (1963), Smith (1973, 1975), and Henderson (1982).

Patterson (1982) presents a review of studies investigating the necessity for phonological mediation in reading as well as evidence from a case study of a patient who had suffered a coronary thrombosis and several weeks later an embolism secondary to myocardial infarct. On the basis of her review of other clinical literature and the empirical data from the study she conducted, Patterson concludes that evidence from studies of subjects suffering from phonological dyslexia points to limited involvement of phonological coding in reading. Further, evidence from the study of the patient who suffered from coronary thrombosis and myocardial infarct, along with data from normal subjects, suggests that recognition of printed words does not require nor in typical cases involve a "phonological code assembled from graphemic information" (Patterson, 1982, pp. 104–105).

Patterson comments on the puzzle of this lack of involvement. Her remarks are applicable to the developmental model we have proposed:

The most common assumption about the apparent puzzle of a system which has such a skill but makes no vital use of it is that *learning* to read requires or is facilitated by phonological assembly. There is indeed some evidence for reliance on phonological recoding in word comprehension by young readers, which diminishes as children grow older. (p. 105)

In a comprehensive review of studies on the place of phonological mediation in reading, Coltheart (1980) reaches conclusions that are in accord with those of Patterson and Henderson (1982). The bulk of the evidence suggests that, in developed stages of reading, phonological coding is optional. It would seem safe to conclude that the same is likely true of the mediational role of phonology in writing.

The evidence from such studies generally supports the transitional model of necessary-to-optional mediation proposed above. The general transition over the course of development (at least in the case of normal populations and in scripts that may be said to be phonetically derived) seems to be from that of linked and interfunctionally mediated systems to partially autonomous systems. We say "partially autonomous," as oral and written manifestations are linked both to a common underlying language code and to each other, as mutually accessible systems of language realization, through the translation rules.

Having considered certain aspects of ontogenesis that argue for the plausibility of our transition model, we now consider the steady-state functioning of such a system to determine if data from other studies of the disruption of such a system due to focal lesions support the conclusion we have drawn. In agreement with what we have said of the relation of oral and written language manifestations as partially autonomous systems, Weigl (1975) speculates,

If it is correct that during the automation of certain functions there is a reduction in the interaction of various partial systems which had to interact during acquisition, then it is possible that these systems might become "protected" as they become independent from one another; this then may clarify the nature of selected losses. In other words, the more autonomous a given partial system, the less likely would an interference of that system implicate other, even related systems, provided, naturally, that the common competence remained intact. Thus it becomes understandable that limitations of comprehension in oral language need not affect comprehension in written language. (p. 390)

To what extent then does neurological evidence from studies of insult support this contention? Schnitzer (1976) undertakes a review of findings on various language disorders due to lesions of cortex. He reviews five major studies of aphasia and alexia in order to answer the question of whether auditory–articulatory mediation is always a necessary component of linguistic performance in any medium in which underlying language competence might be realized.   The populations in the studies reviewed consisted of Japanese aphasics, French-speaking alexics, deaf-mute aphasics, and blind alexics.   These subjects represent an interesting cross-section of pathologies and a population that uses various realizations of language for receptive and expressive communication.   Schnitzer uses the term *mesotic* to refer to the actual means by which communication takes place between an encoder and decoder.   *Mesotic* in this sense parallels the term *substance* used by Hjelmslev and others in opposition to *form,* that is, *langue.*   In this discussion of Schnitzer's analysis we use his term *mesotic.*   Schnitzer distinguishes between various mesotics based on the modality of encoding and decoding.   So for example, speech, that is, oral language, is encoded by the articulatory modality and decoded by an auditory modality whereas writing, that is, written language either phonemic, morphophonemic, syllabic, or ideographic, is encoded by a tactile modality and decoded by a visual modality.   In the case of braille writing, the modality for encoding is tactile as is the modality for decoding.

The first study considered by Schnitzer was that done by Sasanuma and Fujimura (1971) involving two groups of Japanese aphasics.   What is of note here is that the Japanese language is represented in three writing systems, two basically syllabic (hiragana and katakana) and a third (kanji) basically logographic, or perhaps more properly morphemic, to use French's (1976) term based on his analysis of Chinese writing.   The gross distinction between these systems is that the first two, the kanas, involve deliberate phonological derivation, while kanji does not follow a phonemic principle.   Using two control groups of nonaphasics, the authors administered a number of visual recognition and writing tasks involving each of the three systems of written representation.   Control groups generally made no errors in visual recognition tasks in the three writing systems.   Group B aphasics, characterized as having particular phonological impairment beyond the general aphasic syndromes of Group A, scored most poorly in tasks involving the kana scripts (based on a phonemic principle), but better in kanji script (not based on a phonemic principle).   Schnitzer (1976) argues from the Sasanuma and Fujimura data as follows:

> Group B scored as poorly as Group A on all three tests involving kanji words. But on both the visual and writing tasks, they scored significantly worse on *kana* words than on kanji words. . . . If the phonological competence of members of this group was sufficiently impaired, they would not have been able to use it to mediate their transcriptions in the writing tasks or their word recognitions in the visual task. There is additional evidence that this is in fact the case. . . . Group B subjects scored significantly worse on both visual and writing tasks with hiragana words than with katakana words. (p. 146)

Schnitzer argues that this better performance on katakana words further indicates that Group B subjects, with phonological impairment, used a principle of nonphonological processing for these words, as katakana signs are or can be stored as the ideographic kanji words. Schnitzer points out that, as indicated in this study, hiragana words are unlikely to be stored other than phonologically. As a consequence, Schnitzer concludes that Group B aphasics' performance argues that phonological mediation need not always play a role in linguistic communication. This conclusion is in line with the model of the role of phonological mediation we proposed above. Schnitzer summarizes a number of other studies as follows:

> 2. The performance of the French alexics [Dubois-Charlier, 1971, 1972] indicates that there are (at least) two types of alexia. One type of alexic (literal) attempts to read by guessing at ideograms, some of which are poorly known, and does not attempt to relate individual letters to sounds. Another type of alexic (verbal) tries to "sound out" words he is reading, thereby attempting to mediate his impaired reading ability through his knowledge of correspondences between letters and phonological segments.
> 3. The case of the blind alexic suggests that this patient first attempts to read ideographically (employing the strategy of the literal alexic), and upon failure, then proceeds to use phonological mediation to successfully read the word being attempted (employing the verbal alexic strategy).
> 4. The discussion of aphasic deaf mutes [Critchley, 1938; Douglas & Richardson, 1959; Sarno, Swisher, & Sarno, 1969; Tureen, Sunolik, & Tritt, 1951] tentatively suggests (on the basis of only two cases) that whereas those having congenital deafness employ no phonological mediation in finger-spelling tasks, those with acquired deafness may mediate finger-spelling performance through a phonological system acquired prior to the onset of deafness.
> 5. Finally, the discussion of the aphasic with the impaired lexical redundancy system suggests that familiar words are read ideographically without phonological mediation, whereas unfamiliar words (or possible but nonexistent words) are read by means of mediation through the phonological system. Since this system was impaired in the aphasic discussed, he could not read unfamiliar words. (Schnitzer, 1976, pp. 156–157)

The evidence from the studies reviewed by Schnitzer confirms the general model of the relation of phonological mediation to written language that we have proposed above. Hecaen and Albert (1978) comment on certain agraphic syndromes and the evidence they suggest for autonomous systems of language functioning. They conclude that evidence from certain agraphias suggests that the graphic code cannot be considered as a simple transcription of the oral code and that graphic activity is an autonomous model of language performance. Speech is related to writing by a system of translation rules that allows for a consistent mapping between these domains. We know from accounts of the ontogenesis of language that speech is developmentally prior to written and other manifestations of language, at least in normal populations. This ontogenetic priority of speech allows oral language a direct mediating role in the acquisition of expressive and receptive written language. However, once written language is in place and forms a functioning steady-state system, the mediation of oral language is dispensable, and written language functions as an independent manifestation of man's capacity for linguistic communication.

When we consider arguments and data from phylogenetic, structural, ontogenetic, and neurolinguistic considerations of the relation of oral and written manifestations of language to each other and to language itself, the preponderance of evidence suggests that these manifestations are independent but equipollent and mutually accessible instantiations of language. The simple linear model of necessary oral mediation of written language is a true representation of early stages of acquisition of written language but is not an accurate characterization of mature language functioning in fully literate populations. It may be that the model of necessary phonological mediation may more accurately characterize semiliterate populations or instances of limited literacy practice (Scribner & Cole, 1981). We examine this in more detail in the following chapter on functional differentiation of language norms.

3

Functional Differentiation of Oral and Written Language Norms

Introduction

In the Manifesto presented to the First Congress of Slavic Philologists in Prague (1929/1978), the Prague Linguistic Circle affirmed the following position as central to their notions on the analysis of language:

> Language and human activity, from which language results, share the element of intention. Whether language is analyzed as an expression or as information, the intention of the speaker is [the] easiest and most natural explanation. Therefore, the functional aspect ought to be considered in a linguistic analysis. From a functional standpoint, language is a system of instrumental means of expression. No language phenomenon can be understood without considering the system of which it is a part.

These principles of intentionality and systematicity of instrumental means are no less critical for a full appreciation of the role of oral and written language manifestations. Indeed, the structural consideration put forward in Chapter 2 can only be made sense of in light of these principles.

Only by means of functional considerations can we in any reasoned way account for the existence of the two manifestations. The structural differentiation of oral and written means of expression is accounted for in part by the principle of functional differentiation. Within the framework of human communication, social praxis, and indeed higher psychological functioning, spoken and written language can be seen to fulfill separate but complementary ranges of functions. Insofar as spoken and written language fulfill specific cultural needs, are associated with particular social practices, are constitutive of different levels of psychological activity, and are correlated with certain structural means of expression, they constitute autonomous language norms.

By the term language *norms* is to be understood a set of potential linguistic means, structural and organizational, that are correlated with particular communicative ends or functions. Viewed in this sense, norms are to be found on the plane of language code and are instantiated in particular communicative acts that call forth a particular norm. By the term *norm* we do not understand that which is ordinary or customary usage if by this is implied a single type or instance of use of either written or spoken language in a given set of contexts. Written and spoken language norms may have many instantiations, some of which are specialized or restricted, others of which may be more general and hence construed as ordinary usage. So, for example, the written norm may be instanced by a shopping list or a letter to a friend (fairly wide or customary usage) but also by a scholarly monograph. While each of these instances of usage shares certain invariant functional features of the written norm, each also conforms to the particular context of use — either customary or specialized. In psychological terms, written and oral language norms form part of what has been termed the *communicative competence* of an individual. These norms are regimented and constituted by the interaction of *langue* and social praxis. So we find that the Prague group asserted in their Manifesto that every functional utterance is an instantiation of a system of conventions, and as a consequence no one function or functional language is to be associated with de Saussure's term *langue* and all other functions with the term *parole*. This has often been the case in the past when linguistic analysis has privileged the referential aspect of language (Bühler, 1982; Horalek, 1966; Mukarovsky, 1937; Zawadowski, 1956), and psychology has followed suit in ignoring pragmatic and metapragmatic facts as salient to a description of the cognitive organization of language behavior. In this sense also, written and oral language norms constitute equipollent systems at the level of language code and are called forth differentially in particular language acts as determined by particular communicative ends.

This differentiation of oral and written norms, in part constituted and regimented by social praxis and communicative function, places oral and written manifestations in a privative opposition in which the relation between the two norms is one of marked to unmarked order. In this sense the oral norm constitutes the unmarked member and the written norm the marked member. The two norms may be said to form something like complementary distributions with respect to the functions they fulfill and characteristics they exhibit.

As was the case in discussing the nature of the relation of oral and written manifestations of language in light of structural and neurological principles, the existence and relation of the two language norms depend to a large extent on the particular diachronic stage. Clearly, in the case of traditional oral cultures there is no question of a written norm standing in opposition to the oral norm. One might be tempted, in light of such cases, to claim that once again the lack of universality argues against the ontological reality of such norms. But arguments from universality have no more merit in discussing the two norms than they had in structural and neurological considerations. Vachek (1959, pp. 13–15) observes "All languages tend to develop to an optimum stage at which they will have developed their latent structural possibilities in full. And it is this optimum stage alone which can furnish the analyst with materials capable of an adequate evaluation of the two norms" (i.e., oral and written language). Just as it would be misleading to regard the language performance of six-year-olds as characterizing fully developed steady-state language functioning, it would be equally misleading to characterize linguistic performance only in light of preliterate societies. Vachek's remarks assume that language is not a static phenomenon, a functional principle of all linguistic analysis and a critical assumption for any genetic explication of oral and written language.

The principle of functional differentiation claims that the two language norms fulfill different communicative ends and are correlated with specific linguistic means of expression when instanced in any particular usage. The underlying assumption for such a principle is that language is not unifunctional but rather plurifunctional in nature. Conceptions of language that favor a unifunctional interpretation privilege what have been termed the referential aspects of language. Such conceptions could almost be termed afunctional, since they often assume that this referential capacity, central to language, is unique and transparently obvious and in need of no contrast with other functional ends. For such views, function is clearly not a matter of *langue* or language code, but rather a matter of trivial performance constraints.

But the concept of function as we wish to delineate it here is not merely the addition of arbitrary performance constraints to the formal properties of language. Rather, function, that is, purposive use of language in intentional contexts, involves the modification of actual signal form. Indeed, regularities of signal form cannot be understood without attention to function. This view of language does not draw a distinction between language as a self-contained system of formal means and language as a system of signs put to use in the practice of intentional communication. In a diachronic sense, language as a formal system is shaped by the facts of use. Language is not an abstract entity or preformed capacity somehow evolved apart from its intentional use by subjects any more than cognition is preformed and independent of environment and the social order.

The literature on the functions of language is long and varied, and we make no attempt to review it here. For a general discussion of three major approaches to the topic of language structure and function and some consequences for a psychology of language, see Silverstein (1978). Perhaps the scholar whose name is most associated with the study of language function (here understood as the intentional goal-directed use of language means in the act of communication) is the German psychologist Karl Bühler. In a widely cited monograph, Bühler (1934) outlines his now-classic statement on the threefold nature of the functions of speech utterances. In addition to what may be termed a superordinate function of *communication* shared by all speech utterances, Bühler identifies three principle functions: *Darstellungsfunktion,* a referential function that communicates the factual, objective content of extralingual reality; *Kundgabefunktion,* an expressive function that characterizes the speaker of the utterance; *Appelfunktion,* the function of appeal used to influence the hearer of the communication. This last-named function has often been referred to as the conative function of an utterance. Bühler's work served as a point of departure for further work on the nature of intentional speech use and the characteristic means of expression associated with particular functions, especially the work of the representatives of Prague linguistics. One important contribution of the work of Prague School linguists is the recognition by these scholars that Bühler's typology of functions is clearly not exhaustive. To Bühler's typology may be added, for example, the notion of an aesthetic function, dealt with extensively in the work of Mukarovsky (1937), Zawadowski (1956), and others, and the notion of an intellectual function as explicated in the work of Havranek. (For further discussion of Bühler's ideas on function see Horalek, 1966; Mukarovsky, 1937; and Zawadowski, 1956.)

Our purpose is not to undertake an analysis of language behavior in order to arrive at an exhaustive typology of language functions but only to emphasize that the signal form of language is directly correlated with the intentional goal-directed use of language on the part of members of a given linguistic community. The consistency of signal form-to-function relations is in part constituted by and maintained by social praxis in any given community. It is also important to note at this point that we do not wish to suggest that the correlation of signal form to function implies an isomorphic mapping of a particular function to a particular signal form in language. The relation of the means of expression to function is more complex and we discuss this point below. We emphasize here that specific utterances are not usually unifunctional; a given utterance instantiates more than one function in any given instance of use. However, this is not to suggest that the various functions within a given utterance cannot be differentiated or that in a given utterance a specific function does not predominate. Halliday (1975), in a genetic study of his son's language, gave a seminal account of the growth of various language functions. This work provides a useful account of the interrelation of language functions as they become differentiated in a child's speech during the course of language acquisition. Karmiloff-Smith (1979) reexamined the Piagetian view of language acquisition in light of the plurifunctional nature of language. Her work also demonstrates that the language of children is plurifunctional in nature.

An appreciation of this functional dimension of language activity is crucial if we are to make sense of the two major coexisting manifestations of language, that is, oral and written. We cannot hope to make sense of the structural facts of oral and written forms of language without an appeal to a functional consideration of the goal-directed use of language in particular social and cultural contexts. The coexistence of two language manifestations in one and the same linguistic community is hardly to be explained away on grounds of fortuitous development. To do so would amount to denying any intentional character to cultural evolution (McDougall, 1929) and still leave unanswered the question of why oral and written manifestations are to be found existing simultaneously in a given community. In order to make sense of this coexistence of two language manifestations we must find some functional justification that explains roles these two manifestations might fulfill in a given sociocultural context or psychological activity. Clearly the functional justification of the two manifestations on the basis of use in any given culture or even at different points in time within the same culture may vary. However, certain functional features distinguish oral and written language at the level of norm, that is, the sum of means of expression. Such features are generally applicable to oral and written language as options of the language code as a system of form.

Our purpose is to arrive at some functional justification of the two manifestations of language within the context of language as system and to explore the nature of their functional relation to one another within this system. We return to the issue of the actual relation of a functional differentiation of the two manifestations and particular sociocultural praxis in a later chapter. Here, however, we examine the justification for a functional differentiation of oral and written language in terms of the systematicity of language as code. There are certain valid generalizations that can be made about the functional justification of oral and written language apart from particular instances of the use of the manifestations within any specific culture.

These generalizations exist on the level of system, as do other features of language as code, and represent the stock of the means of expression or communication that a particular linguistic community draws on and may modify in particular practice. Further, there is a strong psychological foundation for the functional differentiation of oral and written language manifestations that cuts across particular cultural facts.

At least three generalized features distinguish oral and written media of language: a more-or-less documentary character, more-or-less independence of immediate context, and a greater-or-lesser degree of interactive potential. Each of these features provides some functional justification for the existence of the two language norms.

Functional Features and Language Manifestations

In terms of the documentary character of the two substances of expression, written forms present a degree of permanence or *preservability,* to use Vachek's term, not exhibited by spoken forms. This feature has long been recognized and is captured in the medieval saying, *Littera scripta manet, verba volent* (the written word endures, while the voice flies away). The consequences of this feature have not gone unnoticed by scholars from any number of disciplines. It has been argued that a certain level of progress in cultural and intellectual evolution has been critically tied to the existence of such a preservable form of language. Its role in religion, law, intellectual speculation, and political economy has been detailed by Innis (1951), Havelock (1982b), Clammer (1976), and Goody (1968, 1977). In addition to this interaction of special cultural practices and the documentary character of the written form, we can deduce a further psychological consequence of this preservable character. Whereas oral manifestations of language in discourse present a relatively transparent signal form, written manifestations are less transparent and are in fact foregrounded in consciousness. As Luria (1981, p. 166) observes, written forms of language entail a greater "conscious analysis of the means of expression." We demonstrate below the consequences of this foregrounding in consciousness for the signal form of written language.

The second functional feature, degree of contextualization, is in a sense related to the preservability of the written form.

It is often observed that in a linguistic community in which oral and written forms coexist, written forms are in discourse use relatively more decontextualized. By decontextualized, we understand the degree to which the surface signal form of discourse is self-sufficient to carry unambiguously the communicative goal of the actual discourse. This can be seen in the way the written form is to a large extent devoid of extralinguistic expressive devices. In contrast, oral forms have greater appeal to intonation and gesture to supplement surface signal form. The actual extralingual circumstances, situation, or occasion for production of a given discourse matter more for oral forms than for written forms. On a psychological plane, the implications of degree of contextualization required by oral or written manifestations of discourse are felt in the degree of distance experienced between the three factors in any communicative situation. In written language, both speaker and hearer are farther removed from the actual channel of communication than in oral manifestations. Likewise, speaker and hearer are farther distanced psychologically in written manifestations of discourse.

Tied to this notion of psychological distance in terms of the degree of contextualization of the two manifestations is the notion of interactive potential. Oral manifestations of discourse permit a greater degree of immediate language interaction due to the direct and immediate visual and auditory participation in the act of communication. This interactive potential in oral discourse permits a relatively rapid succession of communicative exchanges not equally realizable in written discourse. Differences in interactive potential relate also to our comments on the degree of preservability of the two forms of language.

All of these features serve to contrast and distinguish between oral and written manifestations of language. On the basis of these functional features, oral and written manifestations of language can be seen to be in complementary distribution with one manifestation fulfilling the requirement for a marked and the other an unmarked member of a privative opposition. Figure 3.1 tries to capture this marked (+) and unmarked (−) distribution with respect to the features discussed.

None of the functional features discussed is exclusively associated with any given manifestation, oral or written. It is not the case, as is at times naively argued, that written manifestation represents decontextualized

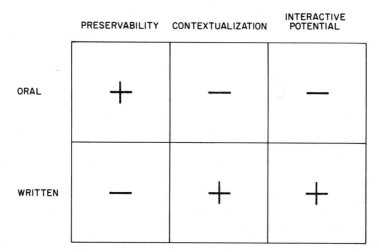

Figure 3.1   Markedness of functional features of oral and written language.

language use and oral language, contextualized language use. The notion of marking indicates that in ordinary or customary cases certain functional features are automatized for certain manifestations and that their range of use with these manifestations exhibits a greater incidence of correlation.

We have only briefly sketched the nature and consequences of these functional features for the two manifestations. The nature and implications of such features for the actual signal forms are discussed in more detail throughout this chapter. At this point we wish only to establish very general grounds for distinguishing oral and written forms of language. Based on our considerations thus far we can conclude that these two manifestations represent distinct functional norms of language, each characterized by functional features that are in complementary distribution.

From this point we term oral and written manifestations of language as oral and written *norms* of language. We use the term *norm* in a synchronic sense, first applied by Vachek, to indicate that oral and written manifestations are realizations or instantiations on the surface level of distinguishable system and code regularities. Oral and written manifestations represent functional norms of language use. Vachek (1959) defines oral and written language norms as follows:

> The spoken norm of language is a system of phonetically manifestable language elements whose function is to react to a given stimulus (which, as a rule, is an urgent one) in a dynamic way, i.e., in a ready and immediate manner, duly expressing not only the purely communicative but also the emotional aspect of the approach of the reacting language user. . . . The written norm of language is a

system of graphically manifestable language elements whose function is to react to a given stimulus (which, as a rule, is not an urgent one) in a static way . . . , concentrating particularly on the purely communicative aspect of the approach of the reacting language user. (p. 12)

These definitions capture many aspects of the features discussed above. The prime motive for distinguishing between the two norms is their differentiation along functional lines in the actual act of communication. However, this differentiation of the two norms is not limited solely to such functional features. We have observed earlier that these functional considerations have consequences for the actual signal form or means of expression of the two norms.

The argument could be made that, whereas oral and written language share the same grammar, they therefore cannot represent autonomous instances of language. On the contrary, we argue that while oral and written language share substantially the same lexicogrammar, functional differences do make for differences in the surface realization of the linguistic means of expression in oral and written language norms. The model of the relation of oral and written language manifestations presented in Chapter 2 indicates that these two norms tap the same underlying system of language form or language code. However, when we come to consider actual language use, the two norms do not realize in equal measure the full range of possible means of expression. This unequal realization is due to the deformation in surface signal form as determined by functional considerations.

When we consider this interaction of function and means of expression we distinguish between two levels of language realization: (1) the lexicogrammatical level, the syntactic, semantic, and pragmatic organization of the act of communication; and (2) the plane of discourse organization, the macro-organization of any communicative act and its means of expression in dialogic or monologic format. We consider each of these planes and their relation to oral and written language in turn.

Oral and written language norms are each particularly correlated with a given discourse organization. Again we emphasize that this correlation is not an exclusive identification of one language manifestation with a given discourse organization but a tendency to a typical and normal pattern. Certain discourse formats are, as it were, automatized for given norms.

We remarked earlier that one functional feature that serves to distinguish oral from written language is the unequal interactive potential of these two norms. Oral language exhibits a greater interactive potential. It is a means of responding to extralingual reality in an immediate sense and is typical of interactive language behavior. About such an interactive potential or situation Yakubinski (1923, p. 117) says, "Corresponding to a direct ('Face to Face') form of human interaction we have direct forms of verbal interaction that are characterized by direct visual and auditory perception of the interlocutor." And about the organization of interaction on the plane of discourse Yakubinski (1923, p. 117) states, "Corresponding to alternating forms of interactions that involve a relatively rapid succession of actions and reactions, we have a dialogic form of verbal social interaction."

Dialogue is typically associated or correlated with language interaction. However, we do not wish to suggest that dialogue is the only discourse format associated with verbal communication. Especially in some oral societies, monologic organization occurs with equal frequency. Typical examples of monologic organization are to be found in narrative modes such as storytelling or the transmission of myths. However, in a linguistic community where both oral and written norms are options for expressing a communicative intention, the use of monologic organization of verbal interaction is more restricted to specialized contexts. When we consider the particular means of expression associated with monologic discourse organization in predominately oral communities and in nonliterate communities, great differences distinguish monologic discourse organization in oral and written norms of language. See, for example, the work of Lord (1964) on oral performance in storytelling contexts. Goody (1968) contains a number of articles documenting discourse formats in oral and nonliterate cultures. Scribner and Cole (1981) further document typical functional variants in oral and nonliterate cultures.

Restricting ourselves for the moment to linguistic communities in which the oral and written norms coexist as fully realized systems (principally Western technological societies), we can contrast the typical discourse organization associated with each of these norms as this organization is called forth by certain typical functional ends. Commenting on the nature of spoken language, Holman (1976) writes:

> Here the roles of communicant and target of communication [the interlocutor] are in constant alternation throughout the transmission of the message. . . . Because of the bi-directional flow of information, spoken communication may be characterized as an extreme form of dialogue or polylogue, organized into structural units or exchanges, which in turn consist of cues and comment. . . . The degree of organization typical of language as spoken is also largely determined by its primary function—the transmission of non-detailed information within the context of social interaction. (p. 127)

One major shaping force for discourse organization in the spoken norm is the physical presence of two or more interlocutors, as Holman suggests. Such copresence results in the shared control of discourse (Zammuner, 1981). Additionally, as Holman points out, the primary or foregrounded

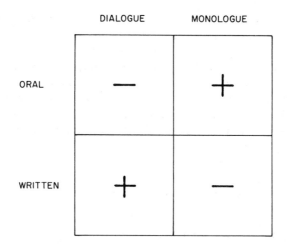

Figure 3.2   Marking relations of discourse organization in oral and written language.

function of communication of nondetailed information plays a role in determining the organization of signal form in the spoken norm. We are not suggesting that the spoken norm is unifunctional. But in a linguistic community with both the spoken and written norm as communicative options, certain functions are foregrounded for particular norms to a degree that might not be true for a community with only the spoken norm. In such a community, it would perhaps be incorrect to speak of the primary function of the spoken norm as "the transmission of nondetailed information." However, by and large for communities with a spoken and written norm, the statement by Holman holds true.

Dialogic discourse organization is more highly correlated with the spoken norm and extended monologue is the more typical pattern or organization for the written norm. This correlation and the range of distribution of the two forms of discourse organization results in the marking relation illustrated by Figure 3.2.

This figure illustrates that the oral norm is unmarked for dialogue and the written norm is unmarked for monologue. These norms are in complementary distribution with respect to discourse organization.

This marking relation serves to distinguish the two language norms, as did the marking relation of the two norms with respect to functional features. Each fulfills a particular communicative function and each is characterized by a typical discourse organization consistent with its communicative function. This differentiation in terms of functional features and discourse organization provides the necessary criterion for justifying the coexistence of the two norms in a given linguistic community.

In Chapter 4 we consider the psychological consequences of this differentiation of discourse organization associated with oral and written norms. Indeed, the acquisition of the written norm can be characterized primarily as the grasp of command over monologic discourse organization. But initially we must consider the syntagmatic plane of functional organization of communication. There is a similar differentiation of the means of expression associated with the two norms on the lexicogrammatical plane. The following documents some examples of the deformation of surface signal form associated with this functional differentiation of the two norms.

Syntactic Differentiation of Oral and Written Norms

No exhaustive study of the lexicogrammatical means of expression that might be typically correlated with the two norms has been undertaken. We cannot hope to fill this void in this work. We can, however, draw out of the literature some illustrative examples of the means of expression and the organization of the lexicogrammar on the syntagmatic plane that are associated with the two norms. In his study of variable word order in oral and written language, Holman (1976) focuses on the role and frequency of topicalization in these two norms. Beginning with the observation of the functional differentiation of oral and written language in the act of communication, Holman then asks if there is any structural difference in the two forms of language that might be attributable to the functional difference observed in the two norms. Contrasting the use of topicalization strategies in oral and written norms of language, Holman writes:

> Because of the primary cognitive nature of the information conveyed by means of written communication, topicalization is a relatively infrequently employed stratagem in them. In contrast to the relative constancy of topic demanded by written communication, the conversational situation, being more an instance of social interaction than of communication of information, requires that the participants constantly be aware of whether a specific rhematic element [contextually nonderivable information] is to be regarded as a new topic, or as the basis for further treatment of the topic under discussion. (pp. 136–137)

Continuing and arguing from this analysis of the oral communicative situation, Holman says of topicalization in the oral language norm:

> In the construction of spoken texts, in contrast, topicalization assumes a primary role in determining not only the ordering of the sentence, but also its acoustic shape, since the construction of microtextual units in language as spoken is as much determined by factors connected with the transmission of interaction management and indexical information in addition to maintaining psychological and spatial contiguity, as with the transmission of purely cognitive information. Because of

the spontaneous nature of language as spoken it is characterized by the use of syntactic structures borrowed from preceding utterances, use of holophrastic constructions, and an overall syntactic laconicity. All of these factors speak for the expression by other means of the communicative subtleties expressed by word order in language as written if they need be expressed at all. (p. 140)

What Holman argues for and what is demonstrated when we look carefully at topicalization in oral and written language use is not that given syntactic or semantic means of expression are to be found only in one of these norms but that each norm adapts, as it were, given lexicosyntactic structures to the communicative functions of any particular instance of discourse. In topicalization of the object of a sentence, for example, surface signal form is transformed from subject – verb – object to object – verb – subject. The referential information carried by either structure may be the same, but in the case of the transformation certain additional information is superimposed on the signal form as dictated by context, particular communicative function, and discourse organization. Such phenomena are more readily observable and less transparent in languages with variable word order. It might be argued that, unless it can be demonstrated that there are syntactic or semantic structures found only in the written norm, the written manifestation does not constitute an independent language norm.

We have tried to demonstrate that there is no need for exclusive identification of particular syntactic or semantic means of language with any particular norm. Rather there are particular structures that are normally correlated with particular norms. By this we mean that, as in the case of topicalization noted above, certain structures are unmarked for particular norms. When used in the context of a norm where they are not typically used, they appear as marked usages. There are regularities of signal form to function that differentiate oral and written language norms, but these regularities are not exclusive association of signal form to function. The fact that certain signal forms appear as marked testifies to this relation.

If we were to restrict our consideration only to the referential aspects, such a principle of differentiation would be less obvious. As noted in the topicalization example, the referential content remains constant in both word orders. Signal form is transformed in the service of other functional ends, which nonetheless react with surface signal form.

There is, as remarked above, no fully developed typology of syntactic, semantic, or pragmatic structures that are particularly associated with the written or oral norm of language. There are certain general characteristics of structures typical of the oral and written norm of language that are discernible; they are most obvious on the level of the construction of discourse and text. Luria (1981) notes that the structure of the written norm when found in extended monologue is particularly systematic in contrast to oral discourse. The written norm in general exhibits more elaborated and expanded grammatical structures, often noted in expanded clause structure. Luria (1981), in a summary comment on oral and written language, states:

> Thus, written speech differs radically from oral speech in that it must be produced on the basis of the rules of expanded (explicit) grammar. That is what makes the substance of written speech comprehensible in the absence of accompanying gestures and intonation. That is also why the structure of monologic, written speech does not approximate that of oral dialogic speech. In written speech, sentence length is usually greater than in oral speech. Also, written speech rarely uses direct quotation, and relies heavily on complex forms of control, e.g., relative clauses, which are rarely encountered in oral speech. (p. 166)

Other structural differences can be documented along the lines suggested by Luria, such as the difference in use of ellipsis in the oral and written norm. All of these differences must ultimately be related to functional, communicative, contextual, and psychological differences, as we have suggested earlier. Tannen (1982) illustrates work on charting structural differences that are correlated with functional differences in the two language norms. (See also Artymovyc, 1932; Havranek, 1929; Vachek, 1948.)

The observation that written language shares the same grammar as oral language has been seen as sufficient reason for considering the written norm as a mere notational variant dependent on the oral and derived from the oral norm. This is in large measure due to the restriction of the level of analysis to the isolated sentence or utterance. Differences in surface-signal form are best revealed at the level of discourse and text. Discourse and text are instantiations of particular communicative acts with particular functional ends. We have argued that it is functional considerations, as outlined here, that are constitutive of the deformation of surface-signal form in the act of communication. It is on the level of discourse organization that we must particularly look for the justification for the coexistence of the two language norms in a given linguistic community. By a careful attention to the level of discourse and text, where propositional and pragmatic functions of language intersect in the act of communication, we can hope to detail the psychological differentiation and cognitive implications of oral and written language norms. Functional language norms constitute systems of conventions. They each instantiate a system of *langue*. On the basis of the distribution of functional features and discourse organization we have tried to show that oral and written language norms constitute just such functionally differentiated languages with consistent systems of conventions and means of expression. In light of such considerations, taken together with the structural and neuropsychological argument presented in Chapter 2, we conclude that oral and written manifestations of language do indeed constitute complementary, mutually accessible, but separate language norms, each having a particular functional role within the communicative system.

On the basis of this differentiation of oral and written language norms, we formulate the principle that guides further considerations on the respective roles these two norms fulfill in the linguistic and cognitive development of children: Insofar as oral and written language norms constitute systematically distinct functional languages, they constitute distinct lines of development over the course of language acquisition and cognitive growth. In light of this principle, the remainder of this work is concerned with exploring the probable nature of the course of acquisition of oral and written language norms and the consequences for the exfoliation of cognitive systems in terms of the acquisition of oral and written language norms.

Chapter 4 examines the question of natural and cultural lines of psychological development and explores some ideas on the comparative development of oral and written language in an attempt to derive some general theoretical principles on the role of such acquisition in the broader framework of mental development.

4

Developmental Models and the Nature of Written Language Acquisition

Introduction

In Chapters 2 and 3 we argued for the need to draw a structural and functional distinction between oral and written norms of language. Having drawn such a distinction at the levels of language as system and language as intentional communicative act, this distinction should have nontrivial implications for any comprehensive theory of language acquisition and mental development. Minimally we should expect that the acquisition of oral and written language constitute overlapping but increasingly, over the course of acquisition, separate lines of development in the child. The developmental model postulated in Chapter 2 of the gradual differentiation of oral and written language at the neurological level and the evidence of functional differentiation of language norms in Chapter 3 suggest such a picture of the acquisition of oral and written language. Insofar as there is, at some level of analysis, the same underlying system of *langue* for both oral and written language, we should reasonably expect that the primary foundations for oral and written language norms are laid down simultaneously. In this sense we can expect no radical discontinuities between the acquisition of oral and written language norms. Yet given the gradual differentiation of the two norms suggested by our original developmental model and based on the principle of functional differentiation, we should also reasonably expect a discontinuity, at some stage, in the acquisition of the written norm. The prediction about the acquisition of the written norm that seems to emerge from the analytic consideration of the differences in oral and written norms of language is neatly captured by Vygotsky (1962):

> Why does writing come so hard to the schoolchild that at certain periods there is a lag of as much as six or eight years between his "linguistic age" in speaking and in writing? . . . A two year old uses few words and a simple syntax because his vocabulary is small and his knowledge of more complex sentence structure nonexistent; but the schoolchild possesses the vocabulary and the grammatical forms for writing, since they are the same [at the level of *langue*] as for oral speech. Nor can the difficulties of mastering the mechanics of writing account for the tremendous lag between the schoolchild's oral and written language. Our investigation has shown that the development of writing does not repeat the developmental history of speaking. Written speech is a separate linguistic function, differing from oral speech in both structure and mode of functioning. Even its minimal development requires a high level of abstraction. (pp. 98–99)

If it were the case that written language is merely a notational variant of oral language, we could reasonably expect that the emergence of written language would recapitulate the ontogenesis of oral language in children. It would not be unreasonable to assume that this emergence of written language would proceed far more rapidly than the ontogenesis of oral language, having as it were a basis for imitation, and should at any stage when oral and written language are available to the child reflect the state of the child's oral language development.

Before examining these predictions about the acquisition of the written norm of language, we must define more precisely what we understand by the written norm or for that matter written language in the context of the acquisition of language. We must be careful to distinguish the various possible levels of analysis of the term *written language* in speaking of its acquisition. Minimally we should distinguish the following levels:

1. The acquisition of and control over the praxic, psychomotor, and motor organization of the actual production of the inventory of graphic forms (de Ajuriaguerra & Auzias, 1975).
2. The acquisition of the translation rules (for both writing and reading) to allow transcoding between acoustic and graphic forms of language and the gradual differentiation of acoustic and graphic forms (Chao, 1961; Ellis, 1982; Haas, 1970; Henderson, 1982; McIntosh, 1961).

3. The acquisition of the structural and functional rules of written discourse organization that allow for a degree of communicative competence in using written language.

Levels 1 and 2 are necessary preconditions, at least in normal development, for the acquisition of level 3. Level 1 relates particularly to motor development, what Vygotsky has termed the *mechanics* of writing. This area we largely ignore, assuming that under normal conditions there is sufficient neural maturation to allow for such development. (For comment on motor development see Callewaert, 1954; de Ajuriaguerra & Auzias, 1975; Lurcat, 1974.) Since it is at the level of structural and functional rules for discourse production that the written norm emerges as a separate line of development, we focus on level 3, since our primary concern is to explicate the unique development of the written norm and its contribution in the general scheme of cognitive development. By *written language acquisition* we understand the ontogenesis of the set of structural and functional features and rules that characterize the ability to produce communicatively adequate written text. At a later point we address the notion that the level of discourse or extended communication is of critical importance in the acquisition of written language norms and in the genesis of certain higher-level cognitive structures. Before we turn to the major focus of this chapter, the acquisition of written language as defined under 3 above, some comment on what Vygotsky termed the *prehistory of writing* is called for. Vygotsky (1978, p. 107) states that "the first task of a scientific investigation is to reveal this prehistory of children's written language, to show what leads children to writing." The goal of writing such a coherent account of the prehistory of writing in children is unrealized, even though Vygotsky's remarks were first published in 1935. We can, as Vygotsky did, only sketch and hint at the probable course of the growth of awareness of visual signs in the child's semiotic development. This course of development from the use of gestures and symbolic play through drawing remains a dark area of child development, illuminated only at certain segments by systematic study.

We argue that what ultimately leads to the child's acquisition of written language is the pressure of a cultural institution. We do not wish to suggest that this line of development is external to the child's general or natural ontogenesis, externally imposed by culture and divorced from natural development. Before this cultural aspect of the acquisition of written language plays its role, there is a period of preparation that can be termed, with Vygotsky and Luria, the *prehistory* of the acquisition of written language. Of what does this initial step in the acquisition process consist? To make sense of any graphic meaning the child must gain an insight into the idea that a visible mark, be it conventional phonetic script, a pictograph, or a drawing, can enter into a "stand for" relation, what Luria calls the transformation of a sign-stimulus to a sign-symbol. Considering this process in the abstract, apart from any particular symbolic medium, the transformation is not unique to written language acquisition. However, when we consider the visible, and hence consciously foregrounded, aspect of the graphic mark, the nature of this transformation is somewhat distinctive. For the mark stands psychologically outside the individual in a way that the voice of the audible stimulus and audible-symbol sign does not. The graphic mark, in the transformation from sign-stimulus to sign-symbol, demands that this transformation be consciously and deliberately attended to. If in the course of acquiring oral language this process of transformation is covert, in dealing with written language it is preeminently overt and set apart from the individual. We return to this point from a somewhat different perspective when we consider the question of the respective roles of learning and development in the acquisition of the written norm of language.

The Prehistory of Writing in the Child

We return at this point to the specific question of the prehistory of writing in the child, specifically the transition of sign-stimulus to sign-symbol. Luria directly takes up this point in his study entitled "The Development of Writing in the Child," first published in 1929 and translated in his selected papers (1978). In this study of the use of writing by preschool children, Luria identifies four stages in the child's developing insights into the nature of visible sign-symbols. The basic protocol used to elicit information on the child's understanding of writing is a recall task in which children are read a number of sentences and asked to recall these sentences after presentation:

> We took a child who did not know how to write and gave him the task of remembering a certain number of sentences presented to him. Usually this number exceeded the child's mechanical capacity to remember. Once the child realized that he was unable to remember the number of words given him in the task, we gave him a sheet of paper and told him to jot down or "write" the words we presented. (Luria, 1978, p. 149)

Based on this procedure, Luria and his associates identified the following stages: (1) undifferentiated-noninstrumental, (2) undifferentiated ostensive sign use, (3) undifferentiated to differentiated transformation of sign-stimulus to sign-symbol, and (4) pictographic use of sign. A child in stage (1) produces a set of undifferentiated scrawls, arranged in some seeming order on the paper. The child does not refer to these marks in the recall task and they produce no increase in the amount of material recalled. This stage is termed *undifferentiated* because the marks produced by the subject are similar for each instance of production, no matter what the material presented to the child for recall. This stage is further termed *noninstrumental* since the child shows no awareness of the functional use to which visible signs may be put. Luria notes two aspects of this stage: the writing is divorced from its immediate objective, and the child is unaware of the function of the graphic marks. By this Luria means that the child is unaware of the functional significance of the marks. Luria speculates that it is as if the child were aware that writing is some kind of motor activity that adults engage in that is productive of visible marks on paper, but that there is only an imitation of certain external features of the act of writing. The child produces the visible marks (in light of their undifferentiated nature it would be inappropriate to label them signs of any kind) but does not grasp their relation to either the task at hand or the "connection with the idea evoked by the sentence to be written; it was not yet instrumental or functionally related to the content of what was to be written" (Luria, 1978, pp. 153–154).

The second stage is in many respects similar to this first undifferentiated, preinstrumental stage in that the marks produced are not externally distinguishable one from the other. Yet there is a subtle shift in awareness on the part of the child as to their relation to the sentences in the recall task. Luria comments on this shift in use:

> We . . . discovered that these scribblings actually were more than just simple scrawls, and were able to show without error and many times in succession which scribble signified which of the dictated sentences. Writing was still undifferentiated in its outward appearance, but the child's relation to it had completely changed: from a self-contained motor activity, it had been transformed into a memory-helping sign. The child had begun to associate the dictated sentences with his undifferentiated scribble, which had begun to serve the auxiliary function of a sign. (p. 159)

Luria considers this transformation to the use of what he calls a *primary sign* an ostensive use of the mark to point to a particular content. We might speculate that this transformation is somewhat analogous to certain developments in the use of gesture in a deictic sense. Luria considers the emergence of this ostensive use of undifferentiated marks the first form of writing in which the functional relation of the mark as an instrumental means is grasped. But Luria does not consider this use of undifferentiated marks as a sign in the symbolic sense nor as an instrumental sign in the fullest possible sense. The true symbolic or instrumental use of a visible mark is characterized in Figure 4.1, where a content A is encoded in a visible and differentiated sign X, which on a later occasion serves to recall the content A in an immediate sense.

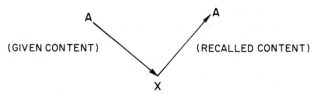

(AUXILIARY SIGN)

Figure 4.1   The nature of sign mediation.   Reproduced from Luria (1978) with permission of M. E. Sharp.

On the use of these undifferentiated marks as ostensive or primary signs at this stage of the prehistory of writing Luria (1978) comments:

> It [the undifferentiated mark] only signals that *some* content written down by means of it exists, but does not lead us to it; it is only a cue evoking some (associative) reaction in the subject. We actually do not have in it the complex instrumental structure of an act, and it may be described by the following formula:
> (Given content) A $\longrightarrow$ X
> X $\longrightarrow$ N(Recalled content)
> (Primitive Mark)
> where N may not have any relation to the given content A, or, of course, to the mark X. Instead of an instrumental act which uses X to revert attention back to A, we have here two direct acts: (1) the mark on the paper, and (2) the response to the mark as a cue. (p. 162)

Even though, as Luria points out, this usage falls short of a grasp of the true nature of visible sign to a given content, this step is a critical one along the path to a fuller grasp of the relation of a particular written sign to particular ideational content.

With the next two stages in this process of development the child begins to move towards the use of a differentiated mark and an awareness of the functional relation of the mark to a given content.   In the third stage there is a double transformation: first, surface differentiation of the mark, and second, use of the mark as a true instrumental sign-symbol.   Luria and his coworkers speculate that this transformation is evoked by the need to attend to several factors in noting down the stimulus material.   These factors are quantity, rhythm, and contrast.   So the need to recall sentence pairs such as *There are two trees in the yard* and *There are many trees in the forest* leads to a differentiation of the marks used to encode or write these sentences for later recall.   Under the pressure to represent such factors as quantity, rhythm, and contrast, what were once undifferentiated marks are transformed into a kind of primitive pictography having definite differentiated contours.   It is interesting to note that Werner (1957), in an attempt to study the symbolic mediation and organization of thought, uses a graphic protocol similar to that employed by Luria. Werner distinguishes several differentiating features in the use of simple line representations for subtle language nuances such as tense and aspect, for example, pressure, length, speed, and position on page. The Werner study suggests that indeed the idea of a rich graphic symbol system may well have deep genetic roots.

The final stage elicited by Luria in his study of the prehistory of writing is more truly pictographic. Luria suggests the child calls on his capacities for drawing to further and more fully differentiate his visible-sign use in writing specific contents. Vygotsky has suggested at various times that this prehistory phase of writing may be linked with the ontogenesis of gesture and drawing in the child.

Luria makes the point, when reflecting on this process of visible-sign differentiation in the child, that the child's understanding is generated by the very act of using signs and that the origin of this primitive use of visible signs is not generated in the first instance by an understanding of their nature. In this connection it is interesting to note the remarks of Werner and Kaplan (1963) on symbol formation and cognition: "The act of denotative reference does not merely, or mainly, operate with *already formed* expressive similarities between entities. Through its productive nature, it brings to the fore latent expressive qualities in both vehicular material and referent that will allow the *establishment* of *semantic correspondence* between the two entities" (p. 25).

In like manner Humboldt (1836, p. 57) states that language as a symbolic vehicle comes into being "in the very act of its production." In a very similar way, understanding of the nature of writing comes about in the very act of its production, as suggested by Luria's study.

Biological and Cultural Lines of Development

Luria's study is not definitive and is certainly not the last word on the developmental prehistory of writing. Clearly a sustained research effort should examine the basic semiotic development of children in the realm of the use of other-than-verbal manifestations of language and symbolic development in other representational media. Gardner's work at Project Zero has provided some seminal insights into such areas (Gardner, 1978; Gardner, Howard, & Perkins, 1974; Wolf & Gardner, 1978). Luria's work itself is of immense interest and significance in pointing to different lines of development in the acquisition of written language. His work concentrates on the natural or organic line of development. The term *natural* is used by Luria and others such as Vygotsky to distinguish development explained by biological or noncultural influences in contrast to development that may be explained primarily by cultural or social factors. This natural line of development is largely unmediated by the intervention of systematic cultural practice, whereas in the cultural line deliberate social–cultural praxis and sociocultural institutions such as language are brought to bear on the developmental process in a conscious way through institutional practice, as, for example, schooling in Western technological cultures. Summing up his treatment of the prehistory of writing, Luria (1978, p. 193) states, "The further development of literacy involves the assimilation of the mechanisms of culturally elaborated symbolic writing and the use of symbolic devices to simplify and expedite the act of recording." Speaking of the transformation from undifferentiated marks to pictographic representation and the further assimilation of cultural practice, Luria comments:

> At the same time this transformation takes place, a fundamental re-organization occurs in the most basic mechanisms of the child's behavior; on top of the primitive forms of direct adaptation to the problems imposed by his environment, the child now builds up new, complex, cultural forms; the major psychological functions no longer operate through primitive natural forms and begin to employ complex cultural devices. These devices are tried in succession, and perfected, and in the process transform the child as well. (p. 193)

This intricate interplay between natural and cultural lines of development is further explored below in the context of explaining the acquisition of written language. Only by fully appreciating the nature of this cultural line of development can we make sense of the acquisition of written language, which is preeminently a cultural creation. Far too often has what is termed *cultural* been rather arbitrarily excluded from developmental accounts of the growth of the mind.

The dichotomy between biology and culture is also found in accounts of ontogenesis. Indeed, the continuity of psychogenesis and biogenesis is often stressed in such accounts. Perhaps the most forceful advocate of such a principle is Piaget. He articulates an explanation of ontogenesis in biological terms in his *Biology and Knowledge* (1971). The central principles to account for change — assimilation–accommodation, equilibration, and self-regulation — are rooted in the very biology of the organism. Indeed, many of the fundamental concepts of mainstream accounts of psychological development appear to be drawn from studies of biological morphogenesis. Without arguing the merits of this treatment, we must point out that this account and indeed much of Piaget's work on genetic epistemology seriously undervalues and underplays any sociocultural explanation of change in the psychogenesis of the individual or the species. (For a well-considered critique of this position and its probable philosophical roots see Russell, 1978.) In light of this lack of attention it is not surprising that accounts of the acquisition of written language, so much a part of man's cultural history, have received less-than-serious attention in accounts of the acquisition of knowledge.

Yet this lack of appreciation or understanding of the place of a cultural line in the explanation of ontogenesis has not always been the case. Hobhouse (1913, p. 90) writes, "From the dawn of language onwards the action of mind on mind is the *leading factor* [emphasis added] in development, and henceforward every phase of thought may be regarded as a social product." Hobhouse defines this cultural factor in development when he states, "This branch of our inquiry . . . is concerned with what we may call the social mind, understanding by that term, the Order formed by the *operation of mind on mind* [emphasis added], incorporated in a social tradition handed on by language and by social institutions of many kinds" (p. 13). This concern with the sociocultural line of development is to be found in the work of Baldwin (1894, 1913) and Romanes (1902) writing at approximately the same time as Hobhouse. Bound up in this cultural line of development is a recognition of the sociocultural basis of knowledge as expressed in Wittgenstein's term *labensformen*. In turn the social basis of knowledge finds its expression in the public symbol system of the group, that is, language. Russell (1978) sums up this argument when he writes:

> The system [conceptual] is the result of the phylogenetic process of conciliance within the species about ways of proceeding, of being forced by our necessarily social life to conventionalize our criteria for what is and is not, can and cannot be the case. The outward and perceptible result of this accretion is our language system, and indeed the existence of a conceptual system is inconceivable without some public signal system. (p. 208)

Any sociocultural principle in the explanation of development is intimately bound up with the whole process of acquisition of the public symbol system of the particular group or society. The social basis of objective knowledge is unthinkable without such a system of representation in mental function and activity. Knowledge is mediated in Baldwin's sense by language. Russell (1978, p. 249) states that "only through a sign system can knowledge be made common and objective so that the child makes the world objective to himself by the utilization of rules engrained in the linguistic-conceptual system . . . , which are also modes of representation." Part and parcel of this process, the drive to objectivity in the acquisition of knowledge, is the growing consciousness or meta-awareness of the sign system and its decontextualization. By *decontextualiza-*

tion we understand the divorce of discourse from immediate perceptual dependence. When we move from speech to writing there is a necessary movement from contextual to more decontextual representation and a growing consciousness of the representational system itself (Donaldson, 1978). The changes to be seen with the appearance of language — first spoken and then written — are best explained by appeal to a cultural line of explanation or Hobhouse's "action of mind on mind." A consideration of the whole course of cognitive development points to the fact that in addition to the principles of explanation of development that may be termed natural or biological there are cultural or social – social-psychic principles that are simultaneously operative in ontogenesis and largely account for change in the organism after the appearance of language.

Culture, Learning, and Development

Much of the time during which the acquisition of written language takes place is a period when the child is particularly subject to the influence of a cultural line of development. This is particularly true for those children in developed technological societies, where the acquisition of writing takes place in a formal school setting. It can be argued that, because of this formal schooling, the acquisition of written language is simply the result of instruction in contrast to the acquisition of spoken language, which is the consequence of development per se. In Chapter 2, instances of this dichotomy were used to argue for the primacy of spoken language and the secondarity and artificiality of written language. Such a dichotomy between learning and development, especially in the domain of language, is simply not justified. If studies of language acquisition reveal anything it is that the child does not construct language on his own in some interactionless vacuum. Studies (Bruner, 1975; Ninio & Bruner, 1978; Trevarthen & Hubley, 1978) have again and again shown that the child's attempts at communicative language construction demonstrate active modeling of primary caregivers and other adults in the child's *umwelt.* This is a sort of instruction, albeit not formal or systematic. It is also clear that learning plays its role in all aspects of development and certainly cannot be limited to the period of formal schooling. While learning in the preschool years does differ in many respects from learning in formal school settings, we should not conclude that learning and development constitute distinct and irreconcilable processes. Nor should one take the other extreme position, as some have, that development is learning. Rather, learning in formal school settings complements and feeds development. We must bear in mind that at the time of entrance into school the child has moved decisively into the phase of cultural development alluded to earlier. On this relation of learning and development Vygotsky (1978) states:

> We propose that an essential feature of learning is that it creates the zone of proximal development; that is learning awakens a variety of internal developmental processes that are able to operate only when the child is interacting with people in his environment and in cooperation with his peers. . . .
>
> From this point of view learning is not development; however, properly organized learning results in mental development and sets in motion a variety of developmental processes that would be impossible apart from learning. Thus, learning is a necessary and universal aspect of the process of developing culturally organized, specifically human, psychological functions. (p. 90)

Written language is a culturally organized function or system subject to learning and development. Clearly, in most cases, the acquisition of written language belongs centrally within the cultural line of development. However, the exclusive role assigned to instruction in the acquisition of written language has been overrated. Such an assertion is likely due to a lack of controlled study of the process of written language acquisition. Gundlach (1981) comments on the role of instruction in this process from the perspective of careful studies of the acquisition of writing:

> Becoming literate seems to depend on instructional support and special conditions of language use associated with school. . . . However, while children's writing develops largely in such contexts, there is at best an indirect relation between what children are taught about writing and what they learn. Indeed, some children learn to write with little or no instruction, while others fail to develop as writers, no matter how much instruction is provided for them. (p. 134)

We would wholeheartedly agree with this comment if what is meant by *taught* is deliberate instruction. Clearly what is taught in this sense is far from what is to be understood by the terms *written language,* or *written language acquisition.* It is a dubious assumption that the acquisition of written language ends with the close of formal schooling; we need only recall the statement of Humboldt about language coming into being in the "very act of its production." In Chapter 5 we explore in more detail the nature of the relation between written language and schooling when we consider issues of social praxis and written language. For the moment we only claim that instruction is not sufficient to account for the acquisition of written language unless what we mean by this is deliberate instruction in the mechanics of graphic-form manipulation or explicit instruction in rules of phoneme-grapheme correspondence and that this acquisition constitutes the domain of an authentic developmental process.

Turning once again to the distinction we have made between a natural and a cultural line of development, the acquisition of written language falls, we have stated, within the cultural line of development. But we do not wish to imply that there is a radical discontinuity between a natural line or cultural line. As we have argued in earlier chapters about natural versus nonnatural capacities in man, we cannot draw a distinction based on a difference between biology and culture. In speaking of phylogenesis it may be valid to speak of change in prehominid periods as directed primarily or exclusively by natural biological-environmental principles and change in posthominid periods as primarily explained by sociocultural principles of change. Yet even this distinction draws an arbitrary line between the biological and cultural when speaking about functional organization and change in the organism. Man's phylogenetic history is a complex intertwining of natural and social factors of change. These two aspects of development are continuous in the sense that the natural line is always intertwined with the cultural line. At various stages of development, either the natural or the cultural line may be particularly foregrounded, but both lines of development are present and operative. Where these lines of development differ is in the organizing and explanatory principles operative within each domain. On this point Vygotsky (1928) writes:

> Cultural development does not create anything over and above that which potentially exists in natural development in the child's behavior. Culture, generally speaking, does not produce anything new apart from that which is given by nature. But it transforms nature to suit the ends of man. This same transformation occurs in the cultural development of behavior. It also consists of inner changes in that which was given by nature in the course of the natural development of behavior. (p. 418)

This remark implies that there is no radical break between the natural and the cultural line. The cultural line does not simply impose something on top of a mammalian foundation of development or just add something that is outside the range of biological development. Natural development is guided by a set of energetic principles, whereas cultural development is driven by a set of nonenergetic principles; herein lies the basis for any difference between these lines of development. (For a challenging account of energetic and nonenergetic causation in the domain of morphogenesis and the insufficiency of solely energetic explanations, see Sheldrake, 1982.) By a natural line of development or the principle of explanation in a natural line of development we understand a principle similar to the assimilation-accommodation principle articulated by Piaget. Such a principle of explanation of change is rooted in the biological (Piaget, 1971) and owes nothing in its first instance to cultural forms. In a fuller statement on the transformation effected by the cultural line of development, Vygotsky (1928) argues:

However that structure [of thought] does not remain unchanged. That is the most important point of all we know concerning the cultural development of the child. This structure is not an outward, ready-made creation. It originates in conformance with definite laws at a certain stage of the natural development of the child. It cannot be forced on the child from outside, it always originates inwardly, although it is modelled by the deciding influence of external problems with which the child is faced and the external signs with which it operates. After the structure comes into being, it does not remain unchanged, but is subject to a lengthy internal change which shows all the signs of development.

A new method of behavior does not simply remain fixed as a certain external habit. It has its internal history. It is included in the general process of the development of a child's behavior, and we therefore have a right to talk of a genetic relation between certain structures of cultural reasoning and behavior, and of the development of the methods of behavior. This development is certainly of a special kind, is radically different from the organic development, and has its own definite laws. It is extremely difficult to grasp and express precisely the peculiarity of that type of development. (pp. 418–419)

In affirming that cultural development is different and has its own definite laws, we have to ask what these laws might be. In the case of the acquisition of written language—an external sign system—the laws of development are partly derived from the properties of written language. The cultural line of development primarily consists of mastering the public sign system, that is, language that is the common coin of cultural interchange and praxis and the repository of *Labensformen.* Mastering of written language introduces two unique features. These features or principles derive from the functional nature of written language considered in Chapter 3. Written language is more external and decontextualized than spoken language. Written language represents a more advanced point along the cultural line of development. If the cultural line of development can be said to appear formally with the mastering of spoken language, it is further radicalized in the acquisition of the written manifestation of language. The principles or features of externalization and decontextualization introduce in the first instance of their appearance a distal principle of control over development. In this respect Bruner (1975) writes:

The sphere in which language provides a new basis for human invention of new modes of thought is beyond either innate linguistic competence or socially reinforced communicative competence. We shall label it—analytic competence—and its principle feature as with Piaget's formal operations . . . is that it involves prolonged operation of thought processes exclusively on linguistic representation, on propositional structure, accompanied by strategies of thought and problem solving appropriate not to direct experience with objects and events but with ensembles of propositions. (p. 72)

The process that Bruner refers to is uniquely instantiated in the acquisition of written language. The feature of decontextualization distances the language user from both the sign system itself and what Bruner refers to as "direct experience" to a far greater degree than does spoken language. All such differences serve to introduce into later stages of development principles of explanation that are discontinuous with those of earlier stages. This should not be particularly surprising, for while development is a continuous process, it is also marked by discontinuities in transition at certain points. In this respect, psychological development is unlike embryological development, whose model is that of a smooth continuous unfolding in time.

We have argued that the acquisition of written language, while occurring under circumstances radically different from those of spoken language, can in no way be simply dismissed as a skill learned solely through some model of formal and deliberate instruction. Such a dismissal would constitute a gross misrepresentation of the role of instruction in the whole of cognitive and linguistic development, and, further, seriously oversimplify the nature of developmental processes. Development, we have argued, consists in both a natural line and a cultural line, each of which admit of discontinuous principles of explanation but are nonetheless not dichotomous processes. As Piaget remarked (1969, p. xvi), "learning is an acquisition which occurs over time and thus, itself, constitutes, a form of development."

The Nature of Written Language Acquisition

The acquisition of written language properly begins with the achievements referred to in categories 1 and 2 listed in the introductory section of this chapter. During this period the child masters the cultural conventions of the script of the linguistic community. But this mastery, even when achieved, if limited to production of the graphic inventory and translation rules for graphic and phonic correspondence, does not constitute what we understand by "written language". Such mastery, while the sine qua non for written language acquisition, constitutes a sort of prehistory, in Luria's sense, of the acquisition of written language. This acquisition is fundamental and foundational and we do not wish to minimize its importance. However, in the past there has been a tendency to associate this stage in development with the central core of what is to be understood by written language acquisition. What was seen to follow this initial step in development has been viewed as a trivial elaboration of this achievement. If we accept the contention that written language is simply parasitic on spoken language for its syntax, semantics, pragmatics, and discourse organization, then it follows that once we acquire the ability to interpret graphic lexical forms via the spoken language, all further development can follow fairly easily aided by some model of instruction. But we have been at some pains to argue that written language is not parasitic in this sense and that the exfoliation of ability in written language is hardly a trivial affair of direct conscious instruction. The simplicity of supposing that written language acquisition simply parallels and is parasitic on spoken language is pointed up by noting the numerous cases of those with a command of graphic production and translation rules and yet with no effective ability to use written language in a communicatively productive way.

While the initial acquisition of graphic and phonic forms cannot be said to constitute or characterize the whole of the acquisition process for written language, it is nonetheless, as we have affirmed above, a necessary precondition for the acquisition process proper. In the review of Luria's study on the prehistory of writing we have singled out those aspects of this process that seem of key importance, at least in the child's growing awareness of the functional sign capacity of the written mark and its transformation into a visible sign-symbol. As Luria argues and other research seems to confirm, this process is prior to the onset of formal instruction. Well before formal schooling, children may be exposed to a wealth of print or written experiences. As Sulzby (1982) has remarked:

> We tend to be far less aware of the written language that surrounds even tiny infants and of the early impact of written language and written language-like forms and functions upon the child's developing language abilities. . . . Printed forms of language are fairly easily recognizable as written language. Story books are used for interaction between parents and children. Embroidered ABC samplers may hang on the wall above a child's crib and as he is tucked in, mama may touch "A" and say, "What's that, Ryan? A." (p. 17)

Children's television programs such as "Sesame Street" and "The Electric Company" expose the child to yet further examples of the written code. Examples could be multiplied, documenting children's prewriting exposure to written language in many contemporary Western cultures. (For further discussion see especially the studies by Clay, 1979; Ferreiro & Teberosky, 1982.) When attended to in a critical and inquiring fashion, the supposedly oral world of the prewriting child emerges as one replete with written language exposure. What the experiences may contribute to the acquisition process for written language is still not fully clear. However, the assumption that written language development is solely the product of formal instruction is seriously challenged by such inquiry into the prehistory of writing acquisition.

We stated earlier we would not give major attention to either psycho-motor and motor development of the ability to produce the inventory of graphic forms or the acquisition of the translation rules for the phonic-graphic lexical forms. Motor development of writing falls clearly outside the scope of our considerations. The acquisition of translation rules for graphic and phonic lexical forms has received extensive treatment in the literature on reading. Further treatments of the acquisition of translation rules from the perspective of writing per se have received a great deal of attention under the rubric of children's "invented spellings" (see Chomsky, 1970; Reed, 1975).

Studies of Written Language Acquisition

At the beginning of this chapter we defined the acquisition of writing as the ontogenesis of the set of structural and functional features and rules that characterize and inform the process of producing communicatively adequate text. Gundlach (1981, p. 138) has observed that "Writing is a process of making, and what the writer makes is not a word or a sentence but a text . . . . Children, if given the chance, compose whole discourses from the beginning of their development as writers." The end of written language development is the ability to produce communicatively adequate text. To characterize written language development in terms of the formation of graphic units, either letters or words, or in terms of translation rules between graphic and phonic lexical items seriously distorts accounts of written language development. The bulk of linguistic and psychological evidence in the domains of oral and written language has confirmed that man's use of language is best characterized by the ability to produce discourse and text. An adequate characterization of either oral or written language development must be built in terms of the discourse or text level. To do less seriously impoverishes our accounts of language functioning in man.

It is unfortunate that most studies of the acquisition or development of written language have ignored the level of text. This is in part explained by linguists' preoccupation with language at the level of the word or the syntax of the atomic sentence. Insofar as psychology has been content to derive its models of language from theoretical linguistics, it has also ignored discourse or text in approaching the question of written language acquisition. Since the early 1970s, however, there has been a veritable explosion of theoretical and applied work in linguistics and psychology on supersentential phenomena in language and knowledge structures, from the efforts to construct text models and grammars in linguistics (see

Dressler, 1978; Petöfi, 1979; van Dijk, 1972, 1977; van Dijk & Petöfi, 1977) to work in artificial intelligence and cognitive science on frame-based notions of knowledge and representation (Metzing, 1980). In Chapter 6 we detail one such model of the acquisition of written language within a text-based framework and present some findings on the development of written language within this framework.

Before turning our attention to a textual approach to written language acquisition, we examine the findings of a number of representative studies of the development of written language based on other frameworks. Due to the great number of studies on writing and literacy we limit this consideration to studies that are representative of the many trends this research has taken and of the various ways the term *written language* is construed. We can characterize studies of written language development as having one of three types of focus: (1) syntactic, (2) sociolinguistic, or (3) psychological – cognitive. Syntactic studies are primarily concerned with detailing the development of linguistic maturity of the written language as measured by the increase in syntactic complexity of written sentences. Such studies focus primarily on the clause or sentence level. Sociolinguistic studies can generally be grouped under the rubric "literacy." These studies concentrate on the social, cultural, or educational factors surrounding the entry of the child into literate practice. By and large such studies pay moderate attention to language itself and concentrate on social-psychological variables. Psychological-cognitive studies have grown out of the field of cognitive science. Their focus is primarily on what is termed the psychological *process* of writing. At their worst such studies ignore or pay scant attention to the variable of language itself. Many of these studies are marginally developmental but are mainly concerned with process in skilled writing.

In general, studies in any of these categories with either a primarily developmental methodology or developmental focus are scant. As a discipline, developmental psycholinguistics has to some extent ignored the domain of written language. This neglect is perhaps not particularly surprising given the misconceptions and prevailing notions about written language that we have attempted to detail in earlier chapters. If written language is seen simply as the product of formal instruction, it is hardly surprising that developmental psycholinguistics has ignored it.

Turning first to syntactic studies, work on the development of written language has been undertaken by Rouma (1913), Lull (1929), Brueckner (1939), Thabault (1944), Perron and de Gobineau (1954), Tondow (1954), Harrell (1957), Fraisse and Breyton (1959), Lurcat (1963), Hunt (1965), and Pellegrino and Scopesi (1978). While the methodology of the majority of these researchers could hardly be termed rigorously developmental, they at least have concerned themselves with either change over time or change by grade level. A second major focus of a number of these studies is a comparison of the oral and written language development of children at various ages or grade levels. Harrell (1957) constitutes one of the major assessments of oral and written language development in children within a syntactic framework. We limit our consideration to Harrell and the Pellegrino and Scopesi studies, as they are fairly representative of the findings in this area.

The Harrell monograph is more exhaustive and far-ranging than other comparative studies of oral and written language development. It describes and compares aspects of oral and written language in school children at 9, 11, 13, and 15 years of age. Harrell (1957) summarizes the sample and design as follows:

> The total sample consisted of 320 children chosen from four age levels . . . . In order to control the amount of practice and instruction in writing, no child who was advanced for his age or retarded for his age was taken; thus only 9-year-olds in the fourth grade, only 11-year-olds in the sixth grade, etc., were taken . . . . To collect the written stories, groups of children were shown a short movie and asked to write the story of the movie. Oral stories were obtained in the same way except that the children were shown a different movie, chosen so as to be similar in content, and were asked to tell their stories independently and privately to the investigator. (p. 63)

On the analysis of data from these protocols Harrell states:

> The data were analyzed to determine
> (a) the length of the composition,
> (b) the length of clauses,
> (c) the number of unrelated words used in oral stories,
> (d) the proportion of subordinate clauses to the total number of clauses,
> (e) the proportion of various clause types to the total number of subordinate clauses, and
> (f) the position of the subordinate clauses in relation to the clause or word they modify or to which they are connected. (p. 63)

Before considering Harrell's findings, a brief comment on the analysis and design is necessary. The measures of linguistic maturity used in the study appear somewhat limited in scope. There is, for example, no appreciation of the discourse or text level. Analysis and comparison of oral and written data are carried out on the unit of the sentence with no questioning of whether the sentence is a proper unit of analysis for oral data. Oral and written language production are compared on the basis of sentence complexity, percentage of sentence types produced, and percentage of types of subordinate clauses produced in the respective language forms. The results must be considered in light of the restricted nature of the analysis to which the data were subjected, bearing in mind that factors such as context, mode of production, word order, and hypersyntax were not taken into account. In this respect the Harrell study is representative of syntactic studies in group (1).

Harrell found significant differences for oral and written production. For measures of length and complexity of sentence type and subordination; written productions are generally more complex in sentence type and exhibit a higher subordination index. In particular, the following differences appear: At all age levels, oral stories are longer than written stories. However, the overall length of clause in written stories is greater at all ages. A significantly greater number of subordinate clauses occur in written productions. These differences increase especially after about 9.5 years of age. This subordination index for written production is seen to be related to subjects' mental age.

In general Harrell's findings seem to indicate that there is a difference in children's written and oral productions of narrative material. However, given the type of analysis employed, it is difficult to conclude whether this difference is a significant one (other than in a statistical sense) or merely trivial. Great emphasis seems to be placed on the differences found for the subordination index, but no adequate reasons are put forth to explain this difference. It might be the case that some of these observed differences can be explained by the functional differentiation of oral and written communication. In the Harrell study, no attempt is made to assess the effect of having an interlocutor present. In any case, asking children to produce sustained monologue in an oral mode may not be the most accurate means of assessing oral communicative competence, given that the majority of oral communications, under ordinary circumstances, take place in shorter dialogic exchanges where the production demands are far different from those of sustained monologue.

Pellegrino and Scopesi (1978) undertook an assessment of the development of descriptive language production, oral and written, in children between the ages of 8 and 14. They hypothesize that within the descriptive framework, which they claim places a premium on the referential function of language, oral language production should evidence less structural complexity but a greater number of sentences as compared with written language production and that observed differences should be less pronounced at younger ages. The untimed experimental task was to have subjects write and verbally produce a description of two polychrome pictures of country scenes. A total of 90 subjects were used and 180 texts analyzed.

The unit of analysis chosen was defined by syntactic criteria:

> In defining such units, punctuation was not taken into account, because of the inadequate use of it frequently found in written texts at the lower age levels, besides its being absent . . . in recorded spoken texts . . . . The verbal phrases located in each text were divided into a series of sentences, each of which was examined in the first place with reference to the presence or absence of explicit nexuses with contiguous sentences. (Pellegrino & Scopesi, 1978, p. 7)

Based on this procedure the authors characterized sentences according to their structural complexity: simple enumeration, expanded enumeration, simple sentence, simple expanded sentence, compound and complex sentences. Comparisons of oral and written productions were carried out on the basis of this structural complexity index.

The authors found that analysis of the texts, oral and written, confirmed their original hypothesis that "oral language presents a greater incidence of sentences as compared to the written at all age levels; poorly structured forms are generally more frequent in the spoken than in the written form" (p. 14). They go on to state that "written and oral patterns do not appear to be highly differentiated at the lowest age level . . . , whereas at [older age] levels an increasing differentiation may be noted, with the most considerable difference at the highest level" (p. 14).

In general the results detailed by Pellegrino and Scopesi seem to agree with the findings of Harrell and others. Pellegrino and Scopesi conclude that oral and written language represent separate linguistic developments, written language evolving in an autonomous manner. It appears that most studies of this kind support the conclusion that written language does not recapitulate nor necessarily parallel oral language development. The two modes do differ, but the nature of this difference is not clearly articulated. Both the Harrell study and the Pellegrino and Scopesi study, as do most, opt for the sentence as the unit of analysis. As we have noted above, the sentence may not be properly applicable to considerations of oral data. It is also questionable whether differences in function and structure emerge on the level of such a unit as the sentence. It seems more reasonable to assume that differences, if they do exist, would be more readily apparent on the level of text and discourse (see Chapter 3 above). However, the studies considered as representative of work in this area do point to differences in oral and written language production that are difficult to ignore.

Studies such as those of Hunt (1965, 1970) and others (Evanechko, Ollila, & Armstrong, 1974; Peltz, 1974) investigate the nature of change in written language ability. All these studies (again using a sentence or clauselike unit as the basis for analysis) confirm that units of written language, that is, the written sentence, increase in both length and complexity during the course of language development. Comparative studies of oral and written language development such as those of Golub (1969), O'Donnell, Griffin, and Norris (1967), and De Vito (1965) consistently report differences in the syntax of sentence and clause units in oral and written language samples. However, generally these studies do not present data that allow for any assessment of differences that might exist at the level of discourse or text, nor do the data allow for any refined analysis of order of acquisition of various structures in speech or writing. (For a useful summary of the major studies in this category, see Ulatowska, Baker, & Stern, 1979.) None of the studies that we can group under our first category articulate a truly developmental account of the acquisition of written language as we have defined the term at the opening of this chapter. What such studies do provide is some documentation for Vygotsky's contention that written language acquisition does not simply or easily recapitulate the acquisition of oral language.

The second category of studies on the development of written language can be grouped under the general rubric "literacy". A great number of studies are at least loosely concerned with the sociocultural facilitating factors in written language acquisition and the necessity for critical attention to sociocultural variables when studying the acquisition of written language. Whiteman and Hall (1981), Nystrand (1982), and Ferreiro and Teberosky (1982) present a comprehensive cross-section of the work in this aspect of written language acquisition. Stubbs (1980) is particularly developmental in focus. Sulzby (1982) presents one of the few major assessments of children's early experience with and initiation into the world of written language using a cross-sectional approach. In all this work there is generally a recognition of the importance of the level of discourse and text and some exploration of systematic differences between the sociocultural organization of oral and written language. These studies do not in general present very sophisticated models of written language at the level of text. By and large the linguistic aspects of written language are deemphasized in favor of an emphasis on sociocultural variables such as the shift away from the multimodality of oral discourse, meta-awareness of written language, factors of decontextualization, functional uses of written language, and differential organization of various communication environments such as home and school. These studies do focus *necessary* attention on this set of communicative and sociocultural variables.

This level of attention to the sociocultural variables within which written language functions addresses an imbalance found in studies of language acquisition in which actual questions of use and social organization are either ignored or given scant attention. While drawing attention to these critical variables of use and organization many of the studies that can be grouped under the rubric of "literacy" fail to integrate data and findings with adequate linguistic models of text or discourse. This is particularly unfortunate since the only hope of arriving at sound conclusions about the acquisition and use of written language is to recognize that linguistic, functional, and sociocultural considerations must be taken into account simultaneously. Models of the acquisition of written language must give due attention to articulating a concept of text function and use. All three factors, linguistic, functional and sociocultural, are interfunctionally defined, and to believe that they can be considered in isolation is an analytic fiction. Genetic studies provide the best opportunity for understanding how each of these factors contributes to mature written language use.

We consider the nature and relevance of developmental literacy studies in Chapter 6 and integrate such studies in a general model of literacy and written language acquisition.

The third type of studies we have termed *psychological – cognitive.* Studies that fall under this rubric are not, properly speaking, developmental. These studies focus on process and plans in the actual production of written text. Such studies are primarily motivated by work in the area of cognitive science. The most representative studies of this sort may be found in Gregg and Steinberg (1980). Flower and Hayes (1980, 1981) is typical of such cognitive-science approaches to written language. Also falling in this group is the work of Bruce, Collins, Rubin and Gentner (1978), Nold (1981), and Scardamalia (1981).

All of these studies seek to discover the cognitive steps or procedures that are implemented in and are constitutive of the process of producing written language. From the point of view of knowledge about the acquisition process, such studies tell us little. However, insofar as they attend to primarily cognitive or psychological variables in an information-processing framework, they advance our understanding of the cognitive constraints on the production process. If such studies are flawed, it is in the lack of linguistic or psycholinguistic sophistication. In one sense such criticism is unfair, since these studies do not set out to provide a comprehensive model of written-language function. Yet the lack of linguistic or psycholinguistic consideration potentially compromises the usefulness of such studies in formulating a model of written-language production at the level of text. As we argued earlier, the analytic separation of psychological, sociocultural, and psycholinguistic variables is a fiction likely to lead to unwarranted conclusions about the acquisition process for written language and inadequate models of written-language use.

This brief survey of representative trends in research on written language demonstrates the paucity of truly developmental studies on the acquisition of written language at the level of text and discourse. What studies there are have either not been concerned with questions of development or not been constructed in light of any adequate model of written text. This trend is not particularly surprising when we consider the lack of any serious attention given to distinguishing written language as an autonomous norm of *langue*. There are a group of studies concerned with the topic of the acquisition of written language that do not fall under any of the categories we have discussed thus far. As they represent attempts to come to grips directly with the issue of development of written-language production, they deserve brief consideration.

Shuy (1981) addresses the question of a genetic model of written-language development. Olson and Torrance (1981) also attack the question of written-language development in an article focusing on language development during the school years. The collection of papers by Freedle and Fine (1983) also contains a number of reviewed papers that address various aspects of written language from a developmental perspective at the level of discourse and text. Shuy's article in particular is notable for its attempt to delineate the requirements for an adequate developmental theory of written language. The Olson and Torrance article is particularly useful for its discussion of the question of text and the need to appreciate the nature of written text in any developmental account of written language.

Shuy (1981) addresses his remarks to two main points: the reasons why developmental theories of writing have not been forthcoming and the criteria for constructing such a developmental theory. Shuy attributes the lack of developmental models of writing largely to a failure to understand the relation of writing to language. Shuy identifies what he feels are basic issues that any developmental model of writing should attend to:

> It is not at all clear what the components are in such a theory. Perhaps some of the same ones used in language learning [oral?] or reading would obtain (e.g., lexicon, morphology, sentences and utterances) but probably not in the same ways, since writing is developed after language *[langue?]* is rather thoroughly learned. It would appear, in fact, that the major components in such a theory would be discourse or utterance components — those aspects of writing which foreground, subordinate, equalize, relate, connect, alternate, open, close, continue, etc. (pp. 125–126)

Shuy's remarks seem to hint that discourse or text levels are the critical feature to be attended to in developmental accounts of writing. We concur entirely with this conclusion but not for the reasons given by Shuy, who seems to propose a distinction between language and writing at the discourse or text level when he says that "writing is developed after language is . . . thoroughly learned." Shuy goes on to comment, "If a developmental theory of writing is to create utterance-building strategies [text creation], it will be necessary for us to determine what these discourse units are and how they are acquired. It will come as no surprise to learn that the science is not yet there" (p. 127).

Shuy places the effort to document how discourse units and strategies are acquired squarely at the core of any developmental account of written language. Again we must agree fully with the central place given to this notion. We seriously disagree with Shuy's contention that we are far from realizing such a model. We present in Chapter 6 one text model that could serve as the basis for an account of written-language acquisition. As we stated earlier, many text models that might serve as a theoretical framework for developmental research have been proposed. In general, Shuy's paper is incisive in its insights about past failures to provide developmental accounts and in its recognition of the central place for text and text-construction factors in any such developmental account of written language.

The Olson and Torrance (1981) paper specifically takes up the topic of written text. The authors discuss at some length the developmental consequences and intellectual implications of the gradual acquisition and command over written-language production during the school years. Many of the variables that Olson and Torrance identify as critical in the language and mental development of school children are drawn directly from the nature of written text. Some of these variables have been discussed at length in Chapter 3 in our efforts to demonstrate the functional differentiation of oral and written language norms. Olson and Torrance address the relation of writing, or in this case, written text, to the notion of *langue*. They attempt to document the possible effects of the nature of this relation for language development during the school years. In Chapter 5 we discuss in detail the nature of this complex interaction among social praxis in schooling, development of written language, and cognitive growth.

Having considered the general conditions for developmental explanations of written language and reviewed representative studies of written-language acquisition, we can single out one serious omission in these accounts of the acquisition of written language. A singular lack of attention is given to levels of discourse organization in the two language norms, namely, what would fall under level "3"; that which is *distinctive* about written language and its acquisition is the nature of its discourse organization. In dealing with written language, the level of text as the proper unit of analysis cannot be ignored, just as in studies of oral language acquisition the level of discourse is critical for accounts of the language-acquisition process.

5

Written Language and
Social Praxis

Introduction

In Chapter 3 we outlined a principle of differentiation that served to distinguish the written norm from the oral norm along structural and functional dimensions. The foundation of this principle of differentiation lies in the functional consideration that language use is grounded in a variety of social practices and that various language uses arise as responses to cultural needs. Only by a consideration of the functional differentiation of language norms and the sociocultural practices that are in part constitutive of such differentiation can we accurately assess the influence of the use of the written language norm on the growth of the mind and understand fully the nature of the acquisition of the written norm. In particular our attention in this chapter focuses on questions of literacy and schooling.

In Chapter 4 we discussed the idea of two intertwined lines of development, the natural or biological and the cultural, and the respective roles of each in contributing to and explaining the nature of the ontogenetic process. The cultural line and its operation as a developmental principle can be best appreciated in the context of the differentiation of the two language norms in the course of social praxis. In particular we examine the place of formal schooling, as it exists in advanced Western technological societies, as a social institution which embodies a given social praxis, in part constitutive of the written norm, and which provides the context for the acquisition of this norm. The arguments in this chapter are addressed specifically to and are based on a consideration of the social practices of Western technological cultures. However, the general principles that underlie this discussion are applicable to non-Western literate cultures, especially those that have adopted institutions such as formal schooling based on Western models.

In speculating on models of development in many domains one general feature of development has stood out that would appear to characterize this process of change over time. Werner (1980) characterizes development as a gradual process of differentiation and integration. This process of differentiation is equally true of language as manifested in an oral or written norm and as manifested in dialogue and monologue on the plane of discourse organization. Tied to this notion of differentiation over time is the fact that differentiation occurs within particular social-cultural settings and is in part constituted by such cultural settings. As language functions differentiate over time, they become correlated with sets of linguistic means and anchored in social practices that in turn condition and define the means and the functions. Karmiloff-Smith (1979) demonstrates such a process of functional differentiation in the domain of early language acquisition.

This model of a gradual differentiation over time suggests that the constructs we have referred to as the oral norm and the written norm of language do not constitute monolithic, unitary phenomena but are themselves further differentiated into functional types. Work on the concept of literacy suggests that it is indeed incorrect to assume that any single notion of a written norm and its associated practice stands in opposition to an oral norm and its associated practice. In particular the work by Heath (1982) and Ochs (1982) strongly suggests that literacy (and by implication the written norm) assumes various forms in connection with varying social practices and cultural institutions. While such work focuses on particular social and cultural practices and the variety of such practices in respect to the concept of literacy, it gives less attention to the question of the specific correlation of linguistic means of expression with given literate or oral praxis.

In Chapter 3 we suggested that the differentiation of the oral and written norm of language is in part constituted by the particular communicative function the norm is meant to serve. In this chapter we argue that these communicative functions are themselves constituted by social and institutional practice. We demonstrate that the communicative function of language norms (in particular the written norm) and social-cultural practice constitute an interfunctionally conditioned and mutually defined system. The acquisition of the written norm of language is at the center of the development process. In order to understand what is meant by a written norm of language we must attend to the communicative function of that norm and the particular cultural practice within which it is constituted. If we are to appreciate the role of the model of text put forward in Chapters 6 and 7 and the implications of the data on development of the written norm generated in light of such a model, we must develop an understanding of the contribution of schooling as a cultural institution to the notion of a particular literate practice. An appreciation of the particular literacy of schooling is indispensable to answering questions about the influence of the acquisition of the written norm on the growth of the mind.

Literacy and Cognition

Scribner and Cole (1981) attack the question of the cognitive consequences of literacy head on. In a massive cross-cultural research effort, the authors question the notion of a monolithic concept of literacy. One major thrust of the Scribner and Cole project is to attempt to assess the contributions of schooling and literacy to cognitive change.

Questions about the written language norm and text have often been formulated in terms of the cognitive consequences of the shift from a primarily oral language use to a dominant written language use. The main thrust of such conceptions is that the use of written language leads to or facilitates the development of higher forms of thought. Oral and written language use are often contrasted as forms of language leading to either a paralogical form of thinking (in the case of oral language) or logical or formal thinking (in the case of written language). The general hypothesis of the transforming effects of such a shift has been formulated by Goody and Watt (1968), Goody (1977, 1982), Havelock (1982b), McLuhan (1967), and Innis (1964) on a global level for culture and society; and by Vygotsky (1978), Luria (1976), Greenfield (1972), Olson (1977), and Bruner and Olson (1977–1978) on the individual psychological plane.

A good portion of Scribner and Cole's (1981) work is devoted to assessing the impact on cognition of the activities of literacy and schooling. Noting that while sweeping claims have been made for the impact of literacy on the course of cognitive development, the authors justly argue that little empirical work has been undertaken to substantiate such claims. Scribner and Cole's work was conducted with the Vai (a people that occupy an area on the border between Sierra Leone and Liberia), a society that incorporates three kinds of literacy: Vai, an indigenous form of the local language used in a limited number of contexts and handed on outside any formal institutional practice of schooling; Arabic literacy, used primarily for recitation of the Qur'an and usually taught in local informal Qur'anic schools; and English school literacy, taught in formal school settings modeled on Western practice. Scribner and Cole assess the impact of each of these literacy practices on cognition. In addition to the variable of written language, Scribner and Cole (1978, 1981) identify the process of schooling as a concomitant variable, which they treat as an independent factor. They observe that:

> Not only does schooling rely on the mediating technology of reading and writing, it does so in settings that fundamentally reorder the motives for carrying out operations on the world . . . . But it is extraordinarily difficult to advance our knowledge of causal mechanisms when all candidate experiences are intangled (literacy and schooling) and co-occuring. Hypotheses about the effects of mastery of a written language, however, can be "untangled." The process of "literacization" is not the same in all countries as the process of schooling; adults as well as children move from preliteracy to literacy in a variety of writing systems and through diversified learning experiences. (1981, p. 13)

Scribner and Cole (1978, p. 452) state very clearly the arguments that lead them to treat literacy and schooling as separable variables: "In all research, literacy was confounded with schooling; yet students are engaged in many learning experiences in school besides learning how to read and write." They observe that "the developmental perspective supports an 'inevitable' interpretation of literacy. It assumes that various components of literacy . . . are likely to have the same psychological consequences in all cultures irrespective of the context of use or of the social institutions in which literacy is embedded" (p. 452). Scribner and Cole set as one of their primary research objectives the identification of the effects of the practice of literacy, that is, possession of a written language, and schooling as separable variables. We argue that this attempt to treat the use of written language and schooling as separable is the result of an unfortunate misunderstanding of the interfunctional correlation of the use of a written-language norm and the process of schooling.

If particular social practice is constitutive of communicative function that itself is constitutive of a particular functional language norm and its associated linguistic means of expression, then an analytic distinction between the practice of schooling and the use of the written norm is unwarranted when the question we wish to ask is about the cognitive consequences of acquisition of the written norm. Posing the question of cognitive consequences in this way can only lead to a distortion of the characterization of the use of the written norm, its acquisition, and its place within a particular cultural setting.

Functional Differentiation and Social Praxis

We have observed that a functional approach to language sees language as the set of linguistic means that are ultimately defined and systematized by the various functions of language. In discussing the distinction to be observed between the oral and written norms of language, we pointed out some of the distinguishing characteristics of the linguistic means of expression associated with each of these language norms. It follows that a command of language must include not only a command over the primary referential system of language but also "the ability to utilize language means [referential, pragmatic, etc.] economically and rationally in accord with *purpose* and *situation* [emphasis added], i.e. developing the capacity to comply best with the specific function of language on specific occasions" (Prague Manifesto, 1929—1978). The implication of this is that we cannot separate consideration of the written norm from consideration of the situational facts of its use. This is particularly true in any examination of the practice of schooling and the written norm, which together constitute a unique functional type of the written norm of language.

In Chapter 3 we distinguished certain functional features that were particularly associated with either the oral or written norm of language. We now consider these functional features in light of the notion of cultural practice as constitutive of communicative function and the consequences of this interfunctional relation among the written language norm, linguistic means of expression (both on the plane of lexicogrammar and discourse organization), and cultural practice for the acquisition of the written norm and cognitive growth.

Within the framework of language as a communicative system, we have seen that Bühler isolated three major functions, which he termed *expressive, appellative,* and *representative.* Mathesius (1947), using Bühler's work as a foundation, distinguishes two principal functions of language, namely the representative and the expressive. Both Bühler's and Mathesius' work have been extended and expanded by Mukarovsky (1937, 1940) in his treatment of the poetic and aesthetic function, Zawadowski (1956), and Havranek (1929). We limit our consideration here, however, to what has been termed the *mental function* or alternatively the *intellectual function,* as it is this aspect of the written norm that can be directly implicated in the formation of structures of formal thought and higher mental functions. This process of the intellectualization of language is defined by Havranek (1964):

> By the *intellectualization* of the standard language, which we could also call its rationalization, we understand its adaption to the goal of making possible precise and rigorous, if necessary abstract, statements, capable of expressing the continuity and complexity of thought, that is, to reinforce the intellectual side of speech. This intellectualization culminates in scientific (theoretical) speech, determined by the attempt to be as precise in expression as possible, to make statements which reflect the rigor of objective scientific thinking in which the terms approximate concepts and the sentences approximate logical judgements. (p. 6)

Two aspects of this intellectualization or scholarization of the standard language need examination: the degree to which this particular functional norm is marked by the functional feature we have termed *decontextualization* and the degree to which the practice and institution of formal schooling foregrounds and indeed is constitutive of the scholarization of the standard language. These two aspects are intimately linked and, as it were, their presences entail one another.

We have observed that each function is correlated with systematic means of expression. This process of differentiation of functions and the correlation of the proper means of expression is accomplished through the processes of automatization and foregrounding. While language as virtual system *(langue)* is the common stock of the means of expression, all potential structures in the system are not instantiated equally within any given functional discourse. The notion of automatization is drawn from the work of the Prague School. In particular, Havranek (1964) defines automatization in the following way:

> By automatization we thus mean such a use of the devices of the language, in isolation or combination with each other, as is usual for a certain expressive purpose, that is, such a use that the expression itself does not attract any attention; the communication occurs, and is received, as conventional in linguistic form as is to be "understood" by virtue of the linguistic system without first being supplemented, in the concrete utterance, by additional understanding derived from the situation and the context. (p. 9)

This automatization is called forth by given social practices or institutions within which a particular discourse occurs. The functional feature that is highly automatized for the written norm as it occurs in the discourse of schooling is in fact decontextualization. Schooled discourse values knowledge insofar as it is objective and depersonalized, that is, knowledge or rules of inquiry into things that are divorced from immediate perceptual experience. The Western institution of schooling sets as its primary task the transmission of the logical in contrast to the magical. Schooling as an institution honors rational and logical knowledge about the world that in its most extreme form is what we have come to call *science.* Goody (1982, p. 209) observes that "The whole process of literate education becomes a matter of absorbing abstracted knowledge through mediators, either directly from books or indirectly from teachers." It is precisely here that the written norm automatized for its scholarly or intellectual function intervenes. School as cultural institution exploits the possibilities of the written norm and provides the essential condition for the intellectualization of the norm. The very functional features of the written norm itself, its documentary and decontextualized character, contribute to this intellectualization.

This process of automatization is in the service of the differentiation of functions within language to achieve given communicative ends as determined by specific institutional demands. We have focused attention on this process to clarify the fact that explications of language that collapse such distinctions falsify the picture of language as a communicative entity and lead to unsound conclusions about its development and use. When Scribner and Cole (1981) test for literacy effects across such domains as Vai script literacy, Arabic literacy, and Western school literacy, they recognize that in each of these cases a different functional load is being carried by the language used. As the functional norms and social practices are different in each of these cases, so are the linguistic means used to accomplish these functions different. Given these considerations, it is by no means realistic to assume that the cognitive consequences that any of these literacy practices may engender are comparable. To argue then that looking at nonschooled literacy allows us to sort out the effects of schooling from those attributable to literacy alone in such domains as memory and classification, is unwarranted. The literacy in school settings, given the thesis of functional differentiation, is not the same literacy as that encountered in Vai script use or Qur'anic learning. The linguistic means associated with each of these functions differs greatly.

The differentiation of language norms should caution us against attributing some unitary function or type in the use of the written norm of language. Any survey of the uses of the written norm confirms that no single function can be exclusively assigned to the written manifestation of language. Further, since at any point in the acquisition of language all functional norms of language are not present in the linguistic repertoire of the subject, there is no reason to suppose that in a given culture or society the full range of functions of the written norm is present. This is clearly evidenced by the limited use of script literacy among the Vai. On the diachronic plane there also may be a gradual differentiation of the standard. The comments of Scribner and Cole (1981) on Vai script literacy illustrate this point:

> [I]t is equally clear that literate practices among the Vai are far more restricted than in technologically sophisticated societies.
>
> In spite of the many different uses of script literacy [among the Vai] we have catalogued, basic productive activities and the workings of the social order do not seem to depend in any critical way on writing.
>
> Even less debatable is the fact that Vai script literacy is not a vehicle for introducing new ways of life. We have called it literacy without education because it does not open doors to vicarious experience, new bodies of knowledge, or new ways or [sic] thinking about major life problems. (p. 238)

This difference among literacy practices is not limited to functional differentiation in terms of social-cultural practice nor to the differentiation of functional norms in ontogenesis. The role and form of the written norm in a given culture is itself subject to a developmental progression and differentiation. Within a given culture or society, the first appearance of script literacy should not be presumed to constitute a fully exploited or implemented norm of language. It would hardly be appropriate to term such a culture or society literate in the full sense of the term. More appropriate would be Goody's term *restricted literacy*. We have seen Vachek (1959, p. 13) caution that in terms of a diachronic consideration not all cultures nor all languages "will have developed their latent structural possibilities in full."

As Scribner and Cole rightly observe, it is incorrect to consider literacy outside of the facts of the social practice in which it is embedded. This notion of social practice is very directly correlated with the differentiation of the functional norms of language. Hence letter writing and the use of the written norm in either journalism or the scientific enterprise constitute very different practices and implement different functional norms. Each calls forth the implementation and automatization of differing linguistic means to achieve their ends. Each in turn is constituted both by the needs of the particular communicative situation and the institution within which it is situated and functions. Communicative goal, automatized linguistic means of a functional norm, and institutional practices are all interfunctionally related and mutually constitutive of each other.

Schooling and the Written Norm

For children within Western technological societies, the acquisition of the written norm must be understood as the acquisition of a particular functional written norm, namely an intellectualized or scholarized written norm. The acquisition of this foregrounded scholarized norm in advanced Western cultures is the foundation for greater social control and economic viability for individuals. This intellectualized written norm is in part constitutive of what we mean by schooling in Western technological society and is itself constituted by the institution of schooling. Goody (1982) speaks of knowledge acquisition with the advent of formal schooling and the written norm as a mediate acquisition through the written norm. In an article on concept formation during schooling, Cole and D'Andrade (1982) comment on the mediate nature of this process:

> We can conceive of schooling as a social process involving activities in two contexts, the "theoretical context between teacher and learner" and the "real concrete context of facts.". . . Within each of these contexts language plays an important, *but different* role. In the theoretical context, one's practices involve manipulations on words. . . . In some instantiations, it teaches that "meaning is in the text". . . and promotes modes of discourse in which the structure of written text enters into the structure of speech. (p.25)

They conclude that

> The structure of communication that characterizes the theoretical context constrains the conceptual process of schooling. It shapes the characteristic cognitive activity of the school context, which leads neo-Vygotskian scholars to declare that "Theoretical thinking is . . . the new psychological structure that emerges at primary school age" (Markova, 1979). (Cole & D'Andrade, 1982, p. 25)

The consequence of this interfunctional conditioning of language norms and functional ends is that literacy practices that fulfill particular communicative and institutional needs are radically different and noncomparable. If we are to accurately determine the cognitive effects of, say, the acquisition of a textual competence, we cannot do so unless we consider seriously the particular functional ends for which the competency is acquired and the particular social-cultural matrix that reinforces and in part determines competence. Given this line of argument, the attempt to assess the cognitive consequence of literacy, at least within Western technological society apart from schooling, or to treat literacy and schooling as separable variables is foolish indeed. The literacy of schooling, the particular textual competence fostered by the schooling process, represents an extreme differentiation of language discourse function to the channel of the intellectualization of written text. The most extreme form of such a differentiation of language function for the purpose of intellectualization results in the decontextualized logical discourse of expository prose, more familiarly known as the scientific research paper. Clearly, to make sweeping claims about the cognitive implications of written text without a proper critical ethnography of writing within the schooling process is unwarranted. However, even without such an ethnography, a consideration of the typical kinds of texts produced and their structural and functional characteristics allows us to draw some tentative conclusions. Further, we can determine, based on a comparison of text types drawn from different cultures and settings, which linguistic means are particularly correlated and therefore automatized for given textual functions and situated within given institutional practices.

Even without a detailed ethnography of text production in schooling, one fact about the process of schooling is clear: It is *par excellence* an attempt to engender knowledge through *mediate* experience. This mediate experience in the case of schooling is *text*. As a consequence, schooling as social praxis is never separable from the medium it employs and exploits in this process. Not only is knowledge extended, but skill and ability in the logic of a particular symbolic system that has its own set of structural, semantic, and pragmatic characteristics (which may exert their own transforming effect on cognitive structure) are gained. Bruner and Olson (1977–1978, p. 149) comment that "each form of experience, including the various symbolic systems tied to the media, produces a unique pattern of skills for dealing with or thinking about the world. It is the skills in these systems that we call intelligence."

Apart from institutional contributions, characteristics of written text and of the process of constructing written texts contribute to the particularized skills spoken of by Bruner and Olson. Two characteristics (detailed in Chapter 3) stand out in particular: the documentary and decontextualized nature of written text itself and the unmarked nature of written text for monologic organization. We have observed that oral and written language differ in that oral language is more contextually dependent, more tied to the actual presence of the producer, and hence more socially vibrant than written language. Written language on the other hand is less dependent on extralinguistic context and hence more objective, in that the producer is removed from the production in a sense that the speaker in an oral mode is not. Spoken language, being more dependent on or sensitive to context (at least in most ordinary usages), is perhaps more elliptical in its structure as communication than is written language, where the need to play out its development as a communicative act is more urgent.

On the function of written language within the communicative act, Holman (1976) writes:

> Language as written typically occurs within an act of communication in which the roles of communicant and target of communication are maintained throughout the transmission of the message. . . . The high degree of organization characteristic of written communication is called forth by its primary function—the transmission of detailed information concerning a severely limited sphere of discourse. In the actual transmission of written communication the factor of spatial contiguity is of

little importance, . . . the factor of psychological contiguity assumes a crucial role in the organization of written communication, since the communicant's choice of an appropriate form for the transmission of his message is governed to no small degree by his ability to utilize the resources the language offers him within the limits set by the content of the message and the nature of its intended target. (p. 126)

In contrast, the oral norm is usually characterized by a dialogic organization. Here there is a give and take in building the discourse, and the discourse itself exhibits a greater degree of interactional management information typical of social exchange.

Additionally, in the written norm the psychological locus of control is situated within the producer of the text; in oral discourse there is a shared interpsychological control of topic between participants. As a consequence, the production of written text demands more elaborate strategies of preplanning. Written language demands the conscious organization of ensembles of propositions to achieve its end. The need to manipulate linguistic means in such a conscious and deliberate fashion entails a level of linguistic self-reflection not called forth in oral discourse. Luria (1981) comments that

Written speech [read *speech* as *language*] becomes a useful means for clarifying thinking because it involves conscious operation with linguistic categories. These can be carried out at a far slower rate of processing than is possible in oral speech. . . . It is therefore obvious why we often utilize written speech not only to convey prepared information, but also to process and clarify our thinking. (p. 166)

The construction of text is itself a complex and conscious analytical activity in which there takes place a logical structuring analogous to higher mental functions.

As Holman (1976) has observed and as we have argued, function as differentiated in oral and written language gives rise to the use of differing linguistic means. One consequence of this selection of means involves the choice of an appropriate discourse organization. On a molar plane, the choice may be between dialogue and monologue. While either of these forms may be appropriate to either the oral or written norm of language, typically dialogue is correlated with the oral norm and monologue with the written norm.

Within the schooling process children are deliberately moved from a primarily dialogic discourse organization to a monologic organization. This is true of instruction in written language use as well as in writing exercises in other curriculum areas. It is equally true that children's oral language is encouraged to assume more characteristics of a monologic organization. Greenfield (1972), for example, comments on the "speak-

ing of the written language." Anecdotal evidence from classroom observations suggests that in a variety of oral activities children are encouraged
to use less context-dependent oral dialogic organization and more fully
explicit monologic discourse. In an article on communication within
classroom settings, Michaels comments (1981) that

> Schooling in this society represents a special set of institutionalized activities that
> center on the acquisition of general purpose skills, the most important of which is
> literacy. As such, classroom activities can be studied as a series of goal oriented
> exchanges between teacher and children in which the overarching concern with
> literacy and literate-like behavior influences the nature of the face-to-face interac-
> tion (wherein the skills of literacy are presumably acquired). . . .
>
> In order to be regarded as literate in school, children must be able to shift from
> the face-to-face conversational discourse strategies appropriate in the home, to the
> more written-like strategies of discursive prose. This entails learning to adopt a
> non-face-to-face perspective with respect to one's audience by making explicit any
> relevant background knowledge (rather than assuming it to be shared), and lexical-
> izing or grammaticalizing all information that in oral discourse would be carried
> over nonlexical channels via prosody, pitch register, nonverbal cues, and so
> on. . . .
>
> Thus in making the transition to literacy, children must learn more than sound/
> symbol skills. In addition, they must acquire new discourse strategies for indicat-
> ing distinctions between new and old information, signaling cohesive ties, topic
> shifts, emphasis, and perspective within and across topics. (pp. 423–424)

Yakubinski (1923) and others argue that dialogue is genetically prior to
monologue and that in some sense dialogue is, in contrast to the "artifi-
cialness" of monologue, more natural. In that ordinary discourse normally takes place on the plane of dialogue and that dialogue is ontogenetically prior in language acquisition, these speculations would appear to
have some merit. In this sense, dialogue is the unmarked member of the
pair. Monologue is reserved for more specialized language functions.

The two functional types of discourse organization, dialogue and monologue, are characterized by structural and psychological differences. Yakubinski details some of these structural differences:

> It is generally known that an answer to a question requires significantly fewer words
> than would be used for the full disclosure of a given mental whole: "Are you going
> for a walk?",—"Yes (I'm going for a walk)." "Maybe [I'm going (for a walk)].",
> etc. Of course dialogue is not an exchange of questions and answers, but to a
> considerable extent in any dialogue there is the possibility for the unsaid, the
> incomplete expression, the nonnecessity for mobilizing all the words that would
> have to be mobilized in order to disclose the same thought complex in monologic
> speech or in the first move of a dialogue. (p. 143)

While writing primarily of monologue in speech, Yakubinski further
points out that written monologue contrasts even more strikingly with
dialogue. Two aspects in particular of written monologic organization

are of critical importance: (1) the absence, in physical terms, of the interlocutor and (2) the need in written monologue for full and explicit linguistic formulation of component utterances. The physical absence of immediately shared communicative context necessitates this full exposition. In terms of production routines for dialogue and monologue there are manifest differences. As we have seen Holman observe earlier, a bidirectional flow of information underlies dialogue, implying that the psychological locus of control in creating the discourse lies in neither interlocutor exclusively. In this sense dialogue is an open semantic system to a far greater extent than monologue, which may be better described as a closed semantic system. Vygotsky (1962, p. 144) observes that "Dialogue implies immediate unpremeditated utterance. It consists of replies, repartee; it is a chain of reactions. Monologue, by comparison, is a complex formation; the linguistic elaboration can be attended to leisurely and *consciously* [italics added]." Luria (1981) similarly observes that

> In oral monologic speech, the speaker is responsible for both the motive of the utterance and for its general scheme. The motive and the scheme must be sufficiently stable to determine the flow of the entire expanded, monologic utterance. This utterance, in turn, can be divided into meaningful chunks. These form an integrated, "closed" structure. (p. 161)

This structure of monologue demands that the person constructing the discourse have command over a fully expanded discourse grammar. Monologic discourse further demands elaborated strategies of preplanning, anticipation of the discourse consumer's potential difficulties of comprehension, and editing in order to accomplish the communicative ends of the discourse. Clearly such cognitive demands are far more explicit, if not more complex, than those of dialogue and involve a level of self-reflection absent in normal dialogic discourse.

When the written norm of language intersects with monologue, the features we have been discussing become further foregrounded and reinforced:

> In written speech, lacking situational and expressive supports, communication must be achieved only through words and their combinations; this requires the speech activity to take complicated forms — hence the use of first drafts. The evolution from the draft to the final copy reflects our mental process. Planning has an important part in written speech, even when we do not actually write out a draft. Usually we say to ourselves what we are going to write; this is also a draft, though in thought only. (Vygotsky, 1962, p. 144)

We have argued that there is a functional differentiation of language norms and of automatization within these norms of given linguistic means of expression (both on the plane of lexicogrammar and the plane of discourse organization) and further that this functional differentiation is correlated with and constituted by social-institutional practice. It remains to ask what the consequences of the acquisition of the scholarized written language are for cognition itself.

Social Praxis and Written Language Acquisition

In light of our remarks on the cultural line of development in Chapter 4 and of our discussion in this chapter of the constitutive nature of social and institutional practices for a written norm, we can begin to clarify the picture of what this cultural line of development entails in the case of the acquisition of the written norm. The acquisition of the written norm largely takes place (we limit these remarks to advanced Western societies with formal institutional schooling practices) in a particular cultural institution, the school, which foregrounds a particular functional mode of written discourse whose chief distinguishing features are the degree of decontextualization and the degree to which the psychological and linguistic responsibility for its production lies with the writer. On this point Cook-Gumperz and Gumperz (1981) comment that

> Developmentally the transition from speaking to writing as a medium for learning about the world of others requires a change from the interpretative principles of *discursive* written language. The move into literacy requires children to make some basic adjustments to the way they socially attribute meaning to the events and processes of the everyday world in order *to loosen their dependence upon contextually specific* information and *to adopt a decontextualized perspective* [emphasis added]. (p. 99)

They detail the nature of such a shift in the following way:

> For children, the essential change between written and spoken language is the change from the multi-modality of speech to lexicalized discursive sequences of written language. Wholly new principles of monitoring meaning and of recognizing the cues for further information, that is linguistic expectations, are necessary for the two modes of discourse. The problem of learning to write lies in learning a new system of what syntactic and semantic alternatives can follow where there are not prosodic cues and in learning about a system of cueing where the distinction between new and given information must by *[sic]* syntactically and lexically expressed rather than through prosody. Furthermore, written language requires a higher concentration of new information, that is a lesser redundancy of lexical choices. (p. 99)

The model of text we detail in Chapter 6 attempts to capture these features of the acquisition of the written norm. Using this model, in Chapter 7 we detail the shifting strategies employed by children for text production during the course of the acquisition process. Such changes during the course of the acquisition of the written norm derive from two poles, the nature of the written norm itself and the social praxis embodied in the cultural institution of school. In terms of the question of development, the forces directing cognitive growth and change in the child at this point are cultural. The child's interaction with the world assumes, during this period, a mediated quality not present during the early stages of the natural line of development. This mediation takes place through the medium of the written norm, which comes to play a critical role in the child's acquisition of knowledge. The principle of change in this cultural line of development is the increasing decontextualization embodied in the mediating nature of text. Indeed, Vygotsky (1956, p. 241) identified this decontextualization as "higher psychological functions whose basic and distinguishing features are intellectualization and mastery, i.e., conscious realization and voluntariness." He considered it the primary factor in development during schooling:

> At the center of development in the school age child is the transition from lower functions of attention and memory to higher functions of voluntary attention and logical memory. . . . the intellectualization of functions and their mastery represent two movements of one and the same process — the transition to higher psychological functions. (p. 242)

This transition is quickened by mastery of the scholarized discourse of the written norm, where the properties of the sign system (written text) present the decontextualization of mediational means in intellectual thought and cognitive activity. Development no longer proceeds through direct action on objects but through the mediation of the written norm. Learning and development are both divorced from action.

We have argued in this chapter that an appreciation of the role of the written norm in general cognitive development and indeed the very process of the acquisition of that norm must be viewed against the background in which it occurs. This background, which is in part constitutive of the intellectualized written norm, is the cultural institution of schooling. We have further argued that Scribner and Cole's (1981) attempt to assess the individual contributions of schooling and the written norm to the course of cognitive growth is misguided in that the written norm and schooling are interfunctionally defined processes partly constitutive of each other. This interfunctional correlation of schooling and the written norm is a cultural line of development, whose driving causal principle is the decontextualization of mediational means of acting on the world, at least the epistemic world. With the advent and acquisition of the written norm within the context of schooling, certain features of written text as foregrounded by the institution of schooling come to play a decisive role in the growth of the mind.

In the following chapter we examine in greater detail the possible nature of this process of textual acquisition and its role in cognitive development in light of the general principles articulated above.

6

A Functional Model of
Written Text

Introduction

In considering the nature of the written norm as constituted in part by cultural practices, we have argued that the written norm is in its discourse organization unmarked for monologue. Indeed, text would appear to be the normal manifestation of the written norm at least within most cultures where the written norm is well established as part of the communicative practice of cultural institutions. In the following pages we present a more-or-less formal account of a model of text that might be used as a framework for explaining the acquisition of the written norm. The model of text presented here has its foundation in the functional-structural principles of language as drawn from the work of the Prague Linguistic Circle. Having outlined this model of text, we present a summary of an initial attempt to look at the acquisition of the written norm using this model of text as an analytic and heuristic tool. The data presented in this and the following chapter represent only an initial attempt to approach the question of the acquisition of written language and the probable consequences for the development of higher cognitive functions. The work summarized here should not be interpreted as anything more than suggestive of some aspects of the development of written language and possible correlations between this aspect of development and the onset of higher cognitive functions. Equally it should be noted that the empirical work reported here must be seen as applicable primarily to an Anglo-American cultural setting.

We have argued in Chapter 3 that the written norm of language is in its discourse organization unmarked for monologue. Written language from a functional and structural point of view is realized in text. We can also observe that even in early stages of the acquisition of the written norm children produce units recognizable as text. Any adequate account of written language acquisition must address itself to the acquisition of the structural-functional rules of text organization. This text level is the proper sphere within which developmental studies of written language must be situated. As Okby (1978, p. 146) has remarked, "Discourse is simply defined as the communication of thought by speech or writing. There is no shying away from the study of language in performance. There is not the slightest doubt that discourse provides the only access to sane conclusions about language as system, or language as code."

We can properly extend these remarks by adding that sane conclusions about the acquisition and use of written language can only come by an attention to text. We cannot suppose that in acquiring the written norm of language the child is charged with the task of acquiring the paradigmatic axis of language in another medium *de novo;* rather, the problem set for the child in acquiring the written norm is to develop the specific syntagmatic semantic, syntactic, and pragmatic properties of the written norm.

The model of text we outline is formulated to capture the discourse organization of the written norm. For contrastive purposes, a model of discourse for the oral norm based on similar principles can be found in Zammuner (1981). We do not present a contrastive account of the acquisition of the oral norm, as the literature on the topic is abundant, but limit ourselves to considerations of written language development.

If, then, the central question for a developmental theory of written language is to explain the acquisition of the rules of written-text production and the cognitive consequences of such an acquisition, we must have some plausible model of written text. Work in discourse and text models provides the possibility of formulating a developmental account of written language acquisition at the level of text. We outline one such text model that has been used as the basis for investigating certain developmental aspects of written language acquisition at the level of text (Scinto, 1982) and present a summary of the findings based on such a model.

Definition of Text

We accept on empirical grounds the ontological status of written language objects, that is, actual instances of the written norm in use, which are traditionally termed *texts.* For arguments justifying the status of such language objects see Petöfi (1979; 1981) and Scinto (1982). By *text* we understand most nearly Batalova's (1977, p. 376) definition: "A text can be considered a semantic-structural-communicative entity, having its own units which we call 'super-phrasal' units. These units differ in the information they contain, since they reflect the logical succession of ideas — ideas which do not carry equivalent information."

We define text in the following way:

> Text is a functional unit of complex meaning, an extended predication that involves the elaboration of ensembles of sentences by a process of composition and concatenation. This process of composition requires the generation of a unifying schema (i.e., an underlying goal-directed communicative intention), the organization of the meaning (i.e., schema) into appropriate information units, and the concatenation of these units through the integration of semantic, pragmatic, and metapragmatic systems of the written language into a coherent linear surface form.

Defined as such, text is a set of linguistic means of expression used to fulfill a particular communicative intention, realized in a given social context, and instantiated through conscious cognitive activity. The developmental task is for the child to realize a command over those particular means of expression as constrained by the set of possibilities of the written norm and a command over the appropriate set of combinatorial possibilities for the concatenation of such means of expression in fulfilling a particular communicative goal.

The definition of text as the result of a process of composition and concatenation implies that the input to this process of composition is units of lower value than the text itself. In acquiring command over the written norm of language, the child has to achieve some awareness of the combinatorial possibilities and the operations of concatenation of these lower-order units. But what are these units and what are the permitted operations of concatenation? Before specifying the nature of these units, we must examine the compositional process itself.

The ultimate goal of the process of composition and concatenation is the conscious production of a coherent linear surface form that fulfills the communicative end of the text. The critical term is *coherent.* The notion of coherence implies that this process is not the mere juxtaposition of units in time and space. Central to the notion of coherence is the concept of dependency. Units composing the text do not merely stand in relation to one another but are rather functions of one another, structured into a closed system that demonstrates necessity. A functional relation between units requires that a specific property of one unit be linked to a

property of other units.   Text construction, given the monologic organization of the written norm, involves the ordering of units and subsequently
coordinating these units into a single series in light of preceding members
in the series.   Bellert (1970) specifies such a functional relation in the
following way:

> A discourse is a sequence of utterances $S_1, S_2, \ldots S_n$, such that the semantic
> interpretation of each utterance S_i (for $2 \leq i \leq$) is dependent on the interpretation
> of the sequence $S_1 \ldots, S_i - 1$.   In other words, an adequate interpretation of an
> utterance occurring in discourse requires the knowledge of the preceding con-
> text. . . . the semantic interpretation of an utterance is the set of consequences or
> conclusions that can be drawn from the utterance.   (p. 335)

Any conception of text must capture this notion of nonarbitrary dependence among the units forming the text.   What is crucial in achieving
coherence is the establishment of this dependency through the creation
of functional relations among units so that the result is an organic whole.

Coherence is the functional relation between successive lower-order
units of meaning such that the entire series of lower-order units forms a
partially ordered set.   This is sufficient to specify the minimal formal
condition for coherence.   We specify the nature of the function that maps
lower-order units to form a text later when we discuss thematic progression in text.   Here we are concerned primarily with the formal structural
properties of coherence.

The text as a functional language object is characterized by a nonarbitrary concatenation of lower-order units.   The constituent units of text
must be derived by an empirical procedure.   However, some preliminary
considerations of a speculative nature are in order.

Units of Text

It is a self-evident observation that written texts are composed of what
are traditionally termed *sentences.* Sentences can in turn be defined on
syntactic or semantic grounds.   For our purposes it is sufficient to note
that the lowest-order units in the composition of texts are characterized
(at least in well-formed texts) by some initial graphic mark (e.g., a capital
letter) and by some final graphic mark (e.g., a period).   Sentences can be
further characterized by their functional organization in the act of communication.   With Daneš (1966), we regard the sentence as being characterized by three levels, namely, grammatic, semantic, and functional sentence perspective (FSP), the level of sentence organization in the act of
communication.   (For a full discussion of the concept of FSP, see Adamec, 1966; Benesova & Sgall, 1973; Dahl, 1969; Daneš, 1964, 1968, 1974,

1976; Firbas, 1959, 1961, 1966, 1974, 1975; Mathesius, 1924, 1939; Svoboda, 1968; Uhlirova, 1977; Vachek, 1955, 1958.)
    Svoboda (1968) summarizes the work on FSP as follows:

> In the first place, the sentence being an act of taking a stand-point towards some reality means that experience occasioned by the new reality is to be classed with some experience acquired before; in other words, the acquiry of new experience takes place through the mediation of previous experience. It follows that every sentence has a basic section, which appears as known or as something that can be easily gathered from, or at least most obviously yields itself as a starting point of communication in the given situation, and a section that brings the very contribution of the given sentence to the development of the discourse. The information communicated by the latter (rhematic — A.S.) section about the former (thematic — A.S.) section cannot be gathered from the situation and constitutes the very essence of the experience towards which the sentence is taking a stand-point. (pp. 52–53)

In this discussion we consider the sentence the most basic unit in the composition of text. The sentence is delimited by the initial capital letter and the final period and characterized by the functional division of theme and rheme. It can be symbolized as $S = T — R$. The process of the composition of these units is articulated by Daneš (1974b):

> Our basic assumption is that text connexity is represented, *inter alia,* by thematic progression (TP). By this term we mean the choice and ordering of utterance themes, their mutual concatenation and hierarchy, as well as their relationship to the hyperthemes of the superior text units . . . to the whole text, and the situation. (p. 114)

Thematic progression takes place on the level of the sentence in written text, as sentences and clauses are the basic field of operation for the theme-rheme division described above.

    It is unwarranted to assume that there are no text-forming units intermediate between the lowest order unit (the sentence) and the highest unit (the text itself). We can reasonably expect that sentences (in the case of text) and utterances (in the case of oral discourse) constitute the sole lower-order text-forming unit only if the structure of text reveals an immediate pairwise concatenation of succeeding sentences or utterances forming the simple linear chainlike lattice structure as shown below:

$$O \longrightarrow O \longrightarrow O \longrightarrow O$$

Here the nodes represent constituent sentences and the arrows the thematic progression spoken of by Daneš. But the TP of texts and their sentence units is not fully ordered in such a successive pairwise fashion

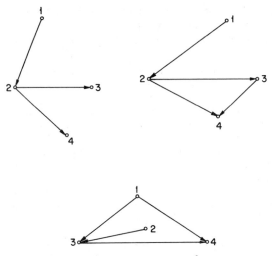

Figure 6.1   Graphic representations of text structure.

(Scinto, 1982). Frequently, patterns of the sort shown in Figure 6.1 are found.

Intermediate between sentences as the lowest-order text-forming unit and the text itself are what we shall term *combinatoric text modules* that are the immediate constitutive units of text. These modules and their distinctive types of structure represent the particular instantiation of the means of expression of the written language norm.

On the function of the sentence in text, Batalova (1977, p. 376) states, "The disclosure of the sentence's function in a text is only possible by investigating the sentence in broader frames, taking into account the much larger text environment. Besides, it must be pointed out that the superphrasal is not merely a sum of sentences but a quite new syntactico-semantic phenomenon." These larger text spans enter into a combinatoric process, the result of which is the text. In light of such a principle, Batalova (1977, p. 376) comments that "the succession of certain units of a text indicates its structure which is revealed by the types of connections between units of text." By articulating the nature and types of these connections between text units as exhibited by their TP as well as by determining the particular TP of the text modules themselves, we can gain an insight into the nature of text structure produced by subjects at various levels of cognitive functioning. This detailing of structural configurations provides a critical insight into the development of the written language norm in children.

Finally, Batalova (1977, p. 377) notes that "it is possible to distinguish in the text certain text-forming units, which we conventionally call predicative-relative complexes. These complexes consist of semantically and structurally bound text spans of different informative value." We can represent this concatenation of combinatoric text modules in the following manner:

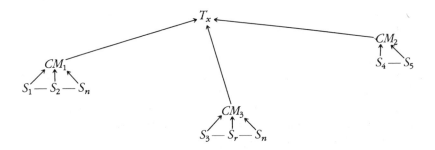

Kukharenko (1979) has observed that texts are constituted in the immediate sense by what she terms *sentence clusters:*

> Indeed, if a word is a sequence of morphemes, and a sentence is a sequence of words then each unit of this word-level or sentence-level may be "dissected" into its constituents and analyzed correspondingly. Proceeding from this, and agreeing that a text is a sequence of sentences it is natural to expect the latter to serve *[sic]* the universal unit of the text level. Alas! Investigations dealing with lengthy texts unanimously claim that sentences as such do not immediately constitute the text, but in the process of text-formation go through an intermediate stage of sentence clusters. (p. 235)

We have observed that the same is true for texts of not so lengthy character. Kukharenko (p. 235) defines sentence clusters as "semantic topical and lexico-grammatical unities of two or more sentences." Langleben (1979) argues similarly that there is at least a triple opposition in the constitution of text, namely, sentence — sentence cluster — text. Langleben goes on to argue that this opposition must by expanded to include simple sentence — nonsimple sentence — sentence cluster — text. This expanded opposition does indeed seem to have some empirical foundation.

Before considering text-forming modules in any more detail, we must first consider the notion of text composition and thematic progression. As observed above, Daneš speaks of text connexity as being represented by thematic progression.

If we are to understand clearly the types of relations that may bind and occur between successive sentences in a text and between combinatoric modules and the reason for the particular manifestations they assume, then we must consider carefully text as a functional unit in a communicative process. As such, the most fundamental requirement of text is that it speak about a particular topic. Text is an extended predication. It sets out to say something, or a number of things, about a particular theme or topic. To this end each successive sentence in a text must contribute to the explication of the topic. It must serve to push forward the communication, that is, the meaning of the text. The result of such a functional requirement is that successive sentences have some relation with sentences that have gone before and sentences that follow. The nature of these relations is determined, in part at least, by the functional requirement of text as stated above. The fact that text is about a particular theme or topic is mirrored in the cross-referential and thematic patterns in a text. Because a text attempts to predicate something about a particular object or set of objects, it must have some means of referring to this object or set of objects through successive sentences. Observed relations between successive sentences and supersentential modules of a text are a result of the TP operative in a text. The individual relations themselves are not the reason for cohesive text but rather are the manifestation of cohesive text as necessitated by the thematic progression and the function for which text is produced, namely extended communication.

The composition of lower-order units to form an extended communication such as the text is accomplished through the concatenation of the theme and rheme structure of those successive units. We can represent this process initially using the notation of Daneš (1974b) with further extensions and modifications by Scinto (1977, 1982, 1983).

Consider the following brief text:

(1) *The book was published by Oxford University Press.*
(2) *It appeared in the autumn.*
(3) *Oxford University Press is second only to Cambridge University Press.*

Assuming that in the first sentence *the book* has been a subject of previous discourse (and as a consequence appears as definite mention), when we apply a *wh-* question-answer procedure as a diagnostic tool to determine theme-rheme components (see Scinto, 1982, 1983), we obtain the following T-R bipartition:

$$T \longrightarrow R$$

The book (was published by Oxford University Press).

Applying this procedure in turn for each sentence in the text we obtain the following patterns of theme and rheme $(T-R)$:

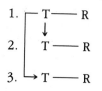

It can be observed that the relation of repeated theme obtains between the first and second sentence of the text. The repeated theme (i.e., the book) appears in the second sentence as *it*. We can represent this relation in the following notation:

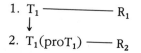

The descending arrow marks the continuation of the same theme (theme progression) while $(proT_1)$ marks it as a pronominalized form of theme 1. Subscripts in the notation are sequential for $T-R$ elements in each successive sentence.

Next consider the first and third sentence in the text. What appears as rheme *(Oxford University Press)* in sentence 1 appears as theme in sentence 3. We can represent this relation in the following notation:

1. T_1 —— R_1

3. $\qquad T_3 (= R_1)$ —— R_3

Again the descending arrow marks the progression of elements in the text and $(= R_1)$ marks T_3 as a lexical copy of R_1.

If these patterns are now ordered as the sentences appear in the text, the following graphic representation of the theme-rheme progression of the text is obtained:

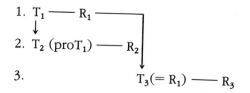

The notation clearly represents the connectivity of the text (the nature of the semantic relations being given in parentheses) and the concatenation of sentences to form the structure of the communicative message.

Using this notation we are able to characterize the thematic structure of texts in order to assess their structural and compositional characteristics. We do not outline the notational system here. (For an extensive discussion, see Scinto, 1982.) A summary of the coding scheme for thematic progression appears in the appendix of this volume.

These remarks on thematic progression and text constitution serve to introduce the major categories for textual analysis (i.e., theme and rheme) and some notion of how their concatenation and progression is observed in text. While no exhaustive typology of possible configurations of thematic progression in text has been compiled, we can suggest several basic types of transition found in written texts: theme iteration, thematization of rheme and rheme iteration.

Through the determination of T-R structure we are able to see how textual combinatorics are employed to achieve the functional communicative product of the text. Ideally we would wish to see how various thematic progressions are employed in the process of composition in order to assess accurately how that process functions. The assessment of the theme dynamics of text allows us a major insight into the actual dynamics of the compositional process and the acquisition of strategies for dealing with written monologic organization.

The basic premise underlying our approach in the discussion and explication of a model of text is the psychological principle that text is the product of an intentional communicative act. As such it is the particular instantiation in performance of a set of linguistic means of expression (of the written norm) in the service of a particular communicative goal or function. Within such a functional and performance model of text we can begin to determine the nature and sequence of the developmental stages. The formal aspects of such a model allow us to detail the operations of concatenation and the nature of the acquisition of such operations as they unfold over time and as they interact with other operative structures of cognition. In order to grasp the nature of the operative structures of written text we need to elaborate this model further. Having characterized a text as a concatenation of lower-order propositional units, that is, sentences, we can assess the combinatorial strategies employed in text construction at different points in development if we have a method of characterizing the combinatorial units or modules actually used in the construction process. We have suggested above that these compositional modules are not necessarily coterminous with atomic propositions, that is, sentences.

In the text model developed above, we have given a rudimentary typology of basic T-R enchainments of sentences. The compositions consisted of a group of possible enchainments between any two successive sentences. But the composition of text is not necessarily limited to such successive paired enchainments. Consider the following text and its TP configurations (for the moment we consider only a simple T-R nexus):

(4) *The essay formed the essence of his argument.*
(5) *This argument was presented at the Society's annual meeting.*
(6) *It was not well received.*
(7) *However, the essay was considered well written.*

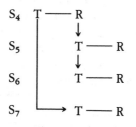

Given this textual pattern, at least two decompositions into constituent patterns are possible. We can decompose the text into $(S_4 \cap S_5)$, $(S_5 \cap S_6)$, $(S_4 \cap S_7)$, giving us the following T-R modules:

T ——— R   T ——— R   T ——— R
    ↓   ↓   ↓
    T ——— R   T ——— R   T ——— R
$(S_4 \cap S_5)$ $(S_5 \cap S_6)$ $(S_4 \cap S_7)$

A possible variant of this configuration would be to replace the final module $(S_4 \cap S_7)$ with $(S_4 \cap (S_5 + S_7))$, giving us

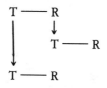

Thus we can decompose the TP configuration of this text into the following modules: $(S_4 \cap (S_5 + S_7))$ and $(S_5 \cap S_6)$. This in turn yields the following T-R module configurations:

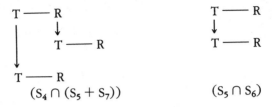

$$(S_4 \cap (S_5 + S_7))$$ $$(S_5 \cap S_6)$$

This second decomposition is preferable to the first in that the two modules exhibit the minimum number of intersections (i.e., shared propositions) of lower-order units while still preserving the greatest amount of information in the two modules necessary for the composition of text. The first decomposition contains a greater number of redundant specifications of propositions in the component modules and is less parsimonious in the number of modules it specifies. In general the principle for decomposition to be adopted adheres to these two requirements: that the component modules preserve the largest informative units and present the least number of redundant intersections of lower-order units. We can define combinatoric text modules in the following manner:

A module M is a set of not less than two constituent S—T between which there exists a functional relation (T-R links). In addition, this module M is not a proper subset of any other module for which the first property is true. (A is a proper subset of B if and only if every element of A is an element of B and there is at least one element of B which is not an element of A.)

The example we have been considering consists of lowest-order units that are simple T-R nexuses. However, it may be the case that these lowest-order units are themselves the product of a process of composition or fusion of simple T-R types. (For a fuller treatment of this topic see Scinto, 1982, and Daneš, 1974b.) Consider now the following text and its TP configuration.

(8) *The manuscript was an example of the late period.*
(9) *It was covered in a neat demotic hand which appeared to be the work of the scribe Kyros.*
(10) *Kyros' work was well known to the professor.*
(11) *This scribe produced a limited number of manuscripts.*
(12) *The manuscript could be dated and placed easily since it came from the workshops at Alexandria.*

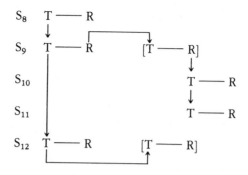

Following the definition of a combinatoric text module given above, we obtain the following decomposition: $(S_8 \cap S_9)$, $(S_9 \cap (S_{10} + S_{12}))$, $(S_{10} \cap S_{11})$. There are three combinatoric modules:

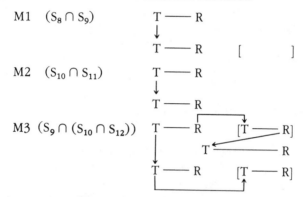

We have still to clarify the treatment of lowest-order units that are a product of fusion or composition. The problem is whether they are to be treated as unitary items for the purpose of module delimitation or as units that may be separable into component parts depending on whether they occur as initial or final elements in a module. This problem is illustrated by (9) in the text above.

This unit consists of two T-R nexuses. For the purposes of the analysis in this study we treat such units as intermediate between the lowest-order units (simple T-R nexus) and combinatoric modules. The consequences of this decision are that such fused or composed T-R nexuses are analyzed as separate combinatoric categories as well as being taken into account as possible members of larger combinatoric modules. In the case where they are taken into account as members of a combinatoric module we have a complex T-R nexus that enters into relation with another T-R nexus. In these cases it is counted as part of the module, but only that portion of the T-R configuration that enters into a functional relation is specified. In the text $(8) - (12)$, we specify M_1 as

$$S_8 \quad T \longrightarrow R$$
$$\downarrow$$
$$S_9 \quad T \longrightarrow R [\quad]$$

The distributional field of lower order given by empty brackets is not specified unless it is functionally related to the T-R nexus of higher order, in this example, S_8. In the case of M_3 we would have

$$S_9 \quad T \longrightarrow R \qquad [T \longrightarrow R]$$
$$S_{10} \quad \downarrow \qquad\qquad\qquad T \longleftarrow R$$
$$S_{12} \quad T \longrightarrow R \qquad \text{etc.}$$

Here the full specification of S_9 is given, as both fields of T-R distribution in this unit enter into a functional relation in the module. However, were it the case that one of these distributional fields did not participate in a functional relation in the module, it would not be specified.

Graph-Theoretic Models of Text and Module Delimitation

In Scinto (1982) we formalized the definition of text in order to develop quantitative measures of coherence and to devise a means whereby we could more easily investigate other functional-structural dimensions of the text-production process. We propose that the connectivity and structure of texts are best modeled by an appeal to graph-theoretic concepts. (For a full discussion of the applicability of graph concepts to modeling text structure, see Scinto, 1982.)

We define a text as a set of lower-order units. In turn, there is a partial-order relation defined over this set; that is, it is reflexive, antisymmetric, and transitive. Given thematic progression, for lower-order units in a text (x, y, z),

$$x \text{ R } x \text{ for some } x \in x = \text{reflexive}$$
$$\text{if } x \text{ R } y \text{ and } y \text{ R } x, \text{ then } x = y = \text{antisymmetric}$$
$$\text{if } x \text{ R } y \text{ and } y \text{ R } z, \text{ then } x \text{ R } z = \text{transitive}.$$

In turn this partial order can be given a graph-theoretic representation: Assume that A is a finite set and denote the elements of A by $a_1, a_2, \ldots,$ a_n. R is a binary relation on A; a graph G or a digraph D represents the relation R on A if the nodes of the graph are elements of A and if an arc $(a_i,$ $a_j)$ exists in the graph if and only if $a_i \text{ R } a_j$. So the graph representation of a relation R on a set A is defined as $G = (A, R)$. The relation and its graph representation are isomorphic.

We define text as a graph characterized by the pair (V, A) where

> V = a set of numbered vertices in canonical order
> A = a set of arcs

Further,

> V = a set of lower-order units (i.e., sentences as characterized by T-R)
> A = the set of arcs representing the functional relation that obtains between the vertices (i.e., T-R nexuses) of the texts as given by the TP coding of the texts.

Returning to the examples of texts given above we can represent them as graphs. Consider the following thematic functional text structure:

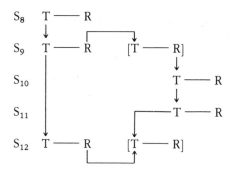

The vertices are the T-R nexuses $S_8 \ldots S_{12}$ and the arcs the relations as illustrated by descending arrows in the coding between T-R nexuses. We obtain the graph shown in Figure 6.2.

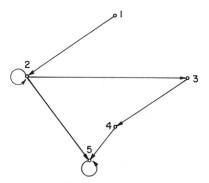

Figure 6.2.   Graph of text coding. The arcs are directed; vertices are labeled in canonical order. Loops at V_2 and V_5 show relation within complex T-R nexus.

Combinatoric Text Modules and Graphs

In order for us to determine the combinatoric modules of the texts from the graphs of the texts we have recourse to the adjacent matrix of the graph of a text. Zierer (1970) defines the adjacent matrix of a directed graph as follows:

> Given the directed graph D, its adjacent matrix $A(D)[a_{ij}]$, is a square matrix with a row and column for each node of the directed graph D, in which the input $a_{ij} = 1$ if the edge v_iv_j is in D, and $a_{ij} = 0$ if v_iv_j is not in D. The order of the matrix depends on the order of the nodes, and upon the direction of the edges. In an asymmetric graph a directed edge v_iv_j implies that there cannot be an edge v_jv_i. In the corresponding adjacent matrix [reproduced below] it is then seen that if the input $a_{ij} = 1$, the input $a_{ji} = 0$. (p. 34)

In Scinto (1982), loops on a graph, namely the entries for a_{ij}, were equal to 1 if a loop existed at that particular node. For this analysis, all entries a_{ij} are by definition equal to 0.

The corresponding adjacent matrix for the graph in Figure 6.3 would appear as follows:

	1	2	3	4	5	6
1	0	1	1	0	0	0
2	0	0	1	0	0	0
3	0	0	0	1	0	0
4	0	0	0	0	1	1
5	0	0	0	0	0	1
6	0	0	0	0	0	0

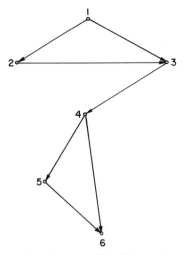

Figure 6.3. Example of graph-text structure.

By inspection of the matrix we see that this graph contains the following edges: (S_1, S_2), (S_1, S_3), (S_2, S_3), (S_4, S_5), (S_4, S_6), (S_5, S_6).

Using this adjacent matrix, we can determine the component combinatoric modules in the following way.   Having constructed the adjacent matrix, we isolate the rows and columns with multiple entries of 1. Drawing out the edges from these rows and columns we obtain the set (S_2, S_3), (S_2, S_5), (S_4, S_5). Since all the members of this set share either a common initial or final node, they constitute a single combinatoric module. We then go back to the matrix and draw out all remaining edges.   In the case above this yields (S_1, S_2), (S_3, S_4).

We next inspect these edges, derived as singletons, to determine if either their initial or final nodes appear also as initial or final nodes in any module thus far derived.   Consider one further example to clarify this procedure, using the graph in Figure 6.3.   The adjacent matrix of this graph is

	1	2	③	4	5	⑥
①	0	1	1	0	0	0
2	0	0	1	0	0	0
3	0	0	0	1	0	0
④	0	0	0	0	1	1
5	0	0	0	0	0	1
6	0	0	0	0	0	0

The rows and columns with multiple entries of 1 have been circled.   The edge sets derived from inspection of these rows and columns are (S_1, S_2), (S_1, S_3), (S_2, S_3), (S_4, S_5), (S_4, S_6), (S_5, S_6).   Next we group together all edges with common initial or final nodes.   This gives two sets:

$$(S_1, S_2), (S_1, S_3), (S_2, S_3)$$
$$(S_4, S_5), (S_4, S_6), (S_5, S_6)$$

Now we extract all singleton edges from the matrix, which gives us the edge (S_3, S_4).   By inspection of the nodes in this edge we see that the initial and final nodes are not also final or initial nodes in either set above.   That is, 3 does not appear as an initial node in any of the other edge sets, nor does 4, the final node in this edge set, appear as a final node in any other edge set.   Hence this edge forms a separate module.   In total there are three combinatoric modules associated with this graph:

$$M_1 = (S_1 \cap S_2); (S_1 \cap S_3); (S_2 \cap S_3)$$
$$M_2 = (S_4 \cap S_5); (S_4 \cap S_6); (S_5 \cap S_6)$$
$$M_3 = (S_3 \cap S_4)$$

The procedure for module detection in graphs of texts can be summarized as follows:

1. For a given graph, construct an adjacent matrix.
2. Isolate all rows and columns with multiple entries of 1.
3. By inspection, list all arcs contained in these rows and columns to determine combinatoric modules with more than one arc.
4. By inspection, partition all arcs derived in 3 so that they form non-overlapping sets according to final and initial vertices of the arcs so derived.
5. From the matrix list all arcs not removed thus far.
6. By inspection of the arcs removed as singletons determine if their initial and final vertices appear also as initial or final vertices in any of the edge sets isolated thus far.
   a. If they appear so in a previously enumerated set, group them with this set.
   b. If they do not both appear so in any previously enumerated set, they constitute separate combinatoric text modules.

The sets of edges thus isolated constitute the combinatoric modules of the text.

Coefficients of Coherence and Compactness

In light of the text model proposed above and the possibility of associating a graph-theoretic representation with the text model, we can generate a set of text indices that allow us to assess the functional-structural characteristics of texts. We outline four such indices. Given the formal definition of a text and its associated graph-theoretic interpretation detailed above, we can define a text as a graph characterized by the four-tuple V, A, D, W, where

$V =$ a set of numbered vertices in canonical order
$A =$ a set of arcs
$D =$ a set of weights
$W =$ a function $W{:}A-D$, which assigns weights to arcs

Further,

$V=$ a set of sentences composing the text

$A =$ the set of arcs representing the functional relation that obtains between the vertices of the texts as given by the T-R coding and defined above

$D =$ the strength of the relation between the vertices, that is, sentences, of the text as given by the coding where $D = 1$, meaning a single T-R element binds the sentences, $D = 2$, meaning two T-R elements bind the sentences, and so on. The weights have a finite upward bound

In order to facilitate inspection of certain graph properties we have recourse to the adjacency matrix of the graph of a text, which we defined above.

Ordinarily on a loopless digraph the entries for the arcs a_{ji} would be 0 by definition. But as we are permitting reflexive relations, some entries for arcs a_{ji} may be 1 indicating that the specified node is adjacent to itself with respect to a loop.

The sum of the rows and columns in the adjacent matrix represents the number of arcs that depart and terminate in each vertex of the digraph (directed graph). Consider the following digraph.

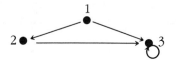

The following matrix would constitute the adjacent matrix for this graph:

	S_1	S_2	S_3	Total of Rows
S_1	0	1	1	2
S_2	0	0	1	1
S_3	0	0	1	1
Total of Columns	0	1	3	

By inspection we determine that the graph contains the following ordered pairs: (S_1, S_2), (S_2, S_3), (S_1, S_3), (S_3, S_3). There are four arcs in the digraph. This number is obtained by summing either the row or column figures. The values of the arcs converging or diverging are always equal.

We can extend the concept of the adjacent matrix to accommodate the weighting of the arcs in the digraph. Instead of entering 1 if an arc is present or 0 if no arc exists, we can substitute the weights associated with the arcs. Nonexistence of an arc is represented by a 0 in the matrix. The sum of the rows or columns gives the value in the formula $\Sigma W(A)$ needed to compute the degree of coherence of the text in question.

Another matrix can be constructed to assess a further characteristic of the text structure. We can weight the arcs as to the type of adjacency they exhibit. We create three categories of adjacency and define them in the following way:

If an arc a_{ji} has a geodesic distance (defined as the shortest path between two vertices) of 1, we term the arc *adjacent*.
If an arc a_{ji} has a geodesic distance of 2, the arc is termed *penadjacent*.
If an arc a_{ji} has a geodesic distance greater than 2, we term it *antepenadjacent*.

To each of these types of adjacency we assign the following values: 3 = adjacent, 2 = penadjacent, 1 = antepenadjacent. We can create a matrix of these values, similar to the adjacent matrix. The sum of the rows or columns gives us a weighted value for type of adjacency.

Based on these concepts we can now formally define indices of two key text-defining properties that may be used to assess and compare the text productions.

We define the degree of coherence of a text by the formula

$$\lambda = [\Sigma W(A)] \div V$$

where

$\Sigma W(A)$ = the sum of the weight of the arcs in the graph text
V = the number of vertices in the graph
λ = degree of coherence

The degree of coherence is a measure of how connected the text is with respect to its structural composition.

We also define compactness using the adjacency weights determined for a text. Compactness is defined by the formula

$$C = [\Sigma W(\text{adj})] \div V$$

where

$\Sigma W(\text{adj})$ = the sum of the rows or columns of the matrix of weighted values for adjacency;

V = the number of vertices in the graph
C = degree of compactness

By compactness we understand the degree to which each successive sentence feeds off an immediately preceding sentence, in building or carrying forward the communication of the text. The greater the number of immediately adjacent vertices the tighter or more compact the structure is as a whole. This successive binding of elements where new information is linked to immediately preceding information insures for the consumer of text a highly predictable and hence easily assimilated structure for decomposition. Such compactness is desirable if a text is to achieve a high degree of cohesiveness. Considering structures as abstract entities, we can observe that the greater the degree of connectivity they exhibit as whole compositions, the closer the binding of their constituent elements. So also for the structure of textual composition.

We can generate two further indices based on the nature of text modules developed above. We can construct two coefficients based on number of modules and arcs in the graphs of texts. These coefficients, which are a measure of a text's structural integrity, can serve as dependent measures in developmental analyses of the acquisition of text-forming strategies. The first coefficient gives a measure of a text's structural integration and the second coefficient a measure of the degree of condensation achieved in the composition of a text.

The coefficient of integration is defined by the formula

$$TM \div A = \alpha$$

where

A = the number of arcs in the text as given by the coding of TP in the text graph
TM = the number of text modules as given by the decomposition outlined above
α = degree of integration of lower order units of the text

The coefficient of integration allows us to determine to what extent the construction of a text has composed the functional relations into coherent ensembles. The fewer the number of component modules in relation to the number of arcs in the graph as a whole, the more integrated is the text in terms of its message.

The coefficient of condensation, hereafter θ, is defined by the formula

$$SL \div V = \theta$$

where:

$V =$ the number of vertices, lower order units in the text as given in the text graph

$SL =$ the number of self loops representing condensed or fused S in the graph of the text

The greater the degree to which a text structure forms the functional links into more structured wholes, intermediate between the lowest-order units, simple TR nexuses, and text modules, the tighter the binding of the information to be communicated by the text.

In addition to these quantitative coefficients of integration and condensation for text modules, we can assess the qualitative type of module employed by individuals in the construction of text. Such a qualitative assessment allows us to determine the correlation between type of module employed in the construction of text and the level of cognition as determined independently. By inspection of typical modules found in the decomposition of text graphs, we can isolate the following typology of modules, which vary along a continuum of structural integration and complexity:

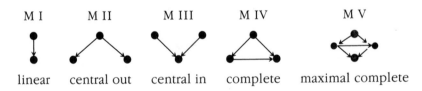

M I	M II	M III	M IV	M V
linear	central out	central in	complete	maximal complete

M I the most basic type, shows a straightforward paired composition of two lower-order units. M II and M III involve lower-order units where one unit is either a common source or common sink for the composition of the module. M IV represents a more complete structure where lower-order units are fully integrated into one ensemble. M V represents a higher type where at least four lower-order units are fully integrated into a single ensemble. The modules may occur in their pure form as given above but are more often found in combination.

The Acquisition of Strategies for Text Construction

The functional model of text we have sketched above provides a frame-work within which we can investigate the central question of the development of written language, namely, the acquisition of the form of monologic discourse organization that is unmarked for the written norm. It is within a monologic discourse organization that the written norm is uniquely realized and the set of linguistic means appropriate to the written norm actually instantiated.

The model we have sketched allows us to probe the structural-functional organization of written text over the course of its acquisition and to delineate those successive strategies of composition that characterize successive stages in the ontogenesis of written language. The model, allows us to explore the relation of written language development and the exfoliation of more general cognitive structures during the developmental process. By exploring various aspects of this relation we can attack the question of the role of oral and written language norms in the ongoing process of cognitive development and acquisition of knowledge.

Before looking at data on the acquisition of written language generated by using this structural-functional text model, we must caution that the model is culture specific in that it represents a model of text that functions in a culture where the written norm has been exploited and developed to an extent not true of semiliterate cultures. The culture to which such a model of text and indeed such a notion of the written norm applies is perhaps best described as a technological-scientific literate culture. More particularly, this model is based on analysis of English and as a consequence restricted to Anglo-American cultural contexts.

The summary of empirical work presented below is, as we indicated at the beginning of this chapter, limited in scope and given only to illustrate certain features of the text model presented above. We formulate certain hypotheses about the acquisition of written text production strategies in children and address the following questions (see also Scinto, 1982):

1. Are there any quantitative or qualitative changes over time in the functional-structural characteristics of narrative and expository texts produced by children? If such changes are observed, are they best predicted by simple maturational differences (age) or by developmental changes in observed cognitive functioning (i.e., concrete and low formal-operational thought)?
2. Are there any measurable quantitative or qualitative differences between narrative and expository text produced by subjects at given maturational or developmental periods? (We assume that narrative

and expository texts constitute general functional types of written text.)

Specifically, the empirical work sought to test the following hypotheses:

1. Narrative and expository texts produced by children between 8 and 15 years of age exhibit quantitative and qualitative functional-structural differences as measured by coefficients of compactness and cohesiveness.
2. These observed differences co-occur with a transition from one level of cognitive functioning to a higher level (concrete operational to low formal-operational) and are not attributable simply to differences in age or in reading ability.
3. Children produce narrative texts that are more cohesive and compact than expository texts produced at the same age or developmental stage.

We use Piaget's characterization of higher cognitive functioning, as his work presents the most fully articulated account of various levels of cognitive development.

To tap the textual production abilities of subjects, two text measures were designed. The first measure (construction measure) consisted of three narrative and three expository texts, graded for structural complexity (using the T-R coding scheme and readability rating), selected from a fable by Aesop, a paragraph adapted from "The Big Two-Hearted River, Part I" by Ernest Hemingway, and various short texts from *Pleasant Books in Easy English Stage 3*. Narrative and expository texts were selected in order to determine whether there were any differences in the ability to manipulate texts representing two functional communicative types that make use of varying compositional structures. Each of the texts was segmented into individual sentences. Each of these sentences was typed on a card and the cards placed, in random order, into envelopes. The task was to assemble the cards in such a way as to make a story or give an explanation of something.

This reconstruction task was employed in order to probe the process of composition where the linguistic and cognitive demand would be on construction or disposition, and not invention, of content. The texts themselves varied, in addition to structural complexity, in the number of units to be assembled. The three narrative texts contained 6, 9, and 12 sentences. The expository texts contained 6, 8, and 10 sentences.

In addition to this text-reconstruction measure, a second measure was used to elicit two examples of actual text production from subjects. In an attempt to reduce variation in the text content produced, the elicitation measure sought to constrain the context of production, at least in a general way. For the narrative text the writer was asked to produce a story for a friend who was ill and in the hospital to read. The opening sentence was supplied. The expository task required that the writers choose an activity they enjoyed and write an explanation of why they enjoyed the activity to a contemporary. Again the opening sentence was supplied. These two functional text types were elicited in order to determine if any differences were discernible in the production of text for varying communicative purposes.

All subjects in the initial sample were given the "Wide Span Reading Test," a sentence-completion task whose range covered all ages in the sample, to obtain information on individual reading ability.

Part of the original sample was given the "Colored Blocks Test" (see Feldman and Stone, 1978) to determine the developmental stage at which subjects were functioning. This test was selected because it is an essentially nonlinguistic measure of cognitive level based on a Piagetian characterization of stages of development; it provides a detailed characterization of cognitive levels of functioning. Further, the materials used, principally colored shapes and cards, were easily adapted to varying settings for administration.

Subjects for this study were obtained through contact with two Cambridge (United Kingdom) schools. They represented three age categories: 8–9, 11–12, and 14–15. In the original sample, subjects represented intact classrooms at the ages specified. Subjects in age category 8–9 were drawn from School A and subjects for the other two categories from School B. There were 16 subjects in the 8–9 category with a mean age of 8.3. There were 27 subjects in the 11–12 category with a mean age of 11.7. There were 30 subjects in the 14–15 category with mean age of 14.4. These numbers represent the original sample drawn. However, due to missing or partial data, 24 subjects were dropped from the original sample. Fifteen subjects were randomly selected from each age category for developmental testing if they scored in the 50th percentile or above on the *Wide Span Reading Test.* Two subjects were found to be at the preoperational level and were omitted from subsequent analysis. Of the remaining 28, 8 were lost because of missing data points. The remaining 20 subjects from the original sample were pooled for use in the analysis on all measures by age and by high and low reading ability.

The hypothesis proposed stated that there should be a qualitative change over time in the functional-structural characteristics of text produced and that this change would co-occur with a shift from concrete

Table 6.1

Group Means for Cohesion and Compactness

Group	Narrative texts		Expository texts	
	λ_1	C_1	λ_2	C_2
CO	1.6920	3.4600	1.7050	3.0450
LFO	2.6660	4.3870	2.0510	3.5800

operational functioning (CO) to low formal operational functioning (LFO), to use Piaget's characterizations. In order to test this prediction, two key text variables, cohesion and compactness, were defined based on the text modeling procedures described above. These notions (Scinto, 1982) are central to defining the nature of written text as a functional-structural entity.

A summary of the results from this developmental assessment of text production follows. For full details see Scinto (1982). The main dependent variables used in evaluating subjects' performance in constructing texts were the indices of functional-structural text features developed above.

The first data subjected to analysis were from a developmental sample. In this sample were 10 CO and 10 LFO children, all reading at age level or above. Each of the elicited narrative and expository texts was first segmented into sentence units, then coded into its theme-rheme structure. From the T-R coding a weighted adjacent matrix and graph were constructed for each text. From the weighted adjacent matrices the values for cohesiveness (λ) and compactness (C) indices were computed using the method described in the text model. The means for CO and LFO groups on each of the variables are given in Table 6.1.

The scores were compared using a Mann–Whitney U test to determine if the texts produced by the LFO group differed from those produced by the CO group. It was suspected that texts of the LFO group would exhibit higher indices for all measures. Results from this analysis, shown in Table 6.2, revealed significant differences between CO and LFO groups on all variables.

To determine if simple age differences contributed to the effects observed above, a Kruskal–Wallis one-way analysis of variance was run on all measures by age. No significant differences for age were found on any of the dependent measures. We concluded that LFO children did signifi-

Table 6.2

Results of Mann–Whitney Test

	λ_1	C_1	λ_2	C_2
U	6.0	13.0	26.5	25.0
P	.00	.00	.03	.02

cantly better in producing both expository and narrative text that was more cohesive and more compact.

While there was a difference in the strength of p values for narrative and expository text between developmental groups ($p = .000$ and $.035$, respectively), we wished to ascertain if there were any differences in performance on narrative and expository text for overall comparisons and within the CO and LFO groups. A Wilcoxon matched-pairs test was used to compare overall sample performance on narrative versus expository text production. A within-group comparison between narrative and expository text on all indices was carried out for both CO and LFO groups, using a Wilcoxon matched-pairs signed-ranks test.

Results indicated an overall difference in production of narrative and expository text on both indices: λ_1 with λ_2, $z = 1.792$, $p = .03$; Compact$_1$ with Compact$_2$, $z = 2.539$, $p = .00$ for all comparisons. Further, a difference between performance on narrative and expository text by the CO group on the compactness measure ($z = -1.682$, $p = .04$), but not on the cohesion measure ($z = -0.153$, $p = 0.43$). Within the LFO group there was a significant difference in performance on narrative and expository text for both cohesion and compactness measures. For the cohesion index ($z = 2.599$, $p = .00$), and for the compactness index ($z = 2.090$, $p = .01$).

Three narrative and three expository texts assembled by subjects in the construction measure were analyzed in the following way. To determine the degree to which subjects' assembly of the various texts corresponded to the original ordering of text sentences, a Kendall TAU was calculated using the original order and the subjects' ordering as the two rankings needed for computation. The TAU coefficient was chosen as it provides a measure of the degree to which the ordering of elements given by subjects conformed to the order given in the original text. Unlike other statistics of correspondence, TAU is based on the number of inversions in order for pairs of objects in the two orderings compared.

Table 6.3

Group Means for Construction Text

	Narrative			Expository		
Group	A	B	C	A	B	C
CO	0.9030	0.7060	0.4520	0.4850	0.4390	0.4120
LFO	0.9170	0.8110	0.5560	0.5040	0.6280	0.7710

TAU was calculated for each subject for each text.   Means for CO and LFO groups on all tasks are given in Table 6.3.

Based on these coefficients, all subjects' performance on the six texts were compared using developmental level as the classifying variable. Results showed a significant difference for developmental level on narrative B: $U = 22.0$, $p = .01$.   Significant differences in performance by developmental groups were also found on expository text B ($U = 26.0$, $p = .03$) and on expository text C ($U = 24.0$, $p = .02$).

As was done for all indices in the text-production measures, comparisons were made using age as a classifying variable for the entire population.   No significant findings emerged from this analysis.   Further, no age differences were found in performance on any of the text-construction tasks when subjects were compared by age within developmental groups.

A second sample was constructed for further analysis on all main text variables, λ_1, λ_2, Compact$_1$, and Compact$_2$.   Thirty subjects were divided into three age categories: 8–9, 11–12, 14–15.   Within each of these groups subjects were evenly distributed as to sex and reading ability.   Five subjects in each age category were reading above the fiftieth percentile, and five were at or below the fiftieth percentile.

The sample consisted of the 17 subjects not used in the developmental sample and 13 subjects selected at random from the developmental sample.   The 17 subjects not used in the developmental sample were first divided into age categories.   At this point it was determined which characteristics of reading ability and sex additional subjects must possess in order to balance the three age categories.

Appropriate pools of subjects were assembled for each age category and from these pools subjects were selected at random using a random number table.   Finally a one-sample runs test was carried out for each major text variable for each independent age category to test for randomness of scores on these variables.   Values of r for all these were found that allowed for the rejection of the hypotheses of nonrandom scores for the variables in each age category.

All performance scores on text-production measures were determined in the same manner as for Sample 1. Subjects' performance on all text measures was compared using reading level as a classifying variable. If subjects were found to be reading above the 50th percentile they were designated as high reading level, at or below the 50th percentile as low reading level. A Mann-Whitney U test was used to test if there were any significant differences in performance between high and low reading groups.

No significant differences were observed in performance on any text measures by reading level. For performance on the Compact$_2$ measure for expository text we found a near significant difference, with low readers performing better as a group than high readers ($U = 68.5, p = .06$). The means for low readers were 3.19, for high readers, 2.69.

In addition to between-group comparisons for age and reading level, within-group comparisons were carried out for each age group, comparing performance of high and low reading-ability groups on all text measures using a Mann-Whitney U test.

Performance on text measures when analyzed within age groups by reading level appears to be equivocal in most cases, with no significant effects. One exception is the 11–12 age group, where there was a significant difference in performance on the Compact$_2$ measure ($U = 0.0$, $p = .00$).

As with the first sample, analysis was carried out on results from the text construction task using a Mann-Whitney test. A significant difference in performance on the second expository text was observed for reading level in the 11–12 age category ($U = 2.0, p = .02$). No other significant effects were observed for within-group comparisons.

A consideration of the results presented above can be parsimoniously interpreted as leading to two conclusions. One, there appears to be evidence to support the contention that there are changes in children's ability to produce narrative and expository texts as measured by the indices of cohesion and compactness. Two, these differences in text production are correlated with differences in level of developmental function as measured by the "Colored Blocks Test" and do not appear to be strongly linked with differences in age. The findings lead to a tentative hypothesis that there should be a difference in narrative and expository texts produced, again as measured by the indices of cohesion and compactness.

Bearing in mind the limited scope of the study on which these conclusions are based, we can draw out their implications a bit further. The results do seem to point to a developmental progression for the unfolding of abilities to deal with the production of written text, as instantiated in narrative and expository texts. The categories *narrative* and *expository* are based on functional differentiation. The narrative mode quite likely incorporates more of the aesthetic function, while the expository mode more clearly incorporates what we have referred to earlier as the intellectual function. The results point to a disparity in ability to deal equally well with these two functional text types at a given age and grade level. The data are suggestive of the fact that ability to produce expository text (the scholarized norm) enters a subject's linguistic repertoire at later stages of development. This inference, if upheld, is not surprising in light of the more specialized nature of expository discourse or the suggestions from studies of oral language development (Halliday, 1975; Karmiloff-Smith, 1979) that not all functions are simultaneously present at a given stage of linguistic development.

While the results demonstrate an association between text-production abilities and level of cognitive function, we cannot exploit this finding to imply any necessary connection between cognitive level and the acquisition of the written norm. These data simply do not disambiguate the nature of this association. In Chapter 7 we present some further work that at least allows us to begin to explore the nature of this association between acquisition of the written norm and the structure of cognitive activity at different levels of development.

The results from the study summarized here have not addressed the issue of differences in oral and written language development at similar ages or levels of cognition. It is not clear that once a child is in school this issue can be meaningfully addressed from a developmental perspective. By this we mean that neither the oral nor written norm exists in isolation from each other, and as a consequence there is an inherent difficulty in disambiguating cross influences, at later stages of development, of one norm or the other. Indeed Greenfield (1972) and Michaels (1981) suggest that schooling and the written norm lead at this period of development to a transformation in the nature of spoken discourse. One thing is clear: At or about the age of eight years oral language development is well advanced and there is no reason to suppose that the task of the child in acquiring the written norm is to develop, *de novo,* in a new domain, the common lexicosyntactic and semantic features that underlie both the spoken and written norms of language.

The study we have summarized in this chapter makes no claim to be an exhaustive examination of the ontogenesis of text production in children. It is limited to a consideration of only one aspect of this production process, the achievement of compositional form as determined by the presence of coherence relations between successive sentences of a meaning unit. However, we have argued that this construction of a compositional whole is at the very core of what is meant by text and hence the written norm, which is unmarked for monologic discourse organization. Before any fruitful speculation about the dynamics of text production models can be undertaken, we must develop an adequate descriptive base for those speculations. The model of text presented marks one such attempt. The work reported here is an initial attempt at providing a descriptive account of one central process in text production. Further work must involve the systematic exploration of the questions this work suggests to deepen our understanding of what is a significant achievement of language functioning. In Chapter 7 we attempt to extend this exploration somewhat further and broach the question of what may be the consequences of the written norm for the development of mind.

7

Text Operations and
Cognitive Functioning

Introduction

In Chapter 6 we presented a functional model of written text that captured the autonomous nature of the scholarized written norm, that is, the propositional structure and decontextualized nature of written discourse in the schooling process. Based on such a model and the operations called forth in order to produce examples of such extended monologic discourse, we summarized some results of a cross-sectional study of the acquisition of the written norm. We now examine more closely the results of this study in an attempt to explore certain aspects of the process of the acquisition of the written norm and what, if any, implications might exist between the process of acquisition of such a written norm and general cognitive functioning.

The central hypothesis of this study is that changes occur over time in the nature of narrative and expository text produced by children and that these changes are associated with differences in developmental level serving as some measure of the organization of cognitive structures. No differences for age were found on the text measures (indices for compactness and cohesion) thus tending to confirm on the basis of the available data the contention that age alone cannot account for observed differences. In contrast, results confirm that LFO subjects produced texts that were both more compact and more cohesive than texts produced by CO subjects.

If changes had been associated with age differences alone, we might plausibly account for them by what Bruner (1978) has termed an *output regulation model*. By the time the child comes to deal with text and has acquired some mastery of reading, he is subjected to a plethora of textual models. Assuming that the child has a fairly well-established command of language (lexical structure and syntax) in the oral norm and perhaps some rudimentary notion of combinatoric strategies from other domains of action, his task in text production is to make his output conform to what he observes in his exposure to text. There is evidence to suggest that text produced for children's use in school and at home is like a baby talk register or motherese geared in terms of its compositional structure and lexicogrammar to the capacity of the child. Given such a model we should expect a linear relation between age, representing exposure to textual models of varying complexity either through school or home, and the type of texts produced. While no assessment was made of the type or variety of textual models to which subjects were exposed, we can at least assume, as there was no age mixing in the schools from which the sample was drawn, that subjects of varying age levels were not exposed to similar textual material in terms of formal scholastic instruction. The lack of clear association with age might argue for a limited role for formal instruction in accounting for the acquisition of a written norm. Further, we might have expected that reading comprehension scores would provide at least a crude estimate of the type and complexity of textual material with which children in the sample might be familiar. However, the data in the study on age difference and reading comprehension do not support the claims made by such an output regulation model. This is·not to suggest that exposure to text types has no effect on the acquisition process, since in the case of the CO group significant differences were observed between subjects at about 8 years of age and subjects at 12 and 14 years. These differences due to age, however, wash out in the LFO group. If the claims of an output regulation model are to be fully explored, an attempt must be made to assess the degree to which the combinatoric text structures found in text spontaneously produced by children at a given age predict or parallel those of the textual models to which they are exposed at equivalent ages either in school or elsewhere. Attention must be paid to developing an ethnography of written language within the schools and other aspects of the child's environment.

By the time at which this study examined the acquisition of the written norm, children had acquired a considerable mastery of oral language in at least two domains, in what Bruner terms a *species-minimum* domain and in communicatively competent language use (oral dialogue). Bruner (1975) argues that going beyond this species-minimum use of language to a context-free elaboration of language use can occasion a transformation in thought itself. He suggests that it may do so by "altering usage of the spoken language by leading to 'speaking of the written language' which is necessarily decontextualized" (pp. 70–71). Data from the study suggest that in the process of acquiring the written norm children do move beyond either a species-minimum level of linguistic competence or a minimum level of communicative competence.

At the time the shift from the almost exclusive use of the oral norm to use of the written norm occurs, and at the time children are beginning this process of acquiring the ability to manipulate successfully the structuring of meaning units into text, we observe a simultaneous shift from CO functioning to LFO functioning in other domains. It might be argued that this co-occurrence is a result of a decalage of general operations to the domain of language. However, there is no reason to assume that such a directional and causal characterization is correct. The data accumulated over a number of years on the question of the relation of oral language and cognition have not provided any compelling arguments about the causal influence of cognitive development on language development (R. Campbell, 1979). It has been argued by researchers such as Piaget that language plays no necessary or sufficient role in the development of higher-level thinking. Such conclusions are often based only on an analysis of the oral norm and, more often than not, are not on discourse levels of language. Before any conclusions can be drawn about the role of language and other factors in the development of mind, due consideration must be given to the written norm.

Textual composition and the production of the scholarized norm involves the child in operating on abstract language units removed from immediate situational and interlocutor support. The actual ordering process or structuring of a text involves the construction of a series of formal propositions (sentences) linked by common properties. The child must learn to link sentences by a process of intension and extension, that is, by looking to what comes first and anticipating what will come next. Such a process is mirrored in the text model presented in Chapter 6. Inhelder and Piaget (1969, p. 283) saw this process of intension and extension and their coordination as the "central problem in the development of classificatory behavior." They argued that only one kind of extension was available to the child at the operational stage, the "spatial or graphic extension of a perceptual whole." Yet clearly the process of text construction presents the child with the necessity of dealing with extension and intension in the domain of written language, certainly representing more general and abstract structures than collections of objects (i.e., physical configurations of blocks). Manipulation of textual objects (the formal propositions of a text and their structuring into communicative wholes), especially during the schooling process, comes to dominate the child's world. Beyond the notion of intension and extension, processes similar to operations of seriation and classification are mirrored in the actual combinatorics of text construction. Careful attention to written language at the level of text should lead us to reexamine the contention that forms of higher-level thinking are autonomous from operations in language in their development and that written language plays little mediational role in the constitution of mind.

Putting aside for the moment the question of the direction of the relation between the shift from CO functioning to LFO functioning and the production of text, what might plausibly account for the emergence of this ability at this particular period? We have argued that the observed changes cannot, given the data, be accounted for in any straightforward way by age or by an output regulation model. However, a possible clue is provided in Beilin's (1975) comment that

> The development of linguistic knowledge undergoes a striking change at about 6–7 years of age. Although the child from about 2½ to 7 years old acquires a formidable repertoire of linguistic rules, enough in fact to have led earlier psycholinguists to claim that the child learned all the essentials of syntax by the age of 4 or 5, a significant capacity is still absent—the ability to treat the sentence objectively, that is, to treat it as an *object capable of direct manipulation*. [Emphasis added.] (p. 371)

More directly on metapragmatic awareness, Bates and MacWhinney (1979) suggest that

> This sort of metapragmatic statement [e.g., I told you that . . . You're not supposed to say . . . , etc.] is related to the onset of connecting terms, reflecting a more general new ability to consider both performatives (speech acts) and propositions as "mental objects" that can be explicitly referred to in speech. The ability to weave sentences together across discourse through the use of explicit connecting terms are viewed as essentially the same thing, even though the particular surface forms involved vary considerably. (p. 198)

This awareness or consciousness of linguistic entities as manipulable appears to facilitate the ontogenesis of text-producing ability. The model of text sketched in Chapter 6 implies that the composition of text involves the conscious ordering of units (sentences and modules) to form integrated wholes. Further, the very practice of schooling foregrounds written language for the child as an entity to be consciously manipulated. Only by being aware of the necessity of ordering to create text can the child penetrate the compositional process and master it.

Contact and experience with written language itself during schooling may be responsible for the reflective consciousness about the linguistic system as something that can be manipulated directly. With entrance into formal schooling and instruction in reading, the child moves from simply using language to becoming consciously aware of language. As Donaldson (1978, p. 93) points out, "being aware of language as a distinct system is relevant to the business of separating what is *said* from what is done." This awareness can be said to give the child a previously lacking measure of control over his language. As one child quoted by Donaldson (1978, p. 95) put it, "You have to stop and think. It's difficult."

Text (the primary instantiation of the scholarized written norm) is relatively late in appearance. This may be explained in part by the necessity for a greater awareness of the abstract nature of the linguistic manipulation involved in the composition of text, a process that depends on the locus of control being situated almost exclusively in the producer of text. The very nature of certain functional features of the written norm as found in text may move the child from operations characterized by interpsychological control (shared by more than one individual) to behavior that is under intrapsychological control (situated primarily within and mediated by the individual).

The child does not come to text wholly unprepared to meet its demands. Before encountering text, the child has considerable command over oral discourse. Text differs from oral discourse in the degree to which contextual and interlocutor support sustains the compositional process. Text has less of this contextual and communicative support and, as a consequence, greater metalinguistic awareness is required to achieve the composition of explicitly context-free components into ensembles. The findings on the text-construction task outlined earlier, while less clear-cut than the assessment of text productions themselves, also tend to support the argument being advanced here. In the text-construction task, subjects were asked to order the scrambled units of various texts. The texts (three narrative and three expository) varied systematically in the numbers of sentences composing them and in the complexity of their thematic structure and overall composition. With narrative texts, a significant difference was found for developmental level for the second text but no differences on either the first or third texts. Analysis of results based on the first text, having a simple thematic structure and consisting of six units, did not show any differences. However, given the simple structure of the text and relatively small number of constituent sentences, the result is not surprising. The third text, the most difficult in the narrative set in terms of its thematic structure and number of sentences (12), again did not show any difference between CO and LFO subjects. It is plausible that with material of a given level of complexity, LFO subjects have not yet achieved sufficient mastery of text operations to distinguish their performance from that of CO subjects.

With the expository text-construction task, results were more clear-cut. The expectation was that LFO subjects should show clear differences in performance. Here the only text on which no differences for developmental level were found was the first text, again the one with the simplest thematic structure and fewest sentences (6). Significant differences were found for the second and third texts.

In the experimental tasks in the cross-sectional study of text ability, subjects generally performed better with narrative texts than they did with expository texts. This result is consistent with the general tenor of our argument that there is a progressive differentiation of functional norms in the course of development. Narrative norms lie closer to models of oral performance than do expository norms. Indeed, expository norms can be more closely identified with an intellectualized written norm. Expository text in its compositional structure further foregrounds the necessity for decontextualized propositional statements. Where narrative composition can in part proceed along a logic that is more closely linked with a construction sequence on the unfolding of concrete events in time, this is less likely in expository text. Narrative text, for example, through its content, lends itself to more real world situational supports such as definite time and space references. It is in its orientation more exophoric. With expository text the producer has to be more acutely aware of the text consumer's point of view in constructing the textual communication. All such factors argue for a later emergence of control over expository text construction.

Differences in performance on the text-construction task are generally consistent with differences observed in text-production tasks, and both tend to support the contention that these differences are cotemporaneous with a shift in developmental level as measured by the Colored Blocks Test. This is not to suggest, however, that the shift from CO to LFO cognitive functioning is causally responsible for the difference in performance, nor does the evidence support any contention that the acquisition of text-producing ability is causally responsible for observed changes in levels of cognitive functioning. There is nothing in the data to support either conclusion. The only sure fact that emerges is that the observed shift in developmental level and observed changes in text production are functionally interrelated in some yet-to-be-determined manner. One mechanism suggested to account for the observed differences in performance is the emergence of a reflective metalinguistic awareness precipitated by operations involving written language and arising as a consequence of school practice.

Function and Relation in Cognition

It could be argued that the ability to produce more cohesive and compact text that occurs with the transition from CO to LFO functioning is accounted for by certain cognitive structures that enter a subject's repertoire at this time. Such very general structures could influence other domains as well. What more general cognitive operations demanded by the text-construction process that might arise during this period and their probable source remains an open question. It is probable, however, that central to the process of text composition is the notion of establishing dependencies between units, that is, sentential propositions comprising text, so that the whole text functions as an integral object not reducible to any of its parts. This involves establishing functions or functional relations between the constituent sentential propositions of text and not merely the arbitrary juxtaposition of such units in time and space. A text is not an arbitrary assembly of random sentences. So any two sentences may be said to be in relation when one occurs either before or after the other in a text. We say there is a relation of priority when A < B. However, if a property of A is linked to some property of B, as when sentences are linked by thematic elements, we say that there exists a functional relation between A and B. It is perhaps this requirement that the constituent units of text be constructed in such a way as to be functions of each other, thereby forming a closed partially ordered set or lattice, that may account for differences in text production of CO and LFO subjects. On the relative difference between relation and function, Piaget, Grize, Szeminska, and Bang (1977) observe that

> Psychological operations involved in relations and functions might also be different. In fact we note that even though two concrete objects can be in relation to one another, (e.g., if one is to the left of the other or if it is produced previously), we cannot properly refer to an object as being a function of another. A function exists only to the degree to which a specific *property* of one is linked to the property of the other. This might lead one to think that the operations for establishing a relation might in some way be more primitive than those establishing functional relationships. (p. 142)

In the case of text composition, this is what must occur. Theme-rheme linking between units establishes just such a functional relation between units of text. A function or functional relation carries with it the notion of dependence. It could be argued that subjects can only deal adequately with establishing dependencies among units of text when they have a clear grasp of the operations of functions. Piaget *et al.* (1977) have in a series of experiments tentatively demonstrated that this notion emerges clearly at about the LFO period.

Whether this grasp of function arises solely in the domain of action on concrete objects or through the coordination of the subject's actions, as suggested by Piaget's work, and then generalizes to operations on written language cannot be supported by the data from this study. However, it can be shown that the kind of combinatory logic that the notion of function leads to is in fact the very combinatory logic that is necessary in operations of text production.

We have suggested above that the tendency of the scholarized written language norm to focus conscious attention on itself might be responsible for observed changes in the production of text. The results from the cross-sectional study at least argue for an interfunctional correlation between what have been termed operational and formal operational structures of thought and the onset of a textual function (i.e., acquisition of the scholarized written norm) in the linguistic repertoire of subjects in the study.

However, such findings leave unexplored the nature of such an interaction between cognitive structures present at particular stages of development and specific textual strategies employed in the course of acquiring a command over the production of written monologic text. In order to explore the nature of this relation, a second study (Scinto, 1984) sought to specifically assess the architectonics of the constituent units employed in the text-construction process to determine what, if any, parallels could be found between the logic of text composition and the logic of cognitive operations as described by Piaget for concrete and formal operational stages of development. Techniques were developed to decompose the texts produced by children into their underlying compositional units (the text modules of the text model presented in Chapter 6) and to examine the actual logic of the structuring of these units into written texts. On the basis of this analysis it was possible to develop a typology of compositional types and strategies and then to examine what parallels, if any, exist between the logic of cognitive operations at concrete and formal stages of development and the logic of text-composition types at or around these stages. Results from this study indicate that there are major differences between the compositional strategies employed by CO children and LFO children. But more interesting for the purposes of our present argument are the parallels between the compositional logic of text production and the logic of cognitive operations in Piaget's sense.

Piaget has stated on numerous occasions (1968, 1970, 1977) that the source for the elaboration of logicomathematical operations is to be found only in the coordination of actions. He argues, "The operations of thought and logicomathematical structures, in the broadest sense, are due to the general coordinations of actions . . . and not to language or to specifically social transmissions; these general coordinations of actions themselves come from the nervous and organic coordinations which have nothing to do with social interactions." (Piaget, 1970, p. 177). Such a statement belies a kind of biological reductionism in which culture and specifically the products of culture, for example, language, are seen as mere accessories to the function of mind that is constituted by primarily biological principles. The function of mind leads to certain seminal psychological principles, which in turn give rise to a social and cultural order. In such an argument, where development and, indeed, the organism itself is viewed as a sort of layer cake with biology as the base, psychology a second layer, and culture the frosting, clearly no constitutive facilitative role can be admitted for language as a formative principle of mind or its workings. Yet this view that man is first a biological being, second a psychological being, and only then a cultural being is belied by a reconsideration of the evolutionary evidence where both neurological and cultural development are properly seen to be synchronous and not serial (Geertz, 1973a). This is no less true of ontogenesis: The neonate is simultaneously a biological and psychological being born into a culture. The child coordinates actions in the context of object manipulations that are themselves partly cultural artifacts; this is no less true of those symbolic objects in the environment into which the child is born. Specifically we would argue that a closer examination of the actual and necessary composition of lower-order units in written monologic text shows a striking parallel to the combinatorial logic of concrete operations. This parallel should encourage us to reexamine the role such cultural-symbolic objects as text may play in the ontogenesis of mind.

In order to explore the nature of the combinatoric logic of text construction and what parallels might exist between such operations and the structure of concrete and formal operational thinking, we present some results from our analysis of text-forming strategies. Using a sample of texts from the cross-sectional study of written language acquisition (Scinto, 1982), we further analyzed the texts produced by CO and LFO children for the actual compositional strategies employed. Using procedures outlined in the text model presented in Chapter 6, we decomposed the texts produced by subjects into their component modules and focused our analysis on the logic of construction in these modules.

The analysis of text construction to be presented attempts to demon-

strate that the act of generating written monologic text involves the subject
in the active and conscious construction of functions and relations between lexicalized abstract meaning entities, that is, linking according to a
combinatory rule of lowest-order propositions to higher propositions to
form a meaning entity. The nature of the links established between these
propositions is not a mere comparison of such propositions and their
juxtaposition in space but implies that the links express and instantiate
syntactic, semantic, and pragmatic dependencies dictated by the logic of
written monologic text itself. Propositions are linked in thematic and
rhematic nets that exhibit functional and relational dependencies. The
text as end product of this process forms a closed meaning system. This is
particularly true of the written language norm, which must function adequately in its communicative goal independently of interlocutor support
and immediate nonlinguistic context.

In their work examining the nature of concrete operations, Inhelder
and Piaget (1958) state that

> in the most general sense concrete logical operations are actions performed on
> objects to bring them together into classes of various orders or to establish relations
> between them. One can distinguish infralogical operations from concrete classifi-
> cations or relational operations; their function is to integrate the parts of objects into
> a spatial-temporal whole—i.e., a permanent object—and to place or displace
> these parts in continuous configurations. (p. 273)

For the term *concrete logical operations* in this characterization one
could easily substitute *text construction*. The objects on which actions
are performed in the case of text construction would be the constituent
propositions of text, that is, the actual sentences of text, that constitute the
most elementary text-forming units. To "bring them together into classes
of various orders or to establish relations between them" is, in terms of
text construction, to mold the lowest-order propositions into text modules by establishing relations and functions of thematic progression between propositions. At about this time, linguistic entities such as sentences come to be seen as objects capable of direct manipulation. Such
parallels cannot be ignored and indeed are likely the basis for the close
correlation between the acquisition of the scholarized written norm and
the characterization of the nature of cognitive functioning in CO and LFO
terms.

Function and Relation in Written Text

Drawing on results from Scinto (1985) of the actual architectonics of
textual compositions, we can illustrate the nature of the parallel between
the logic employed in monologic text construction and the logic of

thought. The most fundamental text-building strategy used by subjects in this study is demonstrated by the regular pairing of successive sentence units in the text. This is clearly illustrated by a number of texts produced by CO subjects. When these texts are broken down into their component modules, the pattern of thematic progression shows that linkages are primarily established by a process of theme iteration, that is, the simple strategy of carrying a single repeated theme throughout the text and successively adding new information to it.

The strategy of construction employed in such texts, that of successively linking rhematic material to a previous thematic element that is conserved through the progression of the text, is analogous to the kind of transitivity and conservation spoken of by Piaget as necessary for the formation of operational modes of thought. While each propositional pair of elements in such texts is constructed successively, it is not constructed without connection to the previous pair. The connection is primitive in the sense of only conserving thematic elements, but the final system as product does exhibit necessity and closure.

In attempting to evaluate the significance of such a strategy of composition, we must ask if the construction is limited to the composition of ordered pairs only, or if it exhibits the properties of a structured whole, which implies a closed system. If the composition of elements were solely limited to paired construction, it would be an instance of what Inhelder and Piaget (1969) call *sublogical operations.* The child in building only successive pairs fails to see that the assemblage must result in a whole.

Indeed, in this sense even the primitive stepwise successive construction as exhibited by the types of texts we have been discussing fulfills the criteria for what Inhelder and Piaget term "logical or pre-logical." Even at these early stages the text forms a meaning continuum and functions as a communicative whole. Clearly this combinatoric strategy exhibits at least a rudimentary notion of the coordination of extension with intension, a factor Piaget deems necessary for the development of operational thought. But while Inhelder and Piaget (1969, p. 283) claim that the only instance of extension available to children is "the spatial or graphic extension of a perceptual whole," clearly the construction of texts in this study also exhibits a basic notion of extension and intension that Piaget claims is not present in language.

The strategy of construction found in the text under discussion does not exhibit a perfect command of reversibility. It is in its basic thrust successive. However, the sense is that the sentences are strictly ordered, in that the system does exhibit a partial order; it is reflexive, antisymmetric, and transitive. The construction may be viewed as forming a simple chainlike lattice structure. Indeed this structure is in a sense guaranteed by the nature of text as a monologic communication. In such simple construction strategies, the child's first experience with producing instances of the written norm may be simply confined to conforming his output to the logic inherent in text itself.

In texts such as the one discussed above, the child in Piaget's sense is dealing with perhaps a limited notion of a combinatorial system in that he is simply bringing objects together by establishing relations and elementary functions between them (Inhelder & Piaget, 1958). Further, in the domain of the written norm, the child may be using a strategy that is limited in much the way Inhelder and Piaget (1958, pp. 273–274) speak of the limitation of concrete operations: "[T]he integrated structures of classes and relations which govern concrete operations are limited to bringing classes or relations together by a class inclusion of *contiguous linkage which moves from one element to the next.*" [emphasis added].

While Piaget has spoken of "objects," it is unclear how children at the CO stage view the predicational units (sentences) of text, as actual objects to be manipulated or perhaps intuitively as formal propositions. Beilin (1975) remarks that these linguistic entities come to be regarded as objects capable of direct manipulation. But clearly the elements of the text, whether we term them propositions, utterances, or sentences, are not given to the child in his immediate environment. The child must invent them, in the sense of "invent" used in traditional rhetorical theory, and then coordinate these units into structural meaning wholes. Such a process implies an ability to deal with a mode of abstraction in a symbolic realm that allows the child to establish the logical-algebraic structures of the text. However these predicatorial elements are viewed, it is evident from the CO texts in our study that subjects were at least operating with some awareness of a combinatorial system. In the CO texts, fully 72% of the constituent combinatoric modules employed can be accounted for by a structure using a contiguous linkage from one element to the next.

Piaget says that a fusion of anticipations and retrospections in constructing a system occurs when the child moves beyond such successive contiguous linkages. This allows a subject to break the constraints of only or primarily forward-linked contiguous items. Piaget (1977, p. 36) notes that "the fusion of anticipations and retrospections . . . implies a closure of the system on itself and this involves an essential innovation: the internal relationships of the system acquire necessity and cease to be constructed successively without connection with the preceding ones."

In producing written monologic text, the subject establishes the theme-rheme articulation that structures the text in just such a manner. The subject must establish a relation aRb between compositional units of text based on the thematic linkage and instantiated in particular semantic and pragmatic relations selected from the particular set of linguistic means foregrounded for this written norm. The establishment of such a set of functional relations characterized by dependency implies that there exists a measure of extension and intension in the combinatory logic of text. Piaget et al. (1977, p. 170) say of such relations: "Even in a given relation aRb the terms *a* and *b* constitute the extensional field of the relation which is in turn characterized by intension." The composition of the text demands that each preceding predicational unit is taken into account and structured into successive predicational units. The composition process for text quickly begins to transcend only immediately linked contiguous predicational units. Longer dependencies begin to be found. For example, one module in Scinto (1985) which involves the integration of propositions in the following manner: $(2 \cap 3) + (2 \cap 5)$ and $(4 \cap 5)$. This results in the structure shown below:

Text Structure   Modules

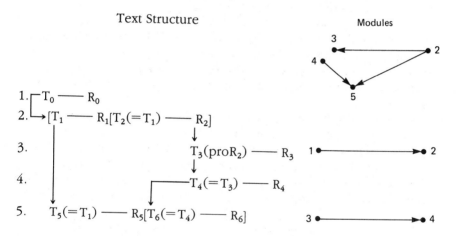

Once the fusion of anticipation and retrospection occurs and is solidified, Piaget states that the relations in a constructed system take the form of two interconnected properties that are general in all operational structures: transitivity and conservation. About conservation Piaget writes:

> The link with transitivity is obvious, for if one has A = C because A = B and B = C, it is because some property is conserved from A to C; and on the other hand, if the subject accepts as necessary the conservations A = B and B = C, he will infer from them A = C by the same arguments. (pp. 36–37)

In the composition of written text the subject must operate with this logic in constructing a coherent communicative whole. Both the outer form of the text's linear arrangement in space and its inner structure as shown by the modular construction conform to such a logic of ordering. In the text, the order relations A – B and B – C imply the further relation A – C. Transitivity and conservation are critical to the text-production process. What is conserved from A – B to B – C to A – C is the thematic progression. So we have, for example, the following kinds of compositions in texts (from Scinto, 1982, p. 185)

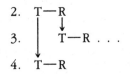

Here thematic and rhematic material is, as it were, conserved throughout the net of necessary relations in the module. Rhematic elements of 2 are integrated in 3 and thematic elements of 2 and 3 are further integrated in 4. The order in the text is transitive.

Some primitive notion of conservation is present even in the most basic (linear) modules in the texts from our study. In examining the typical thematic progression of these linear modules, we see that they are structured by thematic progression, where thematic elements are preserved from unit to unit within modules and from module to module between modules.

The examples of text-composition strategies we have commented on thus far represent those strategies used by subjects functioning at the CO stage. When we examined the compositional strategies exhibited by component modules of text produced by LFO subjects, the compositional strategies quickly transcend even the primitive conservation strategies observed in CO subjects' production. Figures 7.1 and 7.2 give the graph-theoretic representations of the decomposed component modules and the thematic patterns associated with the texts of two LFO subjects.

In these texts A and B it can be observed that there is a more fully developed sense of extension and intension. The thematic progression of the modules of texts A and B shows that the linkage of compositional units is achieved not only by thematic iteration but also involves the concatenation of thematic and rhematic material into more complex compositional nets. At this stage the entire previous composition, not simply immediately prior elements, appears to be available to the subject. The construction of the text shows that the subject reaches farther back into previous elements to continue the construction process.

By examining the compositional strategies of the CO and LFO subjects in this study sample we found three successive stages or types of compositional strategies that appear to follow a regular progression along a hierarchy. Stage 1 involves successive linking of immediately prior elements, a

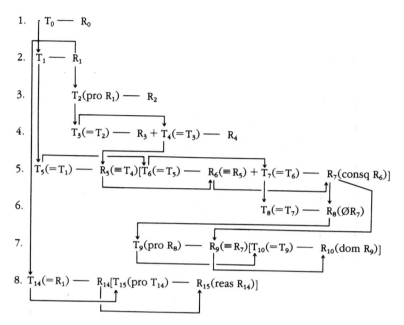

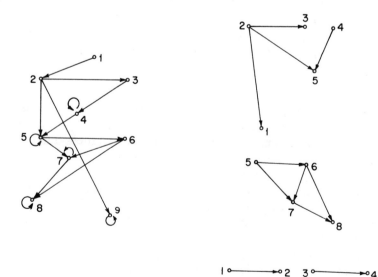

Figure 7.1   Text coding, graph representation, and graph decomposition, LFO subject, text A.

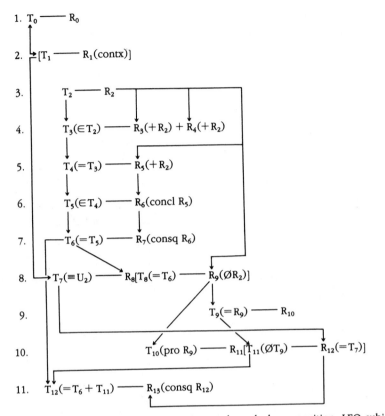

Figure 7.2. Text coding, graph representation, and graph decomposition, LFO subject, text B.

simple pattern of theme iterations. Stage 2 involves compositions with multiple dependencies made by reference to one particular unit in the module that serves as source or sink for other units in the module. This intermediate stage often involves modules of type II or III (see Chapter 6). Stage 3 is illustrated by the complexity of the examples in Figures 7.1 and 7.2, where there are more complete and closed units formed. Clearly the one-to-many and many-to-one mappings of the second stage represent a somewhat transitional strategy between the successive compositions of stage one and the more complex and integrated compositions exhibited by the texts of the LFO group.

All the mappings in these three stages are functional in Piaget's sense, since they are univocal to the right and establish functional dependencies between sentence units and not just comparisons or juxtapositions in a

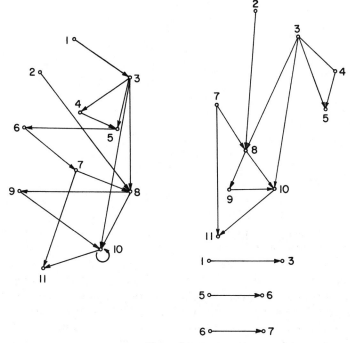

Figure 2 cont.

list.   In particular it is in the second stage, with its many-to-one and one-to-many mappings, that we first see a mature control of reversibility. On a similar point Piaget et al. (1977) write:

> Actions as such are one-way and thus are not operations . . . : the application of E onto F constitutes a correspondence of many to one [Figure 7.3,I] which is a function in that it is univocal to the right.   On the other hand, the one to many correspondence of F to E is, by definition, neither an application nor a function since it is not univocal to the right.   Yet, it is precisely this one to many correspondence (for example, from G to F and from F to E in [Figure 7.3,II]) which characterizes a hierarchical classification . . . , and, to attain it, the subject must be able to go from one direction to the other without difficulty in this system of co-univocal correspondences (one to many or many to one).   It is therefore only in freeing himself from the one-way direction of functions that the subject attains the reversible mobility of operations.   (pp. 182–183)

Unlike what Piaget says of actions, the construction of text is not one way but implies a shuttling back and forth, the notion of retrospection and anticipation.   With the appearance of many-to-one and one-to-many mappings, we see reversibility reflected in the text structure.   This movement of composition strategy from simple univocal functions to the right, that is,

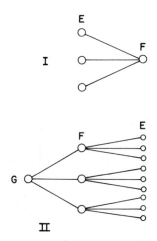

Figure 7.3.   Mapping of one-to-many and many-to-one.   Reproduced from Piaget *et al.* (1977) with permission from D. Reidel.

the successive mappings of the simplest CO texts to the multiple one-to-many and many-to-one mappings and the concatenation of such a strategy in the modules of texts such as A and B in Figures 7.1 and 7.2 demonstrates growth in reversibility and a movement from the notion of functions to that of operations in Piaget's sense.   Of such a transition Piaget et al. (1977) write:

> It is once again reversibility which distinguishes functions from the operating structures of relations. . . .   We can thus generally acknowledge that the basic *decalage* which separates constitutive functions from the development of elementary operatory structures of 'groupings' is due to the gradual formation of the reversibility of class unions and of concatenations or transitive sequences of relations, these reversible operations of union or concatenation thus being the source of the inclusions which are missing in the initial 'categories' of ordered pairs.   (pp. 184–185)

Such a decalage is observable in the gradual differentiation of text-composition strategies to be found in the structure of compositional modules.

The intermediate strategy of Stage 2, one-to-many and many-to-one mappings, bears a resemblance to the early stages of the coordination of anticipation and retrospection.   Inhelder and Piaget (1969) state:

> [C]hildren only begin to abstract a common property when they abandon this kind of successive assimilation and when they show some sign of a retroactive process by remembering the way in which they started a collection.   This enables them to achieve some coherence between the beginning and what comes after. . . .   At first there is no more than a semi-anticipation, partly in the sense that the child cannot foresee what follows as a whole.   (p. 286)

By combining module types I and II, ensembles of a fair degree of complexity are constructed; they fall short, however, of the complexity of the fully integrated module types IV and V. With the appearance of modules of types IV and V and the combination of these module types with others, the subject may be said to have achieved a competent command over operations of reversibility and anticipation and to have begun to weld them into a functional system of compositions. Piaget (1977, p. 47) writes of the stage of formal operations: "It is this power of forming operations of operations which enables knowledge to transcend reality, and which by means of a combinatorial system makes available to it an infinite range of possibilities, while operations cease to be restricted, as are concrete operations, to step-by-step constructions." When we compare the construction strategies of CO texts and LFO texts (Scinto, 1985), we see just such a transition from a predominantly successive step-by-step strategy to the elaboration of a combinatorial logic of fair complexity. While paired successive constructions never fully drop out of the subject's repertoire of compositional strategies, there is a gradual integration of these forms into modules that exhibit a fuller command of a combinatorial architectonics. The operations and structural configuration of text-forming strategies illustrated above are indicative of the construction schemes that children gradually gain experience with and command over in acquiring the scholarized written norm.

The Place of Written Monologic Text in Ontogenesis

The production of written monologic text as a privileged domain in the ontogenetic process may be accounted for by its foregrounding during the schooling process and its self-reflective character. The process of constructing meaningful communications at the level of the text demands that the subject take as the input to the process his own linguistic productions. By this we mean that every successive lower-order unit produced in a text has as its linguistic input the subject's own previous linguistic production. Written text, where control for composition lies primarily with the writer, demands an increased conscious attention (Piaget's reflexive abstraction) to the linguistic context, that is, the previous elements in the unfolding ensemble of the whole text. This self-reflexive aspect of text, combined with a growing self-reflective capacity of the child, acts as a powerful goad in spurring metalinguistic awareness. Such conscious focusing on the process of text creation, indeed on the whole of language use, and the encouragement of self-reflective activity in many domains are principle activities of the schooling process as we know it.   Such activities foreground for the child the self-conscious activity of dealing with language.

Is the gradual elaboration of the linkages and strategies of compositions due in part to the cryptic structure of text or, as Piaget suggests, to the coordination of actions on the part of the subject?   On abstraction Piaget et al. (1977) write:

> Logico-mathematical links are due to reflective abstractions because they are drawn from coordinations of actions and not of objects: even if the contents (in intension) of a class or a relation are drawn from objects (simple abstraction), their form (union, inclusion, order, etc.) is the result of an activity of the subject.   (p. 169)

While we would agree that conscious activity of the subject is necessary for the internalization of a combinatoric text logic, reflective abstraction is likely spurred, in the case of the written language norm, by exposure to written text both at home and within the schooling process.   If the subject is going to coordinate his actions he must first be aware of them.   Such awareness, in the domain of language, is particularly fostered by the child's confrontation with written text and its particular functional-compositional organization.

Given that during the course of the acquisition of the scholarized written norm as exemplified in the production of written monologic text an ever-increasing command over complex schemes for text construction gradually emerges, it remains to be asked from where such strategies of text construction derive.   The argument in this chapter has suggested that one probable source is the act of text production itself and the social practice that calls it forth and supports it.   Yet it may be asked further if there is anything in the textual environment or in the text as object that might in the first instance facilitate the acquisition of the kinds of combinatorial strategies that have been discussed above.   If we adopt a dualist approach to this question we can plausibly argue that the text's structure itself in the first instance imposes an implicit organization that the child must accommodate.   By a dualist approach we have in mind R. Campbell's (1979, p. 420) distinction between "an inner domain of the organism, the contents of which are constantly changing and available to awareness and whose dynamic is rational" and "an outer domain, the contents of which change only slowly and perhaps in some cases not at all."   The outer domain is "not available to awareness," and its "dynamic is causal."   Campbell terms the structure of this inner domain of the organism *phenic* and the structures of the outer domain *cryptic*.   The boundary between these domains, Campbell maintains, is flexible and subject to change.   The structure of the phenic domain deals with operations on representations and explicit knowledge. The cryptic domain typically deals with tacit or implicit processes.

In the area of text, the distinction between explicit phenic processes and tacit or cryptic structure can be viewed as the difference between the external linear arrangement of any text as a simple or total order and the internal order of the texts as represented by the compositional modules that progressively depart farther from the order of the external linear configuration. This deformation represents a shift in control from cryptic to phenic processes. Self-reflection and self-reflexive processes may account in part for the shift we observe. Text composition increasingly departs from control by cryptic structure to manipulation by explicit phenic processes. We have stated that at first the child has available the inherent linear ordering of the text itself. In early stages, textual composition proceeds by a strategy of experiential iconism whereby the order of elements in text is simply given by a sequential arrangement of lower-order units that in large part conforms to some experiential ordering of these units as they might occur in the phenomenal world. However, as practice with text production and exposure to principles of organization that depart from such experiential ordering increase, especially in the case of expository text, the internal logic of cognitive activity is modified more and more. Such a shift is in large part the result of the decontextualized nature of text itself and the learning process the child is subjected to in schooling.

This transformation from cryptic to phenic control, from a natural logic of direct action to the combinatoric logic of text, proceeds through a process of imitative activity fostered by the modeling of discourse types imposed by the schooling process. Commenting on Baldwin's notion of social or cultural factors in development, Russell (1978) writes that

> these [non-preprogrammed behavior patterns] might be developed by imitation, an ontogenetic process of accommodation. So here, because behaviours developed in one generation can be passed on directly through imitation, we have something that mimics Lamarkian inheritance and disposes of its necessity. 'Tradition' is nothing other than the social development and transmission of behaviours, through such agencies as imitation to which young can accommodate. (p. 46)

This process of imitation is neither static not slavish but implies an accommodative and active constructon by the self as agent of that constructive process. What is initially an imitation of an external model of discourse, fostered by the schooling process, is eventually through practice and activity assimilated to the phenic domain of control. Such a process is captured in Popper's remark (1981, p. 45) that "The decisive thing is that we learn to do things by *doing* things, in appropriate situations, including cultural situations." This "doing" in turn rebounds upon the very structure of the conscious cognition of the individual. It can be said that the growing mind of the individual is to some extent the product of cultural practice and the combinatoric logic of text constituted by such practice. The developing mind emerges at least in part through interaction with cultural objects such as text.

This brief account of data that have been presented here and in Chapter 6 has argued for the proposition that written language, not as some abstract entity but as embodied in given cultural practices, is a contributory factor in the growth of the mind. Written language in the sense that it has been defined in these pages is that factor that intervenes to complete the process of linguistic growth begun when the child utters his first words. As such the written language norm is the natural concomitant of the oral norm.

If we properly regard cognition not as something that is out there but as a way of interacting with the material and cultural world and as an entity constructed through such interaction with the objects of the material and cultural world, then we can begin to construe the role that the written norm plays in such a constructive process. The nature of interaction with the world is never direct, except perhaps in very early stages of development, but mediated. What mediates our interaction with the world is the representational system at our disposal. When a shift or change occurs in this representational system, the nature of interaction with the world changes. Such a shift in the nature of representational systems occurs when the child moves from an almost exclusive use of the oral norm to the use of the written norm. Thought becomes truly autonomous when the system of representation that mediates between the individual and the world is characterized by a degree of decontextualization. The prime candidate for such a system is indeed the written norm as instantiated in a textual model of monologic discourse.

8

Written Language and the Growth of the Mind

Introduction

Implicit in most models of cognitive development in children is a bias toward a biological reductionism and a stratificational view of the place of sociocultural facts in such models. Certainly classical accounts of oral language development in Anglo-American psychology have more often than not viewed language as parasitic on cognitive growth. The logical conclusion of such approaches has been to view written language as parasitic on oral (or natural) language development. We have been at some pains to argue that the written norm as instantiated in written text constitutes a unique domain within the ontogenetic process. The failure of past accounts of development to appreciate the two facts, (1) that oral language as cultural artifact plays a constitutive role in ontogenesis and (2) that written language constitutes a further differentiation of the language faculty and so exerts its own formative and facilitative influence on cognitive development, stems by and large from an inadequate appreciation of the functional nature of language and the general formative nature of socioculturally constituted semiotic systems in the development of mind.

An almost exclusive focus on the formal structural aspects of language, whether inspired by Chomsky's work or that of others, has had the inevitable consequence of obscuring the fact of the dual functional-structural nature of language. It is largely in the work of the Prague School (and in Bühler's early work and that of Wundt) that this tendency is resisted. Unfortunately, much of this work is unappreciated by or inaccessible to Anglo-American scholars.

Running parallel to the structural approach to language, divorcing it from its cultural context, is a strongly formal structural approach to the study of the ontogenesis of mind. Such an orientation clearly runs through the work of Jean Piaget, with its biological reductive tendencies and asocial approach to the question of the growth of the mind. When these tendencies are considered, it hardly comes as any great revelation that more functional and sociocultural orientations to the development of mind have received scant attention. The question of the constitutive forces behind the development of consciousness is seen in interest in the 1980s in the work of Russian scholars such as Vygotsky and Luria. However, this attempt is in danger of being swept away by the appearance of another formalist-structuralist approach from cognitive science, with its attendant panoply of esoteric and arcane but certainly timely jargon of flow charts, programs, subassemblies, input systems, input analyzers, and, most recently, the modules of mind. It is perhaps no surprise that such formalist and mechanistic approaches are advocated by the disciples of the new Cartesianism.

Against this kind of mechanistic or perhaps electronic and computational structuralism we would argue that the determinants of the rational mind lie as much in man's sociocultural experience and particularly in his participation in the experience of language as in the experience and accretion of his biological inheritance. We have argued in Chapter 1 that the conception of what is to count as language for a long time precluded any genuine consideration of the formative influence of language on mind. Implicit in the folk view of language presented in Chapter 1 is a structural bias that impeded for a number of years any real progress in attempts to explain the acquisition of the oral norm as well as closing debate in a preemptory fashion on the acquisition of the written norm as an autonomous domain of acquisition or as a formative cause in the genesis of mind.

In Chapter 5 we argued that the written norm cannot be considered as a unitary construct to be contrasted with the oral norm. Rather, a more reasonable characterization of the written norm would differentiate between functional variants, each of which would be correlated with specific sets of linguistic means of expression, each constituted in part by specific social praxis as, for example, in narrative and expository models. As a consequence of this differentiation, each functional variant would entail different consequences for cognitive development. This limited characterization of the written norm allows us to contrast it with particular functional variants of the oral norm and further permits us to properly examine the process and consequences of the acquisition of the written norm.

Developmental Models and Culture

In this characterization of the written norm we have severely limited what we understand by the phrase *the acquisition of written language*. Our focus is restricted to the acquisition of what is termed in Chapter 5 *the scholarization or intellectualization of the written norm*. It may be argued that equating written-language acquisition with the functional variant of the scholarized written norm is far too restrictive to serve as a model for the acquisition of written language. Such criticism would be valid if ours were a cross-cultural consideration of the acquisition of written language in all its functional variants. Scribner and Cole's work (1981) has amply demonstrated the varieties of functional variants that written language may assume in cultures other than our own. However, in the majority of Western cultures two facts are inescapable: (1) the majority of children pass through a process of formal schooling at the time that they acquire the written norm of language, and (2) this schooling both foregrounds and privileges a particular functional variant of the written norm, that is, the scholarized or intellectual function. If our arguments in Chapter 5 have any validity in linking social praxis with a particular functional norm of language, then the conclusion is inescapable that what is meant by the acquisition of written language in such technologically advanced societies is in fact the acquisition of the intellectualized written norm of language.

There are those who may argue that such a process is, for political or philosophical reasons, a basic distortion of some technological ideal of the species. Nevertheless, the fact remains that when we inquire what cognitive development is and what the consequences of such a process are at this particular moment in Western technological society, we have to acknowledge that the process at this time and place values design over production, intellect over action, and mediated means of relating to our particular environmental and psychological niche over direct means. Goody (1982) speculates on alternative paths to knowledge in oral and literate cultures and the consequences for social structure of the alternative paths (mediate or direct, oral or literate). Our concern here has not been to examine the social-structural consequences of such choices but to document some aspects of the process of acquisition along one of these paths, the literate, and to probe the probable consequences for the formation of mind of this acquisition.

In asserting in Chapter 4 that the child is subject to a double line of development, a natural line and a cultural line, our intent is not to establish yet another dualism in characterizing man but to recognize the fact that these lines of development do represent from an analytic viewpoint two irreducible aspects of the child's environment. Perhaps there will come a time when biology and culture may be characterized by a more satisfying unitary construct. But clearly that time has not yet come nor has such a concept emerged, despite the posturings of sociobiology and other reductionist philosophies. The logic of the natural and cultural lines of development differ in significant ways. Yet both must be taken into account in any attempt to explain the genesis of individual mind. Unless we wish to accept the consequences of a biological reductionism (Rose, 1982a, 1982b; Sahlins, 1977), we have to recognize the contributions of a cultural aspect and the particular products of that cultural aspect, tools and symbol systems, to the constitution of mind. Clearly we have to accept that the development of the nervous system is in fact the product (on a synchronic plane) of complex biological processes of morphogenesis (for alternative views see Rose, 1982a, 1982b; Sheldrake, 1981) and that those aspects of human function we reserve to a psychological realm are in some manner related to the central nervous system. But the picture is not complete at this point. At some stage or over a succession of diachronic moments there intervened a second process that we have come to call "cultural." With its appearance, no matter how quickly or slowly, both evolutionary and developmental processes were radically altered. With the appearance of this cultural aspect members of our species were able to alter the course of their development in a Lamarkian way. Acquired characteristics (tool use, language) could be transmitted not only to members of a species existing in the same moment of time but could be passed on across time. Development was not subject only to neo-Darwinian principles (the natural line of development) but also to Lamarkian principles (the cultural line). Evolutionary adaptation of mind follows two lines, the biological and the cultural, and in recent history and in individual development the effects of the cultural aspect have been most manifest. As Olson (1976, p. 191) has observed, "What the mind can do depends upon the devices provided by the culture." Popper (1972, p. 239) argues for an exosomatic principle of change when he states, "But man, instead of growing better eyes and ears, grows spectacles, microscopes. . . . Instead of growing better memories and brains, we grow paper, pens, pencils." These exosomatic characteristics are transmitted by Lamarkian principles.

Olson (1976), arguing for cultural conditioning of the concept of intelligence, states:

> The primary qualities of mind are, therefore, not simply biological in nature. They are the achievement of the coupling of very limited human resources with technologies which, by and large, have been invented to circumvent those limitations. The technologies have the effect of making some particular underlying abilities critical, or at least relevant, to intelligent performance. (p. 199)

These technologies or exosomatic organs mediate between the organism and its transactions with the environment, physical or otherwise. One critical technology or acquired characteristic in the history of cultural evolution is language. The consequences of technology for the development of individual mind have been explored by Vygotsky (1962, 1978) and Luria (1976, 1981). But oral language (which enjoys diachronic priority) undergoes its own evolutionary development during the course of cultural history. The product of this development is the written norm of language. The written norm in time comes to represent a distinct and autonomous acquired characteristic or technology.

What a serious consideration of the nonbiological determinants of the growth of the mind teaches us is that our transactions with our environment are always mediated and become progressively more mediated during the course of development. But the mediated nature of our transactions, whether they be on the level of perceptual processes or at higher cognitive levels, are not simply overlays fused onto a mammalian base. Geertz (1973) argues that such a stratificational model is inappropriate and would "replace the 'stratigraphic' conception of the relations between the various aspects of human existence with a synthetic one; that is one in which biological, psychological, sociological, and cultural factors can be treated as variables within unitary systems of analysis." (p. 44).

Such a synthetic model is possible if we recognize the mediated quality of the whole process of development and the particular contribution each set of mediated means from concrete tools to the various symbolic mediational systems makes to the constitution of mind.

Written Language and Psychological Development

But behavior is not merely ordered by mechanisms of control that lie outside of the organism, rather mind, in the course of development, takes on the characteristics of cultural features, the technologies or Lamarkian characteristics of the mediational means of interacting with the world. A truly interactional account of the growth of the mind must attend to the exogenous forces of development as well as the endogenous ones such as self-regulation and equilibrium, or what Piaget identifies as assimilation – accommodation. The written norm, we argue, represents a critical exogenous force in development, but a force whose role and consequences we little understand.

Given these assumptions about the nature of the developmental process and the nature of mind, what difference do the particular characteristics of the written norm of language make in the developmental process? If indeed the written norm constitutes a significant development of mediational means and therefore a significant characteristic in the developmental field, there should be demonstrable effects or at least significant correlations between characteristics of the written norm and psychological attributes of mind. Having outlined certain basic assumptions about the role of mediational means in the process of the growth of the mind, we examine in greater detail in Chapter 7 some aspects of the correlation between certain characteristics of the acquisition of the written norm and parallel changes in cognitive function during the period of acquisition. Based on the limited data available, there are striking parallels between the nature of text operations and the characteristic structures of cognitive functioning.

The basic conclusion of such an argument is that the acquisition of the written language norm (as delineated in Chapters 6 and 7) is perhaps responsible in part for a functional reorganization of the way the child views and uses language itself as a mediational mechanism in dealing with many domains of thought. In turn this reorganization may facilitate the transformation of cognitive functioning itself in the course of its development.

Olson (1977) and Bruner and Olson (1977–1978) present a detailed discussion of the cognitive implications of text and written language. On the general transforming nature of writing, Bruner and Olson comment, "Our argument is that an important part of intellectual activity is the direct consequence of our learning to reflect consciously upon the structures implicit in our native language, a form of reflection made possible to a large extent by the invention of writing" (p. 5). Such conscious reflection is a powerful mechanism that may well link the domains of symbolic activity of language and general structures of cognition. Bruner and Olson argue that with the appearance of text as an autonomous language entity in the child's world there occurs a fundamental reorganization of operations on reality:

When text becomes autonomous from speech, the construction of reality can proceed on two planes—a plane of intralinguistic logic, and a plane of ordinary experience. Ordinary experience can then be shaped more readily by a logically derived pattern of expectancies. Experience, so to speak, can be pitted against logic. If they do not match, we pause, extract new logical implications, or reexamine experience. In this way we more readily create possible or hypothetical worlds, of which the world as experienced is merely one. This is a power that probably does not rely exclusively upon experience of dealing in autonomous text, but the procedures that we learn for dealing with such text powerfully predispose us in that direction. We honour it as the prototype technique of science; but its main impetus, if not its origin, derives from the habit of reflecting on textualized statements and their entailments. (p. 11)

Other researchers have attempted to detail the likely nature of the transformation that the acquisition and use of written language brings about, notably Greenfield (1972) and Goody, Cole, and Scribner (1977). Goody, Cole, and Scribner write, "The line of theory developed by Vygotsky . . . maintains that when an individual comes to master writing, the basic system underlying the nature of his mental processes is changed fundamentally as the external symbol system comes to mediate the organization of all his basic intellectual operations" (p. 298).

It is perhaps the sustained intersentential organization of text and the construction strategies discussed in Chapter 7 that best demonstrate the impact of written language on elaborated thought or higher-level thinking. It is unlikely that the 16 binary operations of the calculus of Piaget's formal operations are inherent in thought itself. But it is probably the case that the serial order of text, the combinatorics of textual systems themselves are a source of such artificial elaboration of natural modes of thought.

What argument about the formative influence of language can be made on the basis of the expanded structural-functional definition developed in Chapters 3 and 5? What transformational effect can be attributed to such a conception of language? The answers to such questions depend critically on what we view as the end point of development, how we characterize the process of this cognitive development, and to some extent on the culture to which such an answer is expected to apply.

If we assume that one end point of mental development is more or less accurately characterized by something like Piaget's formal operations, then we must further assume that such an end point for development is to a great degree constituted by the particular practice of Western technological society, which as we have said values intellect over action.

Ontogenesis or cognitive development can be viewed as a process of change in the level of consciousness and intersubjectivity. Within such a process, oral and written language play distinctive roles. The end point of such development is the achievement of the capacity of awareness or self-reflection, or in Bühler's term *intentio,* that is, the conscious act of putting to use a system of rules. This, in terms of the cognitive domain, involves the conformation of thinking to certain socially constituted rules for objective knowledge and how such knowledge is used. The development or growth of consciousness implies two things: a loss of automaticity and a focusing in observation, that is, making visible so as to be observable. As the child moves through phases of development there is a progressive differentiation of self from the surrounding environment. An integral part of this differentiation is a progressive distancing of the communicative system from the individual, from gesture to spoken language, and finally to written language.

This progressive distancing of the communicative system from the individual and the progressive psychological differentiation of the individual from the means of communication can be characterized as follows:

$$t_1 \qquad\qquad\qquad t_2 \qquad\qquad\qquad t_3$$

$$\text{P} \longrightarrow \text{C} \text{-----------------} P \longrightarrow C \text{---------------} P \longrightarrow C$$

Gesture and	Vocalization	verbalization
affective	tied to action or	(oral language)
body movement	object	

$$t_4$$

$$\text{----} P \longrightarrow (C)$$

Written language and text

$\longrightarrow$ = distance
P = producer
C = consumer
( ) = consumer not normally present at point of origin of communication

Throughout this process there is not only an increase in psychological distance between the producer and symbol form, but also the distancing of producer and consumer. We can also discern in this process movement from subjectivity to a greater objectivity in the symbol form. Werner and Kaplan (1963) argue that there is over the course of development an increasing distance (or differentiation) in the four elements in any interpersonal communication, that is, addressor, addressee, referent (object), and symbol vehicle. Such a process is characteristic of the whole of development. On the first stage of this process of differentiation, Werner and Kaplan comment that in initial interactions of caregiver and child exchanges have more the character of sharing than actual communication. In Werner and Kaplan's view there is little differentiation among the caregiver, child, and object of reference—the situation is presymbolic. This initial stage out of which symbolic communication develops consists of gesture and affective touching, where the object of reference is in close physical proximity to those involved in the act. Werner and Kaplan argue that such sharing forms the ground for the genesis of symbol and reference and that this genesis is characterized by a progressive differentiation on three planes: addressor and addressee, addressor and objects of reference, and addressor and symbolic vehicle (the acquisition of some conventional symbol system).

If affective sharing lies at the beginning of such a process of differentiation, then the acquisition of written language lies at the other extreme. Written language (again restricting our focus to Western technological society) has as its ideal instantiation the scholarized norm defined in Chapter 5. Such scholarized language is functionally very different in its characteristics from either the initial ground of the development of language (Werner and Kaplan's primordial sharing) or any of the stages on the way to its acquisition.

But does the change in nature of the representational system that an individual acquires and uses make a fundamental difference to the nature of mind? Certainly from the biological viewpoint it would be difficult to argue that the neuroanatomy of the individual is somehow fundamentally altered with changes in the nature of the representational system used. However, as we argue in Chapter 2, it is likely that, with the acquisition of written language, functional neural nets are either established or reordered. Yet the place where the acquisition of a written language norm may make a more noticeable impact on mind is in the nature of consciousness. From infancy to mature adulthood there is a change in the level of explicit consciousness or awareness. There is a progression from behavior controlled by cryptic processes to behavior controlled by phenic processes. The written norm radically restructures consciousness by introducing the objective and the decontextualized. The roots of knowledge and consciousness lie in the nature of sociocultural life forms and the structure of the symbolic representational system.

If a strong link is to be made between the acquisition of this scholarized written language norm and possible shaping of the nature of consciousness and higher mental functions, then it has to be demonstrated that written language and the particular functional variant of the scholarized norm is an integral component of social structure and that this component of social-cultural structure exercises a pressure for adaptiveness on the individual. Written language must be more than an incidental cultural achievement, an optional variant to oral language; it must be an integral outgrowth of particular cultural needs.

Language and Culture

With Vachek, we argue that language as a cultural entity undergoes its own evolutionary process. Written language arises to meet the communicative and social demands of increasingly complex sociocultural institutions. Innis (1964) explores in great detail the interrelation of cultural change and change in the media and technology of communicative systems. Innis' thesis is that changes in the media and technology of communicative systems are directly correlated with growth and change in cultural life forms and institutions. McLuhan (1965), Havelock (1982a, 1982b,) Ong (1982), Clammer (1976), and Goody (1977) make essentially the same argument. A telling example of how different language media (oral and written) arise to meet the differing needs of social structures is given in the discussion of Vai society by Scribner and Cole (1981).

As the information content of a society or culture increases and if such information is critical to the cohesiveness of society in general and for the cultural survival of an individual, effective means for the cultural transmission of such information must be developed. While the oral medium and oral transmission may be adequate to meet these needs of some cultures, others may require a written medium of language — its objectivity, documentary character, its durability and exact repeatability. Imagine the burden imposed on an advanced technological society of transmitting critical information on the design and operation of any complex piece of machinery such as a computer by means of oral language alone. Society evolves institutions such as formal schooling to act as formal channels for the transmission of knowledge necessary for cultural competence and survival and to initiate members of that society or culture into the means of cultural transmission, that is, written language.

If we can make the necessary connection between an increase in the complexity of society and the rise of new media of language, how does such a social-cultural argument translate to one about the impact of a particular language medium (written language) on the growth and shape of the individual mind? To answer this question we have to appreciate that all intellectual development takes place in a social context (Hamlyn, 1983) and that in addition to a biological line in development there is a cultural line, as argued in Chapter 4. The program for mental development is not, to use an analogy, simply a matter of hardwiring (the biological line) but equally a matter of software (the cultural line).

Humphrey (1983) argues for the connection between the social context and the development of individual mind as follows:

> Once a society has reached a certain level of complexity, then new internal pressures must arise which act to increase its complexity still further. For, in a society

of the kind outlined, an animal's intellectual 'adversaries' are members of his own breeding community. If intellectual prowess is correlated with social success, and if social success means high biological fitness, then any heritable trait which increases the ability of an individual to outwit his fellows will soon spread through the gene pool. And in these circumstances there can be no going back: an evolutionary 'ratchet' has been set up, acting like a self-winding watch to increase the general intellectual standing of the species. (p. 22)

Written language is a culturally heritable trait that serves to increase the adaptiveness of individuals in complex technological societies. It does so by opening to the individual that pool of technological and factual knowledge necessary for intellectual prowess and hence social success. In turn, the characteristics of this culturally heritable trait influence that intellectual process itself and as a consequence the forms of life and the morphology of psychological structures.

As Humphrey argues, man's intellectual growth has been and is adaptive for survival in a complex society since intellect arose in the first instance to enable man to cope with an ever more complex social structure. In turn, as society becomes more complex it develops more complex and formal institutions such as schooling and written language. Schooling and written language come, in later stages of cultural evolution and later stages of individual development, to supplement family and oral language as processes fitting individuals to succeed and survive in society. Written language becomes a powerful, culturally heritable trait. Yet this is not to argue that all societies must necessarily pursue such a course of evolution as a process of individual development. There may be alternative paths to the same end. However, once such a solution is chosen there is the ratchet effect that Humphrey detailed. Written language and formal schooling become canalized for particular cultures leading to certain forms of minds. As Hobhouse (1927, p. 95) has remarked, "We have taken language as the distinctive mark of human intelligence because it reflects the conceptions by which empirical data are brought into relation. It not only reflects them, it is the condition of their effective use."

How may a culturally heritable trait such as written language come to be partly constitutive of the morphology of mind? In part, such an effect may take place through a general principle of downward causation. D. T. Campbell (1974) defines "downward causation" in the following terms:

[T]he laws of the higher-level selective system determine in part the distribution of lower-level events. . . . Description of an intermediate-level phenomenon is not completed by describing its possibility and implementation in lower-level terms. Its presence, prevalence or distribution . . . will often require reference to laws at a higher level of organization as well. . . . All processes at the lower levels of a hierarchy are restrained by and act in conformity to the laws of the higher levels. (p. 180)

Written language as such a higher-level product of cultural evolution participates in the organization of lower-level events (the forms of individual mind) by a process of downward causation. We can posit culture as a kind of transmitter of psychogenetic fields (e.g., the written language norm) that are in part constitutive of higher forms of cognitive behavior. Culture itself serves as a kind of functional filter for items in the psychic environment that a child is pressured to adapt to and that—by analogy with biogenesis—have psychic survival value in terms of competence in a particular culture.

Conclusion

George Herbert Mead (1934, p. 50) remarks that "The body is not a self, as such; it becomes a self only when it has developed a mind within the context of social experience," and further (p. 133) that "Out of language emerges the field of mind." These two theses aptly and concisely summarize the argument we have presented on the nature of written language and the genesis of the structure of mind.

Yet while language and, in particular, written language is the focus of our argument, we do not wish to suggest that the development of mind can be accounted for solely in terms of social analysis or an analysis of language. We affirm throughout this account the dual interfunctional nature of the determinants of psychogenesis. Development is a matter of both biology and culture. Biology and culture act simultaneously and in concert to produce that distinctive organism—man. However, having reaffirmed this, the central thesis of this volume is that the explanation of later phases of cognitive development and, in particular, higher mental functions must make reference to the distinctive features of written language for their explanation. If oral language forms the initial ground for the formation of mind and self, written language brings that initial development to a further plane of development. The distinctive form that mind assumes must be seen as arising, within the empirical matrix of social exchange and communication, through a process of successively acquired representational systems that mediate between the individual and reality and that are themselves the product of a social-cultural evolutionary process.

There has been an increasing recognition, as evidenced by the number of studies appearing in the early 1980s, that accounts of language development or of psychogenesis in general are incomplete without a full account of later stages of linguistic development that encompass a consideration of the written language norm. Yet this work has been characterized by a certain lack of coherence and definition in respect to the nature of its object of study, written language itself. As the overview of some representative studies in this area presented in Chapter 4 suggests, there is little broad agreement as to what constitutes written language, what aspects are crucial to any account of its acquisition, or even the nature of its relation to preceding linguistic (oral language) and cognitive development.

We have attempted to address these concerns by presenting a theoretical account of the nature of written language, its relation to oral language, and its constitutive role in psychogenesis. This has been primarily a theoretical consideration and less an empirical study of actual acquisitions of written language. The empirical work presented in Chapters 6 and 7 should not be read as advancing strong claims for a definitive account of the acquisition of written language nor as in any sense "proving" the strong claim that written language is alone constitutive of higher cognitive functions. Rather, these empirical accounts should serve as suggestive approaches for the study of written language acquisition and as suggestive evidence for the partly constitutive role of the written language norm in the development of mind.

The results from the wide range and increasing volume of studies of written language, literacy, or writing can only be properly evaluated in light of some coherent or at least clearly articulated account of written language. This account is presented as an initial essay of that larger theoretical question. Future work in the area of written language must address itself to advancing and refining this discussion of the nature of written language, its place in social-cognitive development, and its relation to oral-language development. Indeed, without further and deeper consideration of such questions, empirical studies will continue to produce results that are at best ambiguous and at worst uninterpretable.

References

Aaronson, D., & Rieber, R. W. (Eds.). (1979). *Psycholinguistic research: Implications and applications.* Hillsdale, NJ: Erlbaum.

Adamec, P. (1966). *Porjadok Slov v Sovrememona Russkom Jazyke.* Praha.

Aristotle. (1973). *De Interpretatione.* In H. P. Cooke (Ed. and Trans.). *Aristotle: Vol. 1, The categories; On interpretation* (pp. 112–179). London: William Heine Mann.

Artymovyč, A. (1932a). *Pysana mova.* Navkovyj Zbirnyk Ukrainskoho Vyssoho Ped. Institua v Prazi 2:1–8.

Artymovyč, A. (1932b). Fremdwort und schift. In *Charisteria Guilelmo Mathesio Quinquagenario a Discipulis et Circuli Linguistici Pragensis Sodalibus Oblata* (pp. 114–118). Prague: Prazsky Linguisticky Krouzek.

Augustine. (1975). *De dialectica.* (B. D. Jackson, Trans & Ed.). Dordrecht, Holland: Reidel.

Ayala, F. J., & Dobzhansky, T. (Eds.). (1974). *Studies in the philosophy of biology.* Berkeley: University of California Press.

Baldwin, J. M. (1894). *Mental development in the child and the race.* New York: Macmillan.

Baldwin, J. M. (1913). *Social and ethical interpretations in mental development.* New York: Macmillan.

Batalova, T. (1977). On predicative-relative relations of text forming units. *Style, 11,* 375–389.

Bates, E., & MacWhinney (1979). A functionalist approach to the acquisition of grammar. In E. Ochs & B. B. Schieffelin (Eds.), *Developmental Pragmatics* (pp. 167–209). New York: Academic Press.

Beilin, H. (1975). *Studies in cognitive basis of language development.* New York: Academic Press.

Bellert, I. (1970). On a condition for the coherence of texts. *Semiotica, 2,* 335–363.

Benesova, E., & Sgall, P. (1973). Remarks on the topic/comment articulation I. *Prague Bulletin of Mathematical Linguistics, 19,* 24–58.

Benesova, E., Sgall, P., & Hajicova, E. (1973). Remarks on the topic/Comment articulation II. *Prague Bulletin of Mathematical Linguistics, 20,* 3-42.

Bruce, B. C., Collins, A., Rubin, A. D., & Gentner, D. (1978). *A cognitive science approach to writing.* Urbana, IL: Center for the Study of Reading.

Brueckner, L. (1939). Language, the development of ability in oral and written composition. *Yearbook of the National Society for the Study of Education, 38*(1), 225-240.

Bruner, J. (1975). Language as an instrument of thought. In A. Davis (Ed.), *Problems of language and learning* (pp. 61-86). London: Longman.

Bruner, J. (1978). Learning how to do things with words. In J. Bruner & A. Garton (Eds.), *Human growth and development: Wolfson College lectures* (pp. 62-84). Oxford: Clarendon Press.

Bruner, J., & Garton, A. (Eds.). (1978). *Human growth and development: Wolfson College lectures.* Oxford: Claredon Press.

Bruner, J., & Olson, D. (1977-1978). Symbols and texts as tools of intellect. *Interchange, 8*(4), 1-15.

Bühler, K. (1934). *Sprachtheorie.* Jena: Fischer.

Bühler, H. (1982). *Semiotic foundations of language theory with Robert Innis.* New York: Plenum.

Callewaert, H. (1954). *Graphologie et physiologie de L'Ecriture.* Louvain: Nauwelaerts.

Campbell, D. T. (1974). "Downward Causation" in hierarchically organized biological systems. In F. J. Ayala & T. Dobzhansky (Eds.), *Studies in the philosophy of biology* (pp. 179-186). Berkeley: University of California Press.

Campbell, R. (1979). Cognitive development and child language. In P. Fletcher & M. Garman (Eds.), *Language acquisition* (pp. 419-436). Cambridge: Cambridge University Press.

Chao, Y. R. (1961). *Language and symbolic systems.* Cambridge: Cambridge University Press.

Chomsky, C. (1970). Reading, writing, and phonology. *Harvard Educational Review, 40,* 287-309.

Clammer, J. R. (1976). *Literacy and social change.* Leiden: Brill.

Clay, M. J. (1979). *Reading: The patterning of complex behavior.* Auckland: Heinemann.

Cole, M., & D'Andrade, R. (1982). The influence of schooling on concept formation. *The Quarterly Newsletter of the Laboratory of Comparative Human Cognition, 4*(2), 19-26.

Coltheart, M. (1980). Reading, phonological recording, and deep dyslexia. In M. Coltheart, K. Patterson & J. C. Marshall (Eds.), *Deep dyslexia* (pp. 97-226). London: Routledge & Kegan Paul.

Cook-Gumperz, J., & Gumperz, J. J. (1976). *Papers on language and context.* (Language Behavior Research Laboratory Working Paper No. 46). Berkeley: University of California.

Cook-Gumperz, J., & Gumperz J. J. (1981). From oral to written culture: The transition to literacy. In M. F. Whiteman (Ed.), *Writing: The nature, development and teaching of written communication* (Vol. 1) (pp. 89-109). Hillsdale, NJ: Erlbaum.

Critchley, MacD. (1938). "Aphasia" in a partial deaf-mute. *Brain, 61,* 163-169.

Dahl, Ö. (1969). *Topic and comment: A study in Russian and general transformational grammar.* Goteborg-Stockholm: Almqvist & Wiksell.

Daneš, F. (1964). Tema//(Zaklad)//Vychodisko Vypovedi. *Slovo a Slovesnost,* 25.

Daneš, F. (1966). A three level approach to syntax. In J. Vachek (Ed.), *Travaux linguistique de Prague* (Vol. 1) (pp. 225-240). Alabama: University of Alabama Press.

Daneš, F. (1968). Types of thematic progressions in texts. *Slovo a Slovesnost,* 29. 125-140.

Daneš, F. (1974). Functional sentence perspective and the organization of the texts. In F. Daneš (Ed.), *Papers on functional sentence perspective* (pp. 106-128). The Hague: Mouton.

Daneš, F. (1976). Czech terminology of FSP. In *Jazykovedne studie*. Bratislava: Slovenská Akademia vied.

de Ajuriaguerra, J., & Auzias, M. (1975). Preconditions for the development of writing in the child. In E. H. Lennenberg & E. Lennenberg (Eds.), *Foundations of language* (Vol. 2) (pp. 311-328). New York: Academic Press.

Derrida, J. (1976). *Of grammatology* (G. C. Spivak, Trans.). Baltimore: Johns Hopkins University Press.

de Saussure, F. (1959). *Course in general linguistics.* (C. Bally & A. Sechehaye, Eds.). New York: McGraw-Hill.

De Vito, J. A. (1965). Comprehension factors in oral and written discourse of skilled communicators. *Speech Monographs, 32,* 124-128.

Dingwall, W. (1979). Human communicative behavior: A biological model. In D. Aaronson & R. W. Rieber (Eds.), *Psycholinguistic research: Implications and applications* (pp. 51-86). Hillsdale, NJ: Erlbaum.

Donaldson, M. (1978). *Children's minds.* London: Fontana.

Dressler, W. V. (Ed.). (1978). *Current trends in textlinguistics.* Berlin: De Gruyter.

Dubois-Charlier, F. (1971). Approche neurolinguistique du problème de l'alexie pure. *Journal de psychologie,* Jan.-Mar., 39-67.

Dubois-Charlier, F. (1972). A propos de l'alexie pure. *Langages, 25,* 76-94.

Ellis, A. W. (Ed.). (1982). *Normality and pathology in cognitive functions.* New York: Academic Press.

Ellis, A. W. (1982). Spelling and writing. In A. W. Ellis (Ed.), *Normality and pathology in cognitive functions* (pp. 113-146). New York: Academic Press.

Evanechko, P., Ollila, L. and Armstrong, R. (1974). An investigation of the relationship between children's performance in written language and their reading ability. *Research in the Teaching of English, 8,* 315-326.

Feldman, C., & Stone, A. (1978). The colored blocks test: A culture-general measure of cognitive development. *Journal of Cross-Cultural Psychology, 9*(1), 3-22.

Ferreiro, E., & Teberosky, A. (1982). *Literacy before schooling.* Exeter, NH & London: Heinemann.

Firbas, J. (1959). Communicative function—Thoughts on the communicative function of the verb in English, German and Czech. *Bruo Studies in English, 1,* 39-68.

Firbas, J. (1961). On the communicative value of the modern English finite verb. *Bruo Studies in English, 3,* 79-104.

Firbas, J. (1966). Non-thematic subjects in English. In J. Vachek (Ed.), *Travaux linguistiques de Prague 2* (pp. 239-256). Alabama: University of Alabama Press.

Firbas, J. (1974). Some aspects of the Czechoslovak approach to problems of functional sentence perspective. In F. Daneš (Ed.), *Papers on functional sentence perspective* (pp. 11-37). The Hague: Mouton.

Firbas, J. (1975). On the thematic and non-thematic section of the sentence. In H. Ringborn, A. Irigleberg, R. Norman, K. Nyholm, R. Westman, & K. Wikberg (Eds.), *Style and text* (pp. 317-334). Stockholm: Skriptor.

Fletcher, P., & Garman, M. (Eds.). (1979). *Language acquisition.* Cambridge: Cambridge University Press.

Flower, L., & Hayes, J. R. (1980). Identifying the organization of writing processes. In L. Gregg & E. Steinberg (Eds.), *Cognitive processes in writing: An interdisciplinary approach* (pp. 3-30). Hillsdale, NJ: Erlbaum.

Flower, L., & Hayes, J. R. (1981). Plans that guide the composing process. In C. H.

Frederiksen & J. F. Dominic (Eds.), *Writing: The nature, development, and teaching of written communication* (Vol. 2) (pp. 39–59). Hillsdale, NJ: Erlbaum.

Fodor, J. A. (1983). *The modularity of mind.* Cambridge: MIT Press.

Fraisse, P., & Breyton, M. (1959). Comparison entre les languages oral et écrit. *L'Année Psychologique, 59.* 61–71.

Freedle, R., & J. Fime (1983). *Developmental issues in discourse.* Norwood, NJ: Ablex.

Gardner, H. (1978). *The development and breakdown of symbolic capacities: A search for general principles.* Cambridge: Harvard University.

Gardner, H., Perkins, D., & Howard, V. (1974). Symbol systems. A philosophical, psychological and educational investigation. In Olson, D. R. (Ed.), *Media and symbols. The forms of expression, communication and education* (pp. 27–55). Chicago: University of Chicago Press.

Geertz, C. (1973a). The growth of culture and the evolution of mind. In C. Geertz, *The interpretation of cultures* (pp. 55–83). New York: Basic Books.

Geertz, C. (1973b). *The interpretation of cultures.* New York: Basic Books.

Golub, L. S. (1969). Linguistic structures in students' oral and written discourse. *Research in the Teaching of English, 3,* 70–85.

Goody, J. (Ed.). (1968). *Literacy in traditional societies.* Cambridge: Cambridge University Press.

Goody, J. (1977). *The domestication of the savage mind.* Cambridge: Cambridge University Press.

Goody, J. (1982). Alternative paths to knowledge in oral and literate cultures. In D. Tannen (Ed.), *Spoken and written language: Exploring orality and literacy* (pp. 201–215). Norwood, NJ: Ablex.

Goody, J., Cole, M., & Scribner, S. (1977). Writing and formal operations: A case study among the Vai. *Africa, 47,* 289–304.

Goody, J., & Watt, I. (1968). The consequences of literacy. In J. Goody (Ed.), *Literacy in traditional societies.* (pp. 27–68) Cambridge: Cambridge University Press.

Greenfield, P.M. (1972). Oral or written language: The consequences for cognitive development in Africa, the United States and England. *Language and Speech, 15,* 169–177.

Gregg, L., & Steinberg, E. (Eds.). (1980). *Cognitive processes in writing: An interdisciplinary approach.* Hillsdale, NJ: Erlbaum.

Gundlach, R. A. (1981). On the nature and development of children's writing. In C. H. Frederiksen & J. F. Dominic (Eds.), *Writing: The nature, development, and teaching of written communication* (pp. 133–151). Hillsdale, NJ: Erlbaum.

Haas, W. (1970). *Phonographic translation.* Manchester: University of Manchester Press.

Haas, W. (1976a). Writing the basic options. In W. Haas (Ed.), *Writing without letters* (pp. 131–208). Manchester: University of Manchester Press.

Haas, W. (Ed.). (1976b). *Writing without letters.* Manchester: University of Manchester Press.

Hall, R. A. (1964). *Introductory linguistics.* Radnor, PA: Chilton.

Hall, R. A. (1966). *Sound and spelling in English.* Radnor, PA: Chilton.

Halliday, M. A. K. (1975). *Learning how to mean: Explorations in the development of language.* London: Edward Arnold.

Hamlyn, D. W. (1983). *Perception, learning and the self.* London: Routledge & Kegan Paul.

Harrell, L. E. (1957). A comparison of the development of oral and written language in school-age children. *Society for Research in Child Development Monographs, XXII*(3, Serial No. 66).

Haugen, E. (1966). Linguistics and language planning. In E. S. Fircherv (Ed.), *1972 studies by Einar Haugen.* The Hague: Mouton.

Havelock, E. (1973). Prologue to Greek literacy. In C. Boulter (Ed.), *Lectures in memory of Louise Taft Semple, Second Series* (pp. 229–291). In University of Cincinnati Classical Studies, Vol. 2, Norman Oklahoma: University of Oklahoma Press.

Havelock, E. A. (1982a). *The literate revolution in Greece and its cultural consequences.* Princeton: Princeton University Press.

Havelock, E. A. (1982b). *Preface to Plato.* Cambridge: Harvard University Press.

Havránek, B. (1929). Influence de la function de la langue littéraire sur la structure phenologique et grammaticale du techèque lettéraire. *Travaux du Circle Linguistique de Prague, 1,* 106–120.

Havránek, B. (1964). The functional differentiation of the standard language. In P. L. Garvin (Ed.), *A Prague School reader on esthetics, literary structure and style* (pp. 3–16). Washington, DC: Georgetown University Press.

Heath, S. B. (1982). Protean shapes in literacy events: Ever-shifting oral and literate traditions. In D. Tannen (Ed.), *Spoken and written language: Exploring orality and literacy* (pp. 91–117). Norwood, NJ: Ablex.

Hecaen, H., & Albert, M. L. (1978). Human neuropsychology. New York: Wiley.

Henderson, L. (1982). *Orthography and word recognition in reading.* London: Academic Press.

Hjelmslev, L. (1963). *Prolegomena to a theory of language* (F. J. Whitfield, Trans.). Madison: University of Wisconsin Press.

Hobhouse, L. T. (1901). *Mind in evolution.* London: Macmillan.

Hobhouse, L. T. (1927). *Development and purpose.* London: Macmillian.

Holman, E. (1976). Some thoughts on variable word order. In N. E. Enkvist & V. Kohonen (Eds.), *Approaches to word order* (pp. 125–143). Finland: Åbo Akademi.

Horalek, K. (1966). Les functions de la langue et de la parole. In *Travaux Linguistiques de Prague 1.* (pp. 41–46) Alabama: University of Alabama Press.

Humboldt, W. von (1836). *Uber die verachiedenheit des menschlichen sprachbaus.* Berlin-Bonn: Dummler.

Humphrey, N. (1983). *Consciousness regained.* Oxford: Oxford University Press.

Hunt, K. W. (1965). *Grammatical structures written at three grade levels (Research Report #3).* Urbana, IL: National Council of Teachers of English.

Hunt, K. W. (1970). Syntactic maturity in school children and adults. *Monographs of the Society for Research in Child Development, 35,* 134.

Inhelder, B., & Piaget, J. (1958). *The growth of logical thinking from childhood to adolescence.* New York: Basic Books.

Inhelder, B., & Piaget, J. (1969). *The early growth of logic in the child.* New York: Norton.

Innis, H. (1964). *The bias of communication.* Toronto: University of Toronto Press.

Innis, R. (1982). *Karl Bühler semiotic foundations of language theory.* New York: Plenum.

Jakobson, R., & Halle, M. (1956). *Fundamentals of language.* The Hague: Mouton.

Johnson, M. K. (Ed. & Trans.). (1978). *Recycling the Prague Linguistic Circle.* Ann Arbor: Karoma.

Karmiloff-Smith, A. (1979). *A functional approach to child language.* Cambridge: Cambridge University Press.

Kukharenko, V. (1979). Some considerations about the properties of texts. In J. Petöfi (Ed.), *Text vs. sentence* (pp. 235–245). Hamburg: Buske.

Langleben, M. (1979). On the triple opposition of a text to a sentence. In J. Petöfi (Ed.), *Text vs. sentence* (pp. 246–257). Hamburg: Buske.

Lenneberg, E. H., & Lenneberg, E. (Eds.). (1975). *Foundations of language development* (Vols. I and II). New York: Academic Press.

Leont'ev, A. N. (1959). *Problemy Razvitiya Rsikhiki.* Moscow: Izdatel'stva Akademii Pedagogicheskekh Nauk RSFSR.

Li, C. N., & Thompson, S. A. (1982). The gulf between spoken and written language: A case study in Chinese. In D. Tannen (Ed.), *Spoken and written language: Exploring orality and literacy* (pp. 77–88). Norwood, NJ: Ablex.

Lock, A. (1978). *Action gesture and symbol: The emergence of language.* London: Academic Press.

Loflin, M. D., & Silverberg, J. (Eds.) (1978). *Discourse and inference in cognitive anthropology.* The Hague: Mouton.

Lord, A. (1964). *The singer of tales.* Cambridge: Harvard University Press.

Lull, H. C. (1929). The speaking and writing abilities of intermediate grade pupils. *Journal of Educational Research, 20,* 73–77.

Lurçat, L. (1963). Langage oral et langage écrit. Passage du langage oral au langage écrit dans une épreuve de rédaction. *Enfance, 4.* 193–207.

Lurçat, L. (1974). *Etude de l'acte graphique.* The Hague: Mouton.

Luria, A. R. (1973). *The working brain.* Harmondsworth: Penguin.

Luria, A. R. (1976). *Cognitive development: Its cultural and social foundations.* Cambridge: Harvard University Press.

Luria, A. R. (1978). The development of writing in the child. In M. Cole (Ed.), *The selected writings of A. R. Luria* (pp. 145–194). White Plains, NY: Sharpe.

Luria, A. R. (1980). *Higher cortical functions in man.* New York: Basic Books.

Luria, A. R. (1981). *Language and cognition* (J. V. Wertsch, Ed.). New York: Wiley.

Manifesto presented to the First Congress of Slavic Philogists in Prague. (1978). In M. K. Johnson (Ed. & Trans.), *Recycling the Prague Linguistic Circle.* Ann Arbor, MI: Karoma. (Original work published 1929)

Markova, A. K. (1979). *The teaching and mastery of language* (B. B. Szekely, Ed.). New York: Sharpe.

Mathesius, V. (1924). Some notes on the function of the subject in modern English. *Pro Moderni Filologie, 10,* 1–6.

Mathesius, V. (1939). On the so-called functional sentence perspective. *Slovo a Slovesnost, 5,* 171–174.

Mathesius, V. (1975). *A functional analysis of present day English on a general linguistic basis.* The Hague: Mouton.

Martinet, A. (1962). *A functional view of language.* Oxford: Oxford University Press.

McDougall, W. (1929). *Modern materialism and emergent evolution.* London: Methuen.

McIntosh, A. (1961). Graphology and meaning. *Archivum Linguisticum, 13:*107–120.

McLuhan, M. (1967). *The Gutenberg galaxy.* Toronto: University of Toronto Press.

Mead, G. H. (1934). *Mind, self and society.* Chicago: University of Chicago Press.

Metzing, D. (Ed.). (1980). *Frame conceptions and text understanding.* Berlin: de Gruyter.

Michaels, S. (1981). Sharing time: Children's narrative styles and differential access to literacy. *Language & Society, 10,* 423–442.

Milner, E. (1976). CNS maturation and language acquisition. In H. Whitaker and H. A. Whitaker (Eds.), *Studies in neurolinguistics* (Vol. 1) (pp. 31–102). New York: Academic Press.

Mukarovsky, J. (1937). O jevistnim dialogu. *Program,* D37, March.

Mukarovsky, J. (1940). Dialog a monolog. *Listy Fifologicke,* 68.

Nasarova, L. K. (1955). Die rolle der kinasthetischen sprechweise beim schreiben. In *Beitrage zur anwendung der lehre pawlows anf fragen des unterrichts.* Berlin: Volk und Wissen Volkseigener.

Nida, E. A. (1975). *Language structure and translation* (A. S. Dil, Ed.). California: Stanford University Press.

Ninio, A., & Bruner, J. (1978). The achievement and antecedents of labelling. *Journal of Child Language, 5*, 1–15.

Nold, E. (1981). Revising. In C. H. Frederiksen & J. F. Dominic (Eds.), *Writing: The nature, development, and teaching of written communication* (Vol. 2) (pp. 67–79). Hillsdale, NJ: Erlbaum.

Nystrand, M. (Ed.). (1983). *What writers know: The language, process, and structure of written discourse.* New York: Academic Press.

Ochs, E. (1982). Talking to children in Western Samoa. *Language in Society, 11*, 77–104.

Ochs, E., & Schieffelin, B. B. (Eds.). (1979). *Developmental pragmatics.* New York: Academic Press.

O'Donnell, R. C., Griffin, W. J., & Norris, R. C. (1967). *The syntax of kindergarten and elementary school children: A transformational analysis.* Urbana, IL: National Council of Teachers of English.

Okby, M. (1978). Transitional dependencies in informal discourse varieties. In M. D. Loflin & J. Silverberg (Eds.), *Discourse and inference in cognitive anthropology* (pp. 145–151). The Hague: Mouton.

Olson, D. R. (Ed.) (1974). *Media and symbols. The forms of expression, communication and education.* Chicago: Chicago University Press.

Olson, D. R. (1976). Culture, technology, and intellect. In L. B. Resnick (Ed.), *The nature of intelligence* (pp. 189–202). Hillsdale, NJ: Erlbaum.

Olson, D. R. (1977). From utterance to text: The bias of language in speech and writing. *Harvard Educational Review, 47*, 257–281.

Olson, D. R., & Torrance, N. (1981). Learning to meet the requirements of written text: Language development in the school years. In C. H. Frederiksen & J. F. Dominic (Eds.), *Writing: The nature, development, and teaching of written communication* (Vol. 2) (pp. 235–255). Hillsdale, NJ: Erlbaum.

Ong, W. J. (1958). *Ramus, method and the decay of dialogue.* Cambridge: Harvard University Press.

Ong, W. J. (1982). *Orality and literacy: The technologizing of the word.* London: Methuen.

Osgood, C. E. (1979). What is language? In D. Aaronson & R. W. Rieber (Eds.), *Psycholinguistic research: Implications and applications* (pp. 9–50). Hillsdale, NJ: Erlbaum.

Patterson, K. (1982). Reading and phonological coding. In A. W. Ellis (Ed.), *Normality and pathology in cognitive functions* (pp. 77–111). London: Academic Press.

Peirce, C. S. (1931–1958). *Collected papers of Charles Sanders Peirce,* 8 vols., (C. Hartshorne, P. Weiss, and A. Burks, Eds.). Cambridge: Harvard University Press.

Pellegrino, M. L., & Scopesi, A. A. (1978). Oral and written language in children: Syntactical development of descriptive language. *International Journal of Psycholinguistics, 5*, 5–17.

Peltz, F. (1974). The effect upon comprehension of repatterning based on students' writing patterns. *Reading Research Quarterly, 9*(4), 603–621.

Perron, R., & de Gobineau, S. (1954). *Génétique de l'écriture et étude de la personalité.* Neuchatel: Delachaux & Niestle.

Petöfi, J. (Ed.) (1979). *Text vs. sentence.* Hamburg: Helmut Buske.

Petöfi, J. (Ed.) (1981). *Text vs. sentence continued.* Hamburg: Helmut Buske.

Piaget, J. (1968). *The psychology of intelligence.* Totowa, NJ: Littlefield Adams.

Piaget, J. (1969). *Mechanisms of perception.* London: Routledge & Kegan Paul.

Piaget, J. (1970). *Epistémologie des sciences de l'homme.* Paris: Galliurard.

Piaget, J. (1971). *Biology and knowledge.* Chicago: University of Chicago Press.

Piaget, J. (1972). *The principles of genetic epistomology*. London: Routledge & Kegan Paul.

Piaget, J. (1973). *The child and reality*. New York: Grossman.

Piaget, J. (1977). *The grasp of consciousness*. London: Routledge & Kegan Paul.

Piaget, J. (1979). *Behavior and evolution*. London: Routledge & Kegan Paul.

Piaget, J., Grize, J-B., Szemenska, A., & Bang, V. (1977). *Epistemology and psychology of functions*. Dordrecht-Holland: Reidel.

Plato (1938). Phaedrus (J. Wright, Trans.). In *Plato: Five dialogues*. London: Dent.

Popper, K. (1972). *Objective knowledge: An evolutionary approach*. Oxford: Clarendon.

Popper, K., & Eccles, J. C. (1981). *The self and its brain*. Berlin: Springer.

Poulton, E. (1963). Rapid reading. *Journal of Documentation, 19*(4), 168–172.

Pulgram, E. (1976). The typologies of writing systems. In W. Haas (Ed.), *Writing without letters* (pp. 1–28). Manchester: University of Manchester Press.

Reed, C. (1975). Lessons to be learned from the preschool orthographer. In E. H. Lenneberg & E. Lenneberg (Eds.), *Foundations of language development* (pp. 329–346). New York: Academic Press.

Resnick, L. B. (Ed.) (1976). *The nature of intelligence*. Hillsdale, NJ: Erlbaum.

Romanes, G. J. (1902). *Mental evolution in man*. New York: Appleton.

Rose, S. (Ed.) (1982a). *Against biological determinism*. London: Allison & Busby.

Rose, S. (Ed.) (1982b). *Towards a liberatory biology*. London: Allison & Busby.

Rouma, G. (1913). *Le langage graphique de d'enfant*. Paris: Alcan.

Russell, J. (1978). *The acquisition of knowledge*. New York: St. Martin's.

Sahlins, M. (1976). *The use and abuse of biology: An anthropological critique of sociobiology*. Ann Arbor: University of Michigan Press.

Sasanuma, S., & Fujimura, O. (1971). Selective impairment of phonetic and non-phonetic transcriptions of words in Japanese aphasic patients: Kana vs. Kanji in visual recognition. *Cortex, 7*, 1–18.

Scardamalia, M. (1981). How children cope with the cognitive demands of writing. In C. H. Frederiksen & J. F. Dominic (Eds.), *Writing: The nature, development, and teaching of written communication* (Vol. 2) (pp. 81–103). Hillsdale, NJ: Erlbaum.

Schnitzer, M. (1976). The role of phonology in linguistic communication: Some neurolinguistic considerations. In H. Whitaker & H. A. Whitaker, *Studies in neurolinguistics* (Vol. 1) (pp. 139–160). New York: Academic Press.

Scinto, L. F. M. (1977). Textual competence: A preliminary analysis of orally generated texts. *Linguistics, 194*, 5–34.

Scinto, L. F. M. (1982). *The acquisition of functional composition strategies for text*. Hamburg: Helmut Buske.

Scinto, L. F. M. (1984). The architectonics of text produced by children and the development of higher cognitive functions. *Discourse Processes, 7*, 371–418.

Scribner, S., & Cole, M. (1978). Literacy without schooling: Testing for intellectual effects. *Harvard Educational Review, 48*, 448–461.

Scribner, S., & Cole, M. (1981). *The psychology of literacy*. Cambridge: Harvard University Press.

Sheldrake, R. (1981). *A new science of life*. London: Blond & Briggs.

Shuy, R. (1981). Towards a developmental theory of writing. In C. H. Frederiksen & J. F. Dominic (Eds.), *Writing: The nature, development, and teaching of written communication* (Vol. 2) (pp. 119–132). Hillsdale, NJ: Erlbaum.

Silverstein, M. (1978). The three faces of function. In M. Hickmann (Ed.), *Preceedings of a working conference on the social foundations of language and thought* (pp. 1–12). Chicago: Center for Psychosocial Studies and University of Chicago.

Simon, J. (1973). *La langue écrite de l'enfant*. Paris: Presses Universitaires de France.

Smith, F. (1973). *Psycholinguistics and reading.* New York: Holt, Rinehart & Winston.

Smith, F. (1975). The relation between spoken and written language. In E. H. Lenneberg & E. Lenneberg (Eds.), *Foundations of language development* (Vol. 2) (pp. 347–360). New York: Academic Press.

Sokolov, A. N. (1967). Unterseochungen ium problem der sprachlichen mechanismen des denkens. In H. Hubsch, F. Klix, & M. Vorwerg (Eds.), *Ergebnisse der sowjetischen psychologie.* Berlin: Academic-Verlag.

Stubbs, M. (1980). *Language and literacy.* London: Routledge & Kegan Paul.

Sulzby, E. (1982). Beginning readers' developing knowledges about written language (draft copy). Evanston, IL: Northwestern University.

Svoboda, A. (1968). The hierarchy of communicative units and fields as illustrated by English attributive constructions. *Bruo Studies in English, 7,* 49–99.

Tannen, D. (Ed.). (1982). *Spoken and written language: Exploring orality and literacy.* Norwood, NJ: Ablex.

Tartaglia, P. (1972). *Problems in the construction of a theory of natural language.* The Hague: Mouton.

Thabault, R. (1944). *L'enfant et la langage écrite.* Paris: Delagrave.

Thornley, G. C. (1975). *Pleasant books in easy English Stage 3.* London: Longmans.

Tondow, M. (1954). Oral and written language of children. *California Journal of Educational Research, 5,* 170–175.

Trevarthen, C., & Hubley, P. (1978). Secondary intersubjectivity: Confidence, confiding and acts of meaning in the first year. In A. Lock (Ed.), *Action, gesture and symbol: The emergence of language* (pp. 183–229). London: Academic Press.

Uhlirova, L. (1977). Optional constituents in theme-rheme structure. *Prague Studies in Mathematical Linguistics, 5,* 308–320.

Ulatowska, H. K., Baker, T., & Stern, R. F. (1979). Disruption of written language in aphasia. In H. Whitaker & H. A. Whitaker (Eds.), *Studies in Neurolinguistics* (Vol. 4) (pp. 242–268). New York: Academic Press.

Uldall, H. J. (1944). Speech and writing. *Acta Linguistica, 4,* 11–16.

Vachek, J. (1942). Psaný jazyk a pravopis. In B. Havranek & J. Mukarovsky (Eds.), *Čteni o jazyce a poesii* (pp. 229–306). Praha: Družstevni Práce.

Vachek, J. (1948). Written language and printed language. *Recueil Linguistique de Bratislava, 1,* 67–76.

Vachek, J. (1955). Some thoughts on the so-called complex condensation in modern English. *Sbornik Praci Filosoficke Fakulty Brnenske University, A3,* 63–77.

Vachek, J. (1958). Notes on the development of language seen as a system of systems. Sbornik Prace Filosoficke Fakulty Brnenske University, A6, 94–106.

Vachek, J. (1959). Two chapters on written English. *Brno Studies in English, 1,* 7–38.

Vachek, J. (Ed.). (1964). *A Prague School reader in linguistics.* Bloomington: Indiana University Press.

Vachek, J. (1965). On the linguistic status of written utterances. In *Omagiu lui alexandru rosetti la 70 de ani* (pp. 959–963). Bucurezti: Editura Academiei.

Vachek, J. (1966). *The linguistic school of Prague.* Bloomington: Indiana University Press.

Vachek, J. (1973). *Written language.* The Hague: Mouton.

van Dijk, T. (1972). *Some aspects of text grammar.* The Hague: Mouton.

van Dijk, T. (1977). *Text and context.* London: Longman.

van Dijk, T., & Petöfi, J. (Eds.). (1977). *Grammars and descriptions.* Berlin: De Gruyter.

Venezky, R. (1970). *The structure of English orthography.* The Hague: Mouton.

Vygotsky, L. S. (1928). The problem of the cultural development of the child. *Journal of Genetic Psychology, 36,* 415–434.

Vygotsky, L. F. (1956). The development of higher forms of attention in childhood. In L. S. Vygotsky, *Collected works* (J. V. Wertsch, Trans.). Moscow.

Vygotsky, L. S. (1960). *Razvitie vysshekh psikhicheskikh funktsii.* Moscow: Isdatel'stvo Akademii Pedagogecheskikh.

Vygotsky, L. S. (1965). Psychology and localization of functions. *Neuropsychologica, 3,* 381–386.

Vygotsky, L. S. (1977). *Thought and language.* Cambridge: MIT Press.

Vygotsky, L. S. (1978). *Mind in society: The development of higher psychological processes* (M. Cole, V. John-Steiner, S. Scribner & E. Souberman, Eds.). Cambridge: Harvard University Press.

Wardhaugh, R. (1976). *The contexts of language.* Rowley: Newbury House.

Washburn, S. L. (1959). Speculations on the interrelations of tools and biological evolution. In J. M. Spuhler (Ed.), *The evolution of man's capacity for culture* (pp. 21–31). Detroit: Wayne State University Press.

Weigl, E. (1964). Bedeutung der afferenten, verlo-kinasthetischen erregungen des sprachapparates fur die expressiven und rezeptiven sprachroigange bei normalen und sprachgestorten. *Cortex, 1,* 77–90.

Weigl, E. (1975). On written language: Its alexic-agraphic disturbances. In E. H. Lenneberg & E. Lenneberg (Eds.), *Foundations of language development* (Vol. II) (pp. 383–393). New York: Academic Press.

Weigl, E., & Bierwisch, M. (1970). Neuropsychology and linguistics: Topics and common research. *Foundations of language, 6,* 1–18.

Weigl, E., Bottcher, R., Lander, H. J., & Metze, E. (1971). Neuropsychologische methoden zur analyse der funktionen und komponenten sprachfunktionaler teilsysteme, ein beitrag zum problem der ionneren und aussesen sprache. *Zeitschrift fur Psychologie, 179,* 444–494.

Werner, H. (1980). *Comparative psychology of human development.* New York: International Universities Press.

Werner, H., & Kaplan, B. (1957). Symbolic mediation and organization of thought: An experimental approach by means of the line schematization technique. *Journal of Psychology, 43,* 3–25.

Werner, H., & Kaplan, B. (1963). *Symbol formation: An organismic-developmental approach to language and the expression of thought.* New York: Wiley.

Whitaker, H., & Whitaker, H. A. (Eds.). (1976). *Studies in neurolinguistics* (Vol. 1). New York: Academic Press.

Whitaker, H., & Whitaker, H. A. (Eds.). (1979). Studies in neurolinguistics (Vol. 4). New York: Academic Press.

Whiteman, M. F., & Hall, W. S. (1981). Introduction. In M. F. Whiteman (Ed.), *Writing: The nature, development, and teaching of written communication.* Hillsdale, NJ: Erlbaum.

Wolf, D., & Gardner, H. (1978). *Beyond playing or polishing: A developmental view of artistry.* Cambridge: Harvard University.

Yakubinski, L. P. (1923). O dialog: ceskoj reci. *Russkaja Rec, 1,* 96–194.

Zammuner, V. L. (1981). *Speech production strategies in discourse planning: A theoretical and empirical inquiry.* Hamburg: Helmut Buske.

Zawadowski, L. (1956). Les functions du texte et les categories de propositions. *Bulletin de la Société Polonaise de Linguistique, 15,* 31–64.

Zierer, E. (1970). *The theory of graphs in linguistics.* The Hague: Mouton.

Author Index

A

Aaronson, D., *175*
Adamec, P., 110, *175*
Albert, M. L., 35, 49, *179*
Armstrong, R., 86, *177*
Artymovyč, A., 32, 64, *175*
Auzias, M., 68, 69, *177*
Ayala, F. J., *175*

B

Baker, T., 87, *183*
Baldwin, J. M., 75, *175*
Bang, V., 145, 146, 151, 156, *181*
Batalova, T., 109, 112, 113, *175*
Bates, E., 142, *175*
Beilin, H., 142, 150, *175*
Bellert, I., 110, *175*
Benesova, E., 110, *176*
Bierwisch, M., 44, *184*
Bottcher, R., 46, *184*

B

Breyton, M., 83, *178*
Bruce, B. C., 88, *176*
Brueckner, L., 83, *176*
Bruner, J., 76, 79, 93, 100, 140, 141, 166, *176, 180*
Bühler, K., 52, 54, *176*

C

Callewaert, H., 69, *176*
Campbell, D. T., 171, *176*
Campbell, R., 141, 158, *176*
Chao, Y. R., 68, *176*
Chomsky, C., 82, *176*
Clammer, J. R., 56, 170, *176*
Clay, M. J., 81, *176*
Cole, M., 3, 50, 60, 93, 94, 97, 98, 99, 105, 163, 167, 170, *176, 178, 182*
Collins, A., 88, *176*
Coltheart, M., 35, 47, *176*
Cook-Gumperz, J., 104, *176*
Critchley, MacD., 49, *176*

D

Dahl, Ö., 110, *176*
D'Andrade, R., 99, *176*
Daněs, F., 110, 111, 114, 118, *176, 177*
de Ajuriaguerra, J., 68, 69, *177*
de Gobineau, S., 83, *181*
Derrida, J., 8, *177*
de Saussure, F., 8, 9, 10, 11, 12, 15, 20, *177*
De Vito, J., 87, *177*
Dingwall, W., 19, *177*
Dobzhansky, T., *175*
Donaldson, M., 76, 143, *177*
Dressler, W. V., 83, *177*
Dubois-Charlier, F., 49, *177*

E

Eccles, J. C., *182*
Ellis, A. W., 68, *177*
Evanechko, P., *177*

F

Feldman, C., 131, *177*
Ferreiro, E., 81, 87, *177*
Fime, J., 89, *178*
Firbas, J., 111, *177*
Flower, L., 88, *177*
Fodor, J. A., 29, *178*
Fraisse, P., 83, *178*
Freedle, R., 89, *178*
Fujimura, O., 48, *182*

G

Gardner, H., 73, *178, 184*
Garton, A., 93, 100, 166, *176*
Geertz, C., 28, 29, 147, 165, *178*
Gentner, D., 88, *176*
Golub, L., 87 *178*
Goody, J., 56, 60, 93, 97, 99, 163, 167, 170, *178*
Greenfield, P. M., 93, 100, 136, 167, *178*
Gregg, L., 88, *178*
Griffin, W. J., 87, *181*
Grize, J. B., 145, 146, 151, 156, *181*
Gumperz, J. J., 104, *176*
Gundlach, R. A., 77, 82, *178*

H

Haas, W., 33, 34, 35, 36, 37, 68, *178*
Hajicova, E., *176*
Hall, R. A., *178*
Hall, W. S., 87, *184*
Halle, M., 14, *179*
Halliday, M. A. K., 55, 136, *178*
Hamlyn, D. W., 170, *178*
Harrell, L. E., 83, 84, *178*
Haugen, E., *178*
Havelock, E. A., 56, 93, 170, *178, 179*
Havránek, B., 64, 95, 96, *179*
Hayes, J. R., 88, *177*
Heath, S. B., 92, *179*
Hecaen, H., 35, 49, *179*
Henderson, L., 35, 46, 47, 68, *179*
Hjelmslev, L., 8, 15, 16, 31, *179*
Hobhouse, L. T., 75, 171, *179*
Holman, E., 60, 62, 100, 101, *179*
Horalek, K., 52, 54, *179*
Howard, V., 73, *178*
Hubley, P., 76, *183*
Humboldt, W. von, 73, *179*
Humphrey, N., 170, *179*
Hunt, K. W., 83, 86, *179*

I

Inhelder, B., 141, 148, 149, 150, 156, *179*
Innis, H., 93, 170, *179*
Innis, R., 56, *179*

J

Jakobson, R., 14, *179*
Johnson, M. K., *179*

K

Kaplan, B., 73, 168, *184*
Karmiloff-Smith, A., 55, 92, 136, *179*
Kukharenko, V., 113, *179*

L

Lander, H. J., 46, *184*
Langleben, M., 113, *179*
Lenneberg, E., *179*
Lenneberg, E. H., *179*

Leont'ev, A. N., 30, 40, *179*
Li, C. N., 41, *179*
Lock, A., *180*
Loflin, M. D., *180*
Lord, A., 60, *180*
Lull, H. C., 83, *180*
Lurçat, L., 69, 83, *180*
Luria, A. R., 29, 30, 39, 43, 44, 45, 46, 56, 63, 64, 70, 71, 72, 74, 93, 101, 103, 165, *180*

M

McDougall, W., 55, *180*
McIntosh, A., 35, 68, *180*
McLuhan, M., 93, 170, *180*
MacWhinney, B., 142, *175*
Markova, A. K., 99, *180*
Martinet, A., 13, *180*
Mathesius, V., 22, 95, 111, *180*
Mead, G. H., 172, *180*
Metze, E., 46, *184*
Metzing, D., 83, *180*
Michaels, S., 102, 136, *180*
Milner, E., 30, *180*
Mukarovsky, J., 52, 54, 95, *180*

N

Nasarova, L. K., 46, *180*
Nida, E. A., *180*
Ninio, A., 76, *180*
Nold, E., 88, *181*
Norris, R. C., 87, *181*
Nystrand, M., 87, *181*

O

Ochs, E., 92, *181*
O'Donnell, R. C., 87, *181*
Okby, M., 108, *181*
Ollila, L., *177*
Olson, D. R., 89, 90, 93, 100, 164, 165, 166, *176, 181*
Ong, W. J., 7, 170, *181*
Osgood, C. E., 18, *181*

P

Patterson, K., 35, 46, 47, *181*
Peirce, C. S., 36, *181*

Pellegrino, M. L., 83, 85, 86, *181*
Peltz, F., 86, *181*
Perkins, D., 73, *178*
Perron, R., 83, *181*
Petöfi, J., 83, 109, *181, 183*
Piaget, J., 78, 80, 141, 145, 146, 147, 148, 150, 151, 155, 156, 157, 158, *179, 181*
Popper, K., 159, 164, *182*
Poulton, E., 46, *182*
Pulgram, E., 33, *182*

R

Reed, C., 82, *182*
Resnick, L. B., *182*
Rieber, R. W., *175*
Romanes, G. J., 75, *182*
Rose, S., 164, *182*
Rouma, G., 83, *182*
Rubin, A. D., 88, *176*
Russell, J., 75, 159, *182*

S

Sahlins, M., 164, *182*
Sasanuma, S., 48, *182*
Scardamalia, M., 88, *182*
Schieffelin, B. B., *181*
Schnitzer, M., 47, 48, *182*
Scinto, L. F. M., 108, 109, 112, 114, 116, 118, 120, 122, 129, 132, 147, 148, 151, 152, 157, *182*
Scopesi, A., 83, 85, 86, *181*
Scribner, S., 3, 50, 60, 93, 94, 97, 98, 105, 163, 167, 170, *178, 182*
Sgall, P., 110, *176*
Sheldrake, R., 78, 164, *182*
Shuy, R., 89, *182*
Silverberg, J., *180*
Silverstein, M., 54, *182*
Simon, J., *182*
Smith, F., 46, *182*
Sokolov, A. N., *182*
Steinberg, E., 88, *178*
Stern, R. F., 87, *183*
Stone, A., 131, *177*
Stubbs, M., 35, 87, *183*
Sulzby, E., 81, 87, *183*
Svoboda, A., 111, *183*
Szemenska, A., 145, 146, 151, 156, *181*

T

Tannen, D., 64, *183*
Tartaglia, P., 14, *183*
Teberosky, A., 81, 87, *177*
Thabault, R., 83, *183*
Thompson, S. A., 41, *179*
Tondow, M., 83, *183*
Torrance, N., 89, 90, *181*
Trevarthen, C., 76, *183*

U

Uhlirova, L., 111, *183*
Ulatowska, H. K., 87, *183*
Uldall, H. J., 32, *183*

V

Vachek, J., 22, 32, 53, 58, 64, 98, 111, *183*
van Dijk, T., 83, *183*
Vygotsky, L. S., 19, 39, 40, 68, 69, 77, 78, 93, 103, 105, 165, *183, 184*

W

Wardharugh, R., 14, *184*
Washburn, S. L., 29, *184*
Watt, I., 93, *178*
Weigl, E., 40, 41, 44, 45, 46, 47, *184*
Werner, H., 72, 73, 92, 168, *184*
Whitaker, H. A., *184*
Whiteman, M. F., 86, *184*
Wolf, D., 73, *184*

Y

Yakubinski, L. P., 59, 60, 102, *184*

Z

Zammuner, V. L., 60, 108, *184*
Zawadowski, L., 52, 54, 95, *184*
Zierer, E., 122, *184*

Subject Index

B

Biology and culture, 28, 39
  development and, 28-29, 73-76, 78, 164
  interactionist position, 28-29
  mutually constitutive principles, 28
  reductionism and, 161

C

Cognitive operations, 145-157, 160
  anticipations, 150-151
  concrete, 140-142, 150-152, 160
  conservation, 151-152
  formal, 139-142
  function in, 148-156
  relation in, 148-156
  retrospection, 150, 151
  reversibility, 149
  and text operations, 139-145, 149
  transitivity, 151, 152
Communicative competence, 52
Cryptic, 158, 159
Culture, 76-80, see also Biology and culture;
  Culture and language
  decontextualization, principle of, 79
  developmental models and, 92, 97, 98, 105,
    163-165
  externalization, principle of, 79
  schooling and, 163
Culture and language, 170-172

D

Developmental models, 92, 97, 98, 105
  cultural line in, 73-76, 78-80, 164
Dialogue, 59, 60, 61, 101, 102-103

F

Functional differentiation, 51-53
  automatization, 96-97
  intellectualization, 96, 105
  signal form, 55, 57, 59, 63
  social praxis and, 95-98, 99, 101, 103-104
Functional features of languages, 56-62, see
  also Functional differentiation
  contextualization, 57
  interactive potential, 57-58, 59-60
  preservability, 56
Functional neural organization, 29-30, 39-40
  social and cultural factors in, 39
Functions in language, 54, 55
  communicative, 54
  Darstellungsfunktion, 54

Functions in language (*continued*)
Kundgabefunktion, 54

G

Glossematic, 15, 21, 32

H

Hiragana, 48

K

Kanji, 48
Katakana, 48

L

Labensformen, 75, 79
Language, 12, *see also* Oral and written language; Written language acquisition
acquisition of, 55
difference in, 11, 12
folk theory of, 11
form, 12
functional approach to, 162
principle of differentiation of, 22–23
psychological definitions of, 16–20
structural approach to, 162
substance, 12, 13
substance neutral definition of, 20–23
substantive manifestations of, 13, 21
trichotomy of, 25
value, 11–12
Langue, 12–13, 16, 19, 21, 52, 67
Linguistic sign, 8, 10–12
Literacy, 3
cognition and, 93–95, 97, 99
schooling and, 93, 94, 97, 98–104

M

Mesotic, 48
Monologue, 59–62, 62, 101, 102–103

N

Natural language, 5, 8, 14, 18, 27
cultural achievement of, 27

manifestations of, 25
Neurolinguistics, 42–49, *see also* Functional neural organization
Norms of language, 52, 53, 58–59, 63–64
oral, 92
written, 92, 93, 97, 158, 162

O

Ontogenesis, 39, 40, 43, 47, *see also* Developmental models
higher mental functions in, 39
priority of speech in, 30–31
Oral and written language, relation of, 25–26, 38
cerebral organization of, 45–46
complementary distribution of features in, 57–58
dependent model of, 32, 34
discourse organization of, 59–62
equipolent status of, 33, 34
genetic model of, 38–42
grapheme–phoneme correspondence, intralingual, 34, 35
independent model of, 33, 34
marking relations of, 58, 61
mediational model of, 45–47, 49–50
structural models of, 31–37

P

Parole, 12–13, 16, 21, 52
Phenic, 158, 159
Phonocentric canon, 1–2, 6–8, 13, 17, 18, 20, 23
Phonological mediation, 46–49
Phonology, 8, 13–15
correspondence, grapheme–phoneme, 33, 34–38
translation, 33–34, 37, 41
Prague school, 22, 32

S

Script, 33
derived, 33, 41
phonetic, 33
Social praxis, 91–106

Sound, 8, 10–12, *see also* Voice
Speech, 9, 12, 13, 14, 19, 21, 25, 26
  phylogenetic priority of, 26–30
Syntactic differentiation, 62–65, *see also* Functional differentiation

T

Text construction strategies, 148–154
  acquisition of, 139–145, 150–152, 153–157
Text models, 107
  architectonics, 148–149
  coherence of, 110, 125–128, 130
  combinatoric logic of, 157, 159
  combinatoric modules, 112, 113, 122–124, 128
  compactness, 125–128, 130
  definition of, 108–110
  expository, 129, 130
  function in, 148–156
  graph–theoretic modeling, 122–124
  narrative, 129, 130
  ontogenesis and, 157–160
  relation in, 148–156
  sentences in, 111, 112
  thematic linkage in, 150, 151
  thematic progression, 111–112, 113–121
  units of, 110–120

V

Voice, 7, 19

W

Writing, 25, 26, *see also* Phonology; Script
Written language, 1–2, 8, 12, 13, 14, 21, 91–106
  decontextualization, 96, 100–101, 104
  differentiation of, 91, 92, 97–98
  social praxis and, 104–106
Written language acquisition, 2–3, 17–18, 26–27, 42, 46, 47, 67–70, 76–78, 80–82, 163, *see also* Text construction strategies
  cultural line in, 92, 105–106
  developmental models of, 73–76
  levels in, 68–69
  metapragmatic awareness and, 142–143
  prehistory of, 69
  stages in, 70–73
  schooling and, 143, 157–158
  studies of, 82–90
    psychological, 83, 88–90
    sociolinguistic, 83, 87–88
    syntactic, 83, 84–87
Written language and psychological development, 165–170